Persecution and Morality

Valerie Oved Giovanini

Persecution and Morality

Intersections and Tensions between
Freud and Lévinas

Valerie Oved Giovanini
Department of Philosophy
California State University, Northridge
Northridge, CA, USA

ISBN 978-3-030-64663-9   ISBN 978-3-030-64664-6 (eBook)
https://doi.org/10.1007/978-3-030-64664-6

© The Editor(s) (if applicable) and The Author(s), under exclusive license to Springer Nature Switzerland AG 2021
This work is subject to copyright. All rights are reserved by the Publisher, whether the whole or part of the material is concerned, specifically the rights of translation, reprinting, reuse of illustrations, recitation, broadcasting, reproduction on microfilms or in any other physical way, and transmission or information storage and retrieval, electronic adaptation, computer software, or by similar or dissimilar methodology now known or hereafter developed.
The use of general descriptive names, registered names, trademarks, service marks, etc. in this publication does not imply, even in the absence of a specific statement, that such names are exempt from the relevant protective laws and regulations and therefore free for general use.
The publisher, the authors, and the editors are safe to assume that the advice and information in this book are believed to be true and accurate at the date of publication. Neither the publisher nor the authors or the editors give a warranty, expressed or implied, with respect to the material contained herein or for any errors or omissions that may have been made. The publisher remains neutral with regard to jurisdictional claims in published maps and institutional affiliations.

This Springer imprint is published by the registered company Springer Nature Switzerland AG
The registered company address is: Gewerbestrasse 11, 6330 Cham, Switzerland

Early Reviews for Persecution and Morality

This quite original and engaging book sets up an encounter between Levinas and Freud in order to pave the way towards an ethics at once capacious and discerning. Centering on the primacy of "persecution" in the lives of both Freud and Levinas, Giovanini tracks the way this term surfaces at the level of fantasy and ethical understanding. The "persecutory" structure of Levinasian ethics establishes the involuntary ways we are affected by others, including the ethical demand that is conveyed by alterity itself. Querying the historical resonance of persecution in the wake of the Nazi genocide against the Jews, Giovanini shows how the psychic consequences can lead to delusional states that break with all ethical relationality. However, she also shows how it can lead to an ecstatic and relational understanding of others, one that is alert and responsive to difference. In her reading, the historical circumstances or persecution can lead to practice of responsibility that limits egoism in the name of a non-appropriative relationality. Few books weave their way between biography, fantasy, and ethics with the urgency and clarity that this one does.

—*Judith Butler, Ph.D., University of California, Berkeley, USA*

In her first book, Valerie Giovanini delivers an ambitious canvassing of persecutable objects. As if conducted by a split-off Israeli part, the work is propelled by the unbearable knowledge of relentless brutalizations visited upon the Palestinian people. Pained by acts of blind hatred, Giovanini explores on a large scale the infectious spread of overmoralizing zeal and falsifications historically inscribed. In a mashup of autobiographical and quasi-biographical scenes of disrupted development, she argues that even the most lucid contenders fall short of their own emancipatory insights, egregiously betraying their premises and archive of rigorous investigations. To her credit, Giovanini opens a dossier on the psychotic overuse of "ethics" in contemporary American theories that depend on Lévinas and Freud's pooled fates for securing faux assumptions and condemnatory stances, uncritically maintained. Importantly, the study tracks how love turns to hate, calling on readers to identify their *particular other*—object of obsession and shadow part—if only to observe when one becomes vulnerable, in a genuinely Levinasian sense, to the foreclosure of ethical relation.

—*Avital Ronell, Ph.D., University Professor of the Humanities at New York University, New York, USA*

In this intriguing book, Valerie Giovanini pairs Sigmund Freud and Emmanuel Levinas, strange bedfellows, perhaps uncanny ones, both haunted by violence. She challenges us to compare and contrast their attitudes toward ethics and vulnerability, as well their life stories. She makes us ask if, or how, psychoanalysis and radical ethics can fit together in the face of personal trauma. Best of all, she leaves us with more questions about the passivity inherent in persecution. An important contribution.

—*Donna M. Orange, Ph.D., Psy.D., NYU Postdoctoral Program and the Institute for the Psychoanalytic Study of Subjectivity, New York, USA*

Dr. Giovanini posits her work as a "retelling" of the works and lives of Freud and Lévinas which foregrounds her sensitivity to the intimate relationship between *reading*, *testimony*, and the possibility of *fictionality*, thus allowing her to both perform readings of their lives and their works — in all of their multiplicities, complexities, incongruities — whilst, at the very same time, be reflexive about the fact that her text might well be running those very same risks. Focusing on *persecution* as an entry point into her exploration is both philosophically intriguing and strategically very sound: there really aren't many texts out there which address this urgent issue. Philosophically speaking, the way in which she unveils the persecutory gestures in the works of those who have been persecuted in their lives (whilst not exonerating herself from the possibility of doing so) is intriguing. I'll go so far as to say that this work might well be responsible for initiating a new generation of reflections that make our philosophical — and ethical — certitudes tremble. I can well imagine Dr. Giovanini's book being on the reading lists in English, gender studies, philosophy, art, and media studies departments, as well as quite possibly the general public. I certainly will be looking forward to the possibility of including her text in a seminar I run, entitled *Writing Women*. Her writing style is clear, welcoming, and very engaging.

—*Jeremy Fernando, Ph.D., Jean Baudrillard Fellow at The European Graduate School, Switzerland*

Photo courtesy of Dan Lenchner's collection

Acknowledgments

I would like to thank Scott, my partner in life and love. Many thanks to the University in the White Mountains and the many conversations there that began this journey of writing this book. It was there that Judith Butler's and Avital Ronell's smashing wings let these ideas soar. I appreciate Judith Butler and Donna Orange who took time to review the manuscript and send me their input. I would like to acknowledge several editors, Lilith Dorko, Christina Lowe, and Carolyn Laubender, through whose hands and eyes this work passed. As Carolyn wisely put it, a piece of writing is never done alone. Though it often felt like this work was done alone in the stacks and at conferences, in bars, on planes, trains, and in automobiles, there are far too many more contributing voices to name. Finally, it is worth acknowledging the lives of Freud and Lévinas that inspired this necessary but difficult reflection on aspects of my moral life.

Contents

1	**Introduction**...	1
	Situating This Work: Persecution Not Only as a Social Phenomenon, But Also as a Psychic Mechanism and Ontological Obligation.......	4
	Methodology, Field Interventions, and the Yields of this Work.......	12
	References...	24

Part I Sigmund Freud

2	**Freud's Life and Work: A Historical Horizon**..................	27
	References...	36
3	**Getting Personal: Persecution in Freud's Personal Life**...........	37
	References...	52
4	**The Uncanniness of Conflicting Moral Norms**..................	53
	References...	69
5	**Freud's Vulnerability to the Social Ideals of His Time & Moral Skepticism**	71
	References...	87
6	**A New Kind of Psychotherapy for Ethical Subjectivity**...........	89
	References...	96
7	**From Freud to Lévinas**......................................	99
	References...	104

Part II Emmanuel Lévinas

8	**Lévinas's Life and Work: A Historical Horizon**.................	107
	References...	122
9	**Epistemic Gaps: Freedom and Mutual Dis-identification**.........	123
	References...	129

10	**Freedom and Existential Vulnerability: Lévinas's Vulnerability to His Cultural Ideals**	131
	References	146
11	**Intentionality of Search: Vulnerability, Persecution, and the Ethical Bind**	149
	References	163
12	**Conclusion**	165
	Ethics Reconsidered: Always Only a Proximate Response	165
	Reference	171

Postscript ... 173

Bibliography ... 175

Index ... 181

Author Biography

Valerie Oved Giovanini, Ph.D., is an independent scholar based in Los Angeles, California, and an affiliate faculty member in the Department of Philosophy, California State University, Northridge. Her doctoral research under the guidance of Dr. Judith Butler at The European Graduate School traced the close relationship between persecution and ethics in the works of Sigmund Freud and Emmanuel Lévinas in order to develop an ethics of alterity. Her most recent work on alterity is published in *Hypatia: A Journal in Feminist Philosophy*, and she is a contributing editor on the special issue of *Free Associations* titled "Aesthetic Subjects." Her more general interests include the intersection of new media with philosophy, phenomenology, and aesthetics.

Chapter 1
Introduction

Abstract The first section begins with a personal anecdote about my life as an Israeli Jewish woman who is morally obligated to remember historical persecutions, but who must also remain sensitive to the possibility of persecuting others to secure a future life in Israel. The anecdote speaks to the manuscript's more general proposal to think anew about relations of persecution in what are considered our moral obligations.

I provide details about phenomenological hermeneutics, a method that I use to untangle the relation between ethics and persecution. I also present the theoretical yields from the book's two major sections dedicated to each author respectively: Sigmund Freud's moral skepticism and Emmanuel Lévinas's new moral horizon.

Keywords Emmanuel Lévinas · Sigmund Freud · Theory of persecution · Ethical relation · Relational subjectivity · Ethical subjectivity · Relations of persecution · Hermeneutical phenomenology · Biographical retelling · Distantiation

A siren. *Amidat Dom*. I got up from the auditorium seat and stood at attention at the sound of a national alarm. We waited a minute in remembrance for all those who perished in the *Shoa*. Never forget all those who did not survive. With the gesture, we were taking an implicit vow never to forget perished family members and what was done to them all those years ago. Never to forget the echoes of our traumas that persist today. A metaphoric stand is taken never to let this happen again. This tradition was new to me, but it seemed to mark an important reminder. It was a good one, never to forget the barbarism, a natural barbarism that seems to exist from time immemorial. Why then does it seem, so many years later, that we can fall prey to the same kind of thinking, to a barbarism of a kind like our persecutors?

"They drink the hate from their mother's breast," I was told around the Shabbat dinner table years later about Palestinians. "They are born to hate and then they are educated to kill." These two kinds of moments make me wonder: which is it? It is important that we understand which it is. Is my enemy born this way, or are they taught, and so unteachable? Do they have an unshakable quality for being evil? The argument that some are born innately unclean, bad, immoral, or wrong leads me to a frightening thought, flashbacks to "they are vermin." The Jew is born dirty, greedy, conniving and so deserving of eradication, conversion, and assimilation. Jews also could not shake their image as vermin. What is the difference between this image and the image of the milk of one's breast, milk that contains hate unavoidably consumed at birth? My enemy cannot shed their image "as full of hate," just as Jews could not apologize and redeem themselves as people. Today the image as objectionable Zionists persists to justify our persecution.

How can "our" persecution seem like such a violation that it is worthy of commemoration, while at the same time we paint the persecution of "our" enemy with the same racist strokes? Does any amount of security justify this blind hatred and unshakable image of these others? It may be time to start wondering about this error in thought, as Hannah Arendt might have called it. But what if the banal capacity to hold inconsistent values, as she argued, does not reflect an error in thought or the content of beliefs, but in fact makes up the constitutive elements of thought itself?

Human history has shown what we can do when an innate quality is attributed to another, as a different and threatening "other." The epistemic error in thought becomes an ethical trespass when some are innately considered worse than others—evil, bad, and bearing detestable qualities, which no forgiveness can excuse. Implicit in the claim that another is detestable is a presumption about what is good. How the other is in error becomes a rationalization and justification for feelings of hate, or worse, physical abuse. The other is persecuted in the name of what is deemed good, whether it is for civic, religious, psychological, or social well-being.

History attests that generally individuals (as much as full populations) take pleasure in zealously pursuing and persecuting what is found to be fearful. For example, the cover photo of this book shows a crowd laughing at an object that is unknown, standing outside the frame. We see fingers pointing, bellies grabbed in laughter, couples whispering at what cannot be seen. Can you sympathize with their feeling? Have you witnessed or experienced this kind of enjoyment? It is easy to imagine a lynching, a burning, or a float with caricatures of the despised other outside the frame. Their expressions are legible to anyone. The familiarity of this scene implicates our complicity and ability to participate in and enjoy the persecution of a threatening other.

What in the conditions of knowledge makes the tendency to persecute possible for any person who always stands in proximity to others? Both Sigmund Freud and Emmanuel Lévinas lived through persecutions. Each, however, reached divergent, hyperbolic conclusions in their theoretical work on the ethical relation considering an acknowledged relation with the other. Given psychological topologies, the ethical relation is impossible for Freud, while Lévinas argues that ontological proximities necessitate the ethical relation. Readers who are familiar with Freud's work in trauma studies, clinical practices, and literary theory, and on how each is influenced by others through processes of identification, introjection, projection, and transference and who are concerned, as he was, with the question of morality will find interest in Lévinas's work. Lévinas takes Freud's moral skepticism for living an ethical life into overdrive. Lévinas concludes that there must be another more fundamental to the self because of these inter-relational processes. Their lives during the World

Wars and after included persecutions that made their moral concerns fluctuate in meaningful ways that interestingly illuminate their disparate positions.

Interweaving the personal lives of Sigmund Freud and Emmanuel Lévinas can help illuminate the strength of their hyperbolic but robust theories of persecution, ethics, and where human failing may arise. Freud and Lévinas developed a view of subjectivity that is persecutory in nature against itself and in relation to others. Even if Freud does not reach the same conclusions about the ethical subject as Lévinas, this project looks toward relational, or intersubjective, approaches in psychoanalysis to find converging ideas and useful differences on a subjectivity that persecutes. Their view that a subject must negotiate their relations on psychic and ontological grounds has led to the view developed here of an embodied, relational person who is limited in knowledge of itself and existentially vulnerable to the delusion of an individuated ego while at the same time bound to ethical demands, obligations, standards, and negotiations. The following work, however, does not aim to integrate their biographical information as a method to substantiate their arguments or to demonstrate the function of their concepts. Rather, there is a systemic analysis of the intersection between Freud and Lévinas about persecution illuminated through the meaning and events of their lives.

Either by the force of psychological mechanisms or ontological and existential conditions, Freud and Lévinas fell victim to the machinations of their reason despite understanding those same machinations. What is the source of this vulnerability to these machinations, even when these mechanisms are in some part understood? If we set aside the question of whether the truth of their theories corresponds with any objective reality or general structure of subjectivity, we can move forward in the true belief that, from their perspective, their theories were ultimately meaningful at least for these two individuals. So, it must be asked: How could they commit the very same "errors in thought" about which they theorized?

Persecution is functionally defined as an affective state that both Lévinas and Freud attribute to an embodied subject who always stands in relation to another but who cannot explain away, apologize for, or give value to psychic ideations or totalizing identifications. The notion of persecution used in this work, therefore, looks at their psychological and moral affects in order to rethink the term philosophically about vulnerability, identity, and ethics. A contrast between Lévinas's and Freud's ideas on persecution is useful because both are suspicious of self-proclaimed motivations, the insufficiency of abstract and universal moral injunctions, and an inability to calculate consequences for arbitrating moral goodness. In other words, both their hermeneutical approaches trace the development of meaning in given contexts to question the role of a self-sufficient subject, to consider the ethical implications of depending on others for a self, and wonder about a subject who is always caught in social or psychological demands that are asymmetrical.

Both Freud and Lévinas came to understand moral impossibilities, and their lives show how they were both guilty of perpetuating similar forms of persecution, while also suffering them. The following work does not condemn either for these ethical shortcomings, but rather explores their life and work to consider the all-too-human tendency to persecute oneself and others in the very formation of identity. These two figures were chosen for their unique and honest admission of the inability to avoid persecuting relations in each's attempt to follow moral standards. The work concludes with the insight that where there is a tendency to persecute another, then so comes a moral concern that is zealously pursued. Whether in delusions of persecution or in the everyday conditions of life where another is perceived to take one's place in the sun, the other is not proverbially seen. Where there is persecution, there is also a moral concern and the possibility of a difficult but ecstatic ethic that can eventually see the other.

Situating This Work: Persecution Not Only as a Social Phenomenon, But Also as a Psychic Mechanism and Ontological Obligation

The following study takes up an old dispute between John Fiske and Henry Thomas Buckle on whether the persecuting spirit is reduced when intellect increases. Does giving moral praise for zealously pursuing personal convictions ensure the permanent use of persecution, as they agreed? John Fiske wrote *The Philosophy of Persecution* (1881) on the historical decline of using persecution as a means for individual and social reform that seemed to follow from a decline in the warlike spirit. He argued that the expansion of civilization and intellect proportionately develops the moral character of those who live in those civilizations. First, this was because resources became more abundant, which led to a decline in conflict over scarcity. Second, industrialization newly grouped workers together in close proximities to each other. In these larger cities, Fiske argued, individuals became less dogmatic and thus less likely to persecute others for what were once believed to be innate qualities. The prevailing belief through developing civilizations was that no one dogma could be trusted to deliver absolute truth. As a result, persecution reduced significantly. The genocidal World Wars of the twentieth century, however, proved that these zealous pursuits were not a thing of a "primitive" past. It seems that the development of industry, luxury, manners, and elegance was not enough to totally remove the enthusiastic persecution of people in various societies. Civilization, in other words, hardly guaranteed civility.

Fiske was responding to Henry Thomas Buckle who wrote, a few years earlier in a *History of Civilization in England* (1878), that the apparent and great improvement of intellectual pursuits has no influence on moral improvement. Although Buckle acknowledged that there had been an increase in intellectual activity, which delivered a blow to the persecuting spirit, he maintained that it is the sincerity, dedication, and unflinching zeal to one's religious or social duty that preserves the possibility to persecute. In his survey of texts on the Inquisition and on persecuting leaders such as Marcus Aurelius, moral virtues are ascribed to those leaders who kept order (Buckle 1878, p. 186). Those who persecuted with pure intentions others who were believed to bring chaos, and fought with admirable courage, were deemed good leaders. Moral virtue was attributed to those who zealously persecuted what they deemed the true and good; these were the qualities, according to Buckle, that constituted better leaders.

Buckle finds that the source of a persecuting spirit is absorption in one's strong conviction of some higher good, with the belief that those who reject that higher good are doomed in some way. The stronger the sincerity, dedication, and conviction, the stronger his spirit will be to persecute the other. With these, one must have enough power—and a great enough ignorance of the consequences of one's actions—to be successful in what Fiske mockingly called a persecutory spirit that is an "unselfish philanthropy" (Fiske 1881, p. 3). Fiske uses this term to caricature Buckle's position on the unimpeachable motives and admirable morality of the persecutor.

Both Fiske and Buckle admit there is an obvious confluence between moral worth given to zealous motives, even if they lead to dogmatic and exclusivist acts of violence. They also agree that the fancies and enthusiasm of imagination always make one vulnerable to persecuting another and honoring with moral praise a persistent intention in the one who commits these acts. Mass scales of persecution perpetrated in the twentieth century confirm the truth of Buckle's position more than Fiske's that intellect cannot reduce the persecuting spirit, although Fiske is vindicated in Freud's study on the ignorance of the mind to calculate the moral consequences for committing violent acts.

In the twentieth century, some of the most ruthless forms of persecution were developed by means of increased intellectual and industrial capacity. Those intellectuals who engaged in the development of industrialized concentration, re-education, or slave-labor camps—including nuclear bombs and strategic warfare—were just as vulnerable to fanciful and solipsistic justifications as Saint Paul, Augustine, or Hobbes, who held dogmas of exclusive salvation in a Christian God or civic state. In circular logic, the perpetrators of persecutions believe that they are the victims of those groups that threaten their culture or risk their salvation.

To shed light on how political philosophy has justified persecution of whole populations, Ronald Christenson argues in "The Political Theory of Persecution: Augustine and Hobbes" (1968) that, for these two, persecution was legitimized by the state as a method to secure religious or civic unity. Christenson finds in Augustine a defense of righteous persecution for a divine order. Hobbes, on the other hand, argues that the sovereign is justified to persecute his enemies in the interest of the commonwealth. While Augustine relies on theological support for his political system, both develop their political philosophies out of a concern for ordering the public by tyrannical enforcement of private standards. These political theories legitimized the zealous pursuit and persecution of those who were believed to threaten or pervert norms that order the public good. Chaos is perceived as an evil that needs a call to order at all costs.

Like the agreement between Fiske and Buckle, for both Augustine and Hobbes positive merit is given to those who persecute for the ends of a religious or civic order. Christenson concludes from these two accounts of political philosophy that taking persecutory measures is justified when the other is villainized as the one who is acting out of irrational or selfish motives. Augustine justified pursuing and persecuting Donatists, for example, for the division they brought to a united church. Hobbes also justified the sovereign's use of persecution against those who threaten the commonwealth. To avoid the chaos of their actions, mercenaries or the sovereign would persecute certain others in order to achieve a greater divine or common good. Zealous desires often motivated persecuting groups to act violently against those they feared. On the other hand, heretics among them who did not uphold their doctrines needed to be dutifully injured by persecuting measures since they were also believed to be evildoers disrupting the social order. In this logic, removing a disruptive group restores social harmony.

These examples of good intentions used to organize a growing civilization did not create more tolerance, but rather increased what Buckle called aggressions turned inwards, "hidden from the public gaze." Ethnic cleansing in Bosnia of the Muslim population, the Armenian population in Turkey, and Jewish people during World War II are some examples of persecutions perpetrated well into the twenty-first century. The more recent persecution perpetuated against the Rohingya people in Myanmar begs to understand what this gaze that turns inwards means if this gaze secures the possibility of using persecution as a means of maintaining social or individual order.

To understand more about this aggression turned inwards, I turn in the following work to Freud's deliberations on how the internalized desire to persecute amplifies its force when it is hidden from public view. Freud shows how aggression can be amplified for the individual psyche when repressed from conscious awareness. Internalized and amplified aggression is the cost of participating in a growing civilization.

Freud began his career as a positivist, but one that was also interested in more conceptual questions such as the general origins of life. He began studying neurology with those who were sure that empirical sciences could map the psyche. The term Psyche, or Psychical Apparatus, was used by Freud to describe the whole apparatus of that which will get divided into its many component parts. It is a concept that assists in the "attempt to make the complications of mental functioning intelligible by dissecting the function and assigning its different constituents to different component parts of the apparatus" (Freud 1900, pg. 536). Ultimately, however, his work would suggest that the psychic life was made up of so many layers of imaginative interpretation that no objective truth and ideal knowledge of moral good sits at its core.

Freud uncovers drives that serve one's ego that must also be negotiated with a drive to live with others.[1] Through a psychoanalytic perspective, Freud is investigat-

---

[1] The concept of the ego underwent many changes in its definition. Freud at times stresses the heteronomy of the ego, while at others emphasizing its relative independence. The ego is treated essentially as a mediator attempting to reconcile contradictory demands. The ego is "a poor creature owing service to three masters and consequently menaced by three dangers: from the external world, from the libido of the id and from the severity of the super-ego …. As a frontier-creature, the ego tries to mediate between the world and the id, to make the id pliable to the world and, by means of its muscular activity, to make the world fall in with the wishes of the id" (Freud 1923a, pg. 56).

ing a moral question about how one comes to live a bounded life with others. More than just looking at what kinds of behavior count as moral, psychoanalysis aims to understand how broader sexual bonds, also called libidinal attachments, influence individual mental functioning. The distinction between morality and ethics is not a hard and fast one in Freud's writing. The following work will mimic how each of these terms was used by their authors, and save the important conversation about the relation between ethics and morality for another time.

Exploring whether a moral possibility exists, defined as a concern with how one should live with their impeding relation to others, Freud doubted that morality could be free of the harsh admonishment of a primary masochism in the form of a super-ego.[2] If the super-ego is the agency that watches the ego against its ideals, then the figure of an adult telling me to play nice becomes part of this psychic agency that reminds me of this social expectation in the absence of a parental figure. According to Freud then, the internal ethical sense develops out of this first renunciation of power to an external force. Given the psychological cartographies and distribution of psychic energy that Freud imagined, he further wondered whether a ubiquitous moral concern for others is even desirable. Freud's doubt about a morality that is free from aggression is paradigmatic for the end of an enlightened Modern era that thinkers like Fiske prized.

Freud's work on delusions of persecution also shows how persecution arises from within the psyche's structures and not just from external social forces. Freud calls the super-ego an agency that derives pleasure from persecuting a prohibited desire in representational consciousness. One's desire for an object that is unacceptable, unattainable, or restricted by whatever norms a culture holds for itself can create the delusion of feeling persecuted by the desired object. Delusions of persecution make use of the circular reasoning that Ronald Christensen finds in Augustine's and Hobbes's political theories. Perpetrators of persecutions believe they are victims of those groups that threaten their moral norms, their culture, or risk their personal salvation. Freud elucidates the psyche's instruments in paranoiac delusions of persecution that use a logic of contradiction. His work on conflicting psychic drives developed into what is called a "hermeneutics of suspicion." Early in his career, Freud sought therapies such as the talking cure to untangle some of the id's desires from the admonishing super-ego but abandoned the attempts as hopeless later in life. The differences between real persecutions that come from an external social reality and delusional or moral persecutions that come from an internal sense of guilt cannot be reflected on by the mind experiencing these feelings, which is why the following work, taken from the perspective of a mind capable of deluding itself, will bracket the truth of a corresponding reality for how they are justified in representational consciousness. Insights from fictional accounts of literature and autobiographical remarks are especially helpful for illuminating relations of persecutions and the concerns for moral obligations despite their author's own blindness to these processes in their personal life.

---

[2] See Freud's *Civilization and Its Discontents* (1930, pg. 134). Also see Freud, "The Economic Problems of Masochism" (1923b, pg. 170).

Social and historical accounts of persecution show the varied ways in which persecution manifests in and among individuals. Historical and political taxonomies of persecuted populations help explain the phenomenon of persecution. For example, what forms of torture have been used by persecutors? What different kinds of justifications have been used in the zealous pursuit of different forms of virtue, justice, or salvation? And which eras have used these means more than others? The pursuit of a goal can become entangled with moral praise for those who zealously pursue and persecute whoever comes in the way of achieving the end goal, such as social unity and harmony in the earthly kingdom of God for Saint Paul and Augustine, or social harmony in Hobbes's political treatise.

This work aims to address not the varied phenomena of different persecutions in social and political histories, but how persecution, as such, is possible. What about the embodied subject always necessitates the possibility of becoming persecutory toward others as a means for assuring something about oneself? The endeavor here is similar to the way in which Hannah Arendt found that the theoretical history of violence was never addressed as its own phenomenon. Violence is an important enough phenomenon to warrant its own study, but until then it did not even have an entry in the encyclopedia. The phenomenon was too ubiquitous; it went unseen, until she began making conceptual distinctions between violence, force, and power, for example. Until her work *On Violence* (1970), it was surveyed incidentally in studies on war and warfare in historical or political analyses.

The main goal for using the term *persecutory* is to avoid the binary distinction normally made between the persecuted and the persecutor. Implicit in the binary distinction between persecuted and persecutor is the fact that one starts with questions of who is intentionally, knowingly, and willingly acting on another, and who in consequence receives the abuse. The term persecutory avoids the tradition of binary questions that arise from concerns with intentionality, agency, and consequences for a subject who becomes both victim and active persecutor. There is always the necessity of finding those reasons why certain minority populations were persecuted over any other for granting social asylum. While these distinctions are important for finding legal, social, and historical justice, they miss the mark of addressing how it is possible for anyone based on the contingencies of their lives to become either persecuted or persecutor. Given the psychological mechanisms that bring about this phenomenon, everyone has been both the persecutor and the persecuted. None are free of this guilt, and all are equally worthy of possible redemption from it at different times.

I begin with the assumption that everyone can become the persecutor, either from internal psychological or biological causes due to external conditions in social and political life. As a thinking subject, another is believed to take my breathing space, which is enough to start relations of enmity between one and the "usurping" other. Another body always takes my place in the sun, as Lévinas quotes Blaise Pascal's *Pensées*. Given the necessary possibility of a persecutory relation, the ability and need to respond to the entailed suffering is also always given. The Greek verb *diokos*, to pursue, is an activity all human life engages in and will be conjoined with the Latin *orios*, made into the suffix *ory*, which means belonging to or connected with.

The shift can lead to the concern for safeguarding all human life against a self that is vulnerable to zealous pursuits of the self and others as a fact about existence. Every day, there is the need and responsibility in one's response to a world that can abandon, destitute, delude, mistreat, and persecute another. The functional definition of persecution used here, therefore, goes beyond its legal, political, or psychological uses.

A persecutory subjectivity includes an inherent possibility for acting both as persecutor and persecuted. My discussion will not focus on how certain minorities can or have been persecuted, which important sociological taxonomies of vulnerability and historical analysis have conducted. My attempt here is to work outside the norms of self-sufficiency, independent control, power, and mastery, which cater to paternalistic and patriarchal moralities. Additionally, I will find that for the ethical subject, a new type of vulnerability comes to light, the vulnerability to obsess over individual identifications, categories, and labels that can never become fixed for an identity that is infinitely pluralistic.

My use of the term vulnerability extends thinking done by contributors to the edited collection *Vulnerability: New Essays in Ethics and Feminist Philosophy* (2013). The following analysis shares their identification of vulnerability as an ontological condition of embodied life. However, in contrast with those collected essays, which primarily aim to find who is responsible for different vulnerable populations and to seek justice for their neglect, I argue that accompanying existential conditions of unknowability and relationality prevent the possibility to find clear lines of accountability for vulnerability in most lives. Instead, illuminated is an existential form of vulnerability that leads to a reaction formation of totalized identities and risk justifications for ontic forms of persecution.

A note then is required about how the word *vulnerability* is used in the context of moral philosophies. Vulnerability denotes here a human condition that results from having a corporeal body that is open to injury and wounding from elsewhere—be it other people, a social-political and legal reality, the environment, or self-injury. Implicit in this use of vulnerability is the assumption that a mind is not capable of reflecting on all its vulnerabilities and those of others. This implicit inclusion begs that each question their moral behavior and possibility for its abuse considering this inherent, mutual, and universal condition of vulnerability.

This argument is informed by my understanding of subjectivity as never totally rational and self-knowing. It may not be possible to separate the vulnerable from the abuser, the persecutor from the persecuted. Judith Butler's claims are extended here that include the "conception of bodily life considered both finite and precarious, implying that the body is always given over to modes of sociality and environment that limit its individual autonomy" (Butler 2004, pg. 31). Similarly, I start with a subject who in its "knowledge" exceeds all normative claims that moral theory can conceive and demand, for example in a Kantian categorical imperative or utilitarian calculus. How do you perform a calculus, or find one's moral duty, when all relevant moral factors are not ready at hand or, worse, distorted? An additional problem is that representations based on veridical perceptions and perceptions based on illusory ones are not always distinguishable to the mind. Rational machinations cannot account for these various distortions in the processes of knowledge production that both Freud and Lévinas each warn about in different ways.

The work also tries to think through new possibilities for ethical responsiveness that Butler states in *Giving an Account of Oneself*, where the impingement of an address from the other can be the voice of no one, the voice of God, understood as infinite and pre-ontological, that makes itself known in the "face of the Other" (2005, pg. 90). I want to take this reading that incorporates Lévinas's notion of the face in place of Butler's reading of the other as belonging to a social category in an idealized dyad, which deceptively appears fixed by the concreteness of social life. For me, ontologies of social constructs lead to more polemical discussions of justice. As much as these are important, I would like to find the conditions that make any person vulnerable to a pre-ontological address by another person, such as simply standing beside another, how the address is evaded because it is risky, and then consider how impoverished the ethical aspect of self becomes because of this evasion.

The impingement of persecuting relations and the ethical address are possibilities for all human beings if it is a pre-ontological condition. In other words, and to follow Lévinas's lead, in order to become a person at all, ethical and as such persecuting possibilities must be presupposed from their very beginnings. By turning away from an isolated subject that is charged with mastering itself, its bifurcated individuated distance from vulnerability and relationality is undone. Vulnerability and relationality can be taken as primary after showing their proximity to the masterful isolated agency. The unbearable and persecuting responsibility to remain bounded to others and cherish proximate, non-reciprocal relations encourages prizing the difficult obligation to live otherwise and critiquing one's private will as the most decisive for moral life. Self-preservation is not the highest value nor are individuated identifications the most urgent need for preserving the self. After all, no one develops in total isolation, while at the same time each bond is necessarily held precariously with others. The primacy of leading an ethical life can shift to an enthrallment with each's relationality to others. While this condemns all to a mutual vulnerability and common exposure, prioritizing the ability to see the other as such prevents suppressing this vulnerability in violence.

I begin with the assumption that the Germans who lived under the National Socialist regime, for example, were not any different from anyone else. The contingencies of their lives demanded a particular vulnerability to the possibility of acting and killing for an Aryan ideal. By taking a step back from taxonomies that aim to understand the economic or social conditions that made them persecute, I look for those conditions that make persecution, or persecutory relations, possible in the first place. Only after addressing what about human existence makes it possible to persecute for moral ideals can a new horizon appear for moral theories that reduces the ever-present, and prevalent, phenomenon of persecuting and being persecuted. My limited focus on Jewish persecution has to do with its appearance in Freud and Lévinas's life. Certainly, however, the Jews were not the only group persecuted in the twentieth century that warrant their own study.

The method and conclusions reached here are like those developed in Abi Doukhan's book, *Emmanuel Lévinas: A Philosophy of Exile* (2012). The first section of Doukhan's work is dedicated to the biographical experiences and life of Lévinas in exile and, in it, Doukhan argues that Lévinas's lived world, *Lebenswelt*, influences his thinking on exile. Doukhan finds that the disruptive experience of living in exile and the need to confront the other is not only paradigmatic for an ethical relation, but that Lévinas can be shown to make the stronger claim where subjective identity, as such, is made,

> The encounter between subjectivity and the exiled other thus constitutes, according to Lévinas, the original ethical moment and encounter with otherness from which will be derived common principles and shared worldviews serving to preserve and protect that newly found other… it is precisely this disruptive intrusion of the exiled in a given society or world that constitutes the original moment of an awakening to the ethical dimension. (2012, pg. 4)

The scope of Doukhan's work on exile and social justice in Lévinas marks the difference between his study and the scope of this study on persecuting relations between individuals who seek to become ethical. Social relations of exile, for Lévinas, engage one, the other, and the unseen third. The ethical relation engages only two and focuses narrowly on individual attunement to the particulars of the other that one faces in an intersubjective relation.

More than Doukhan's scholarship on social exile, Robert Bernasconi's work on the nonphilosophical experience of persecution and the possibility of pluralism in Lévinas's ethics comes closer to my own work in this regard (1995, pg. 84). Bernasconi's focus on substitution as a lack of ontic freedom to choose the ethical relation, being one-for-the-other, shows how Lévinas challenges concepts of moral freedom and identity for a new approach in ethics. Accepting the invisible universality of persecution that makes each capable of responding to the face of the other, Bernasconi notes the particular attention Lévinas gives the Jewish experience of persecution. Bernasconi also notes Lévinas's scandalous favoritism of Greek and Hebraic philosophies for generalizing his understanding of ethical subjectivity. After asking how Lévinas can generalize from his particular experiences of persecution—anti-Semitism—to an "ontic fundament" for concepts of identity and ethics, Bernasconi returns to Lévinas's challenge to the Western approach on personal identity "as this or that." Various types of persecution can replace that to which only Lévinas can testify, his experiences of the persecution he suffered as a Jew. These created the particular biases and admittedly narrower scope in Lévinas's thinking, but which I would like to explore for general conditions of a self that is preoccupied with its particularities especially as it stands in a necessary relation to a threatening other.

Finally, the yield of this analysis in relation to Bernasconi agrees that Lévinas's reflection on his particular experiences can serve "other peoples as a model of how philosophy arises from nonphilosophical experiences. This is of particular importance to those people whose voices have been suppressed by the dominant language and logic of the tradition, especially to peoples who have also suffered persecution but whose philosophical presentation of it might be different from that found in Lévinas" (Bernasconi 1995, pg. 85). Lévinas can only give testimony to his own embodied experiences to develop a pre-ontological condition for his concept of ethical subjectivity, but by shifting the focus here that begins with particular social and historical experiences of persecution to the pre-ontological conditions of unknowability, relationality, and existential vulnerability, varying unphilosophical experiences of these impinging relations can begin to be heard. Still, there will need to be further work on the quantitative impact of an ontological incapacity to determine when persecuting means are used for personally conceived ethical ends in political, social, and legal frameworks.

Methodology, Field Interventions, and the Yields of this Work

In contrast to traditional moral theories that develop explicit standards and central categories of power and knowledge, Freud's hermeneutics of suspicion and Lévinas's post-phenomenology of trust work to "challeng[e] 'idealized models of man' that take exaggerated views of human capacities and autonomy, and which overlook the mundane realities of dependence, poverty and frailty" (Craig 1998). The ethical obligation reflects an inherent state of vulnerability when responsibility struggles to be known or reflected on. Given all that one is capable of formulating in reason, there always remains a surplus source of abuse, ethical superfluity, and always only arguably a superfluity of goodness. Freud and Lévinas conceive of this persecutory subjectivity which cannot be totally known, which is vulnerable in an impressionable constitution, and as such they are left wondering to what one remains obligated. Traditional notions of identity and moral freedom will be challenged, and the use of a phenomenological hermeneutics will yield three conditions for an ethical subjectivity that persecutes itself and others.

First it is helpful to understand that in Levinas's work, persecution is characterized by an accusation, and the persecuted one cannot offer a defense since they are "identified from the outside." In this ethic, a pre-ontological obligation forces an individuated self to go toward the other (Lévinas 1998, pg. 107). Disqualification of the apology, of language, or of what he significantly calls *logos* is the characteristic of persecution that for Lévinas also opens a space of one in the other.

Another significant relation between one with another beyond the mediation of logos is the ethical relation for Lévinas. Both persecution and the possibility of an ethical relation, therefore, come before the imperialism of any logic, economy of state authority, linguistic expression, or even normative moral rule. Similarly, for Freud guilt follows from an aggressive drive without the possibility of explaining the guilt away before its arrival. Lévinas makes an exception, however, by arguing that it is always possible in this confrontation between one and another that the other, who is also reflective of oneself, has the potential to destroy and recall one's absolute responsibility to preserve their life.

For Lévinas, an ethical relation arises when one is elected to witness the vulnerability of the other. The ethical relation occurs when the *visage* or face of another appears before any spoken word is even uttered. Persecution in this sense is defined "as the form in which the ego is affected, a form which is a defecting from consciousness" (Lévinas 1998, pg. 101). The effect of persecution is ethical subjectivity as such, and not, as Freud argues, an affect that a subject experiences when that subject feels hatred by or for another. Subjectivity as an empty site, a *non-lieu*, contains a constitutive obsession that aims at all neighboring thoughts, objects, and other subjects (Lévinas 1998, pg. 8). Accordingly, obsession characterizes the relational position as one of persecution, as one in which each is always affected before an individual decision is made.

Like the competing drives in Freud (1918, pg. 120),[3] for Lévinas infringements that come from others cannot be chosen or avoided and are decided from *otherwise* (Lévinas 1998, pg. 106). The otherwise is similar to that source from which we are granted existence and thrown into the world and to which we are taken after death; however, Lévinas preserves the distance of the other person, or "otherwise," when approached in a proximate relation to another person. Egoistic acts of deliberation and choice that are driven by individual desires remain suspended, or *passive*. The term "egoical" is introduced and stands to contrast "egoistic" since the latter implies a heightened, narcissistic involvement that cannot welcome the other beyond one's representations of them. For the egoical aspect of self, there is a refusal to allow any realization of a trace in what is concretely described as "the neighbor." What makes the neighbor so troubling for both these authors is the need to preserve an obligation to those who cannot be totalized in any labeled description, identification, or empirical quality while each also pursues their individuated interests. The balance between represented ideals and the bare address of the embodied suffering of another can be shown through the individual lives of Freud and Lévinas.

The goal of using their biographies is a hermeneutical one, for interpreting how events in their personal lives were significant for the development of their thought. The objective truth of their theories is bracketed, as much as the truth of their theories relative to psychoanalytic methodologies for Freud, and moral theories for Lévinas. For example, Freudian psychoanalysis is contentious in feminist literature for its occlusion of the female perspective, body, and, as such, psychoanalytic insight. His views will be repeated here not in agreement with them, but as reflecting a commitment to those social norms even as he challenged them. By bracketing the question of objectivity and arguable misogynistic tones of Freud's work, I can place the subversive method to which he was committed in conversation with the expectations and moral norms of the time to glimpse his personal sense of deep ambivalence and psychological unrest.

The truth of these theoretical approaches was trustworthy for the men who spent their life's work articulating them, which will be the focus of the investigation here.

---

[3] It is important to note that here Freud develops this instinct-like knowledge in *From the History of an Infantile Neurosis* by using the German word for a more biological *instinktiv* rather than *triebhaft* to speak about "some sort of hardly definable knowledge, something, as it were, preparatory to an understanding" that is particularly concerned with sexual life. He does offer an analogy for this knowledge to the instinctive knowledge of animals. It is "the nucleus of the unconscious, a primitive kind of mental activity, which would later be dethroned and overlaid by human reason … which retain the power of drawing down to it the higher mental processes," 120.

How plausible is it to hold to the truth of one's personal convictions against broader social demands? After grasping the reasons for which each person is inherently vulnerable (such as their condition of unknowability and relationality) and constitutionally predisposed to the persecutory relation, by developing Lévinas's notion of intentionalities of search I explore what ethical safeguards are available to prevent egregious acts of violence against oneself and others in the name of personal convictions. The hermeneutical and phenomenological methods are used in sections that look at the personal lives of Sigmund Freud and Emmanuel Lévinas alongside their theoretical writing on the persecutory self. Through their personal and social alienation during the Nazi occupation of France and Germany, both Freud and Lévinas pursued the topic of persecution as a central theme in their theoretical reflections on the moral individual in relation to social life.

Both Lévinas and Freud work through a world in which, for them, the *Deus* has absconded from the everyday world. In human failure, in pathologies of mourning, and in great loss, there is no transcendental guarantee. Freud wrote about the increasingly persecutory spirit that took different forms before World War I and up until World War II. Where Freud stops, stutters, and reformulates what he sees as the destructive future in making cultural bonds, Lévinas can be seen to pick up the reformulation despite fundamental differences in their thought. Like Freud, Lévinas asserts that the ethical moment is neither the result of an individual desire nor conscious choice. Lévinas describes the ethical relation as anarchical, lacking any mode of intentionality, an infinitude. Through moments of this impossibility, Lévinas concludes that human beings become obligated to each other. Even with the infinite gap that exists between each individual, language can carry one over these disabled states of being.

According to the historical timeline, Lévinas wrote *Otherwise Than Being, or Beyond Essence* in 1974 after he saw the historical devastation that Freud already started to predict in the 1930s. The horrors of the *Shoa* penetrated Lévinas's personal life: he was sent to a work camp as a French soldier and most of his immediate Lithuanian family was murdered. Threatened by anti-Semitism that tended to alienate his Jewish identity from the definition of humanity, Lévinas aimed to restore the significance of a subjectivity that is always ethically obligated. For him, secular humanism could not ensure that one would always be responsible for the other to prevent the horrors he witnessed. When ethics is the first order of philosophy, as Lévinas famously declares, subjectivity can be understood as the unique possibility to give thanks, teach, and become responsible for another in ways that are not reduced to economies of liberal decision-making, erotic pleasure, and instinctual aggression (Lévinas 1998, pg. 128).

Writing on the ontological condition of persecution after living through the horrors of World War II, Lévinas uses simplified terms of "self," "other," and "the third." While each individual is rooted to a sensing body, no one is ultimately separate from any other. The self, Lévinas argues, can only be itself in relation to a threatening other. Living in proximity to others will always break the security and safety of an isolated self. There is no way to decline or remain indifferent to this relation. Persecution is characterized as an anarchic possibility where the other exercises a power over the self. This interruption leaves the persecuted one speechless. The worst forms of persecution are left unnamed and unnamable in this ontological interruption of the aspect of self that fancies itself isolated from others. In the final chapters, I show that when the impinging relation is faced with a welcome, then the language of the persecutory individual turns to ethical subjectivity.

More than reparations that one may deserve for justice, Lévinas's sense of pre-ontological persecution recognizes the inherent vulnerability of this relation to appear at any time, for anyone, and without apology. Persecution for a moral ideal expels one from their place without an ability to apologize for whatever is their "fault." One's zealous pursuit of the other does not consider the particular individual who is persecuted, but only sees a represented quality of the threatening other. Strategies will be suggested such as doses of intellectual humility or empathy that can remove the zeal attached to idealized representations.

Looking at Freud and Lévinas's historical circumstances can be helpful for understanding their theoretical work, for each wondered what could remain of a moral life when developments in technology were used mostly as a means to plot mass genocide, de-humanization, and acts of persecution against whole facets of society. In a time when dominant progress narratives in Western society correlated a rise in intellectual virtues with a rise in moral virtue for a more benevolent and social humanism, it was devastating for many to realize that the enlightened cultural environment of the time was not sufficient to prevent the atrocities of both World Wars. Many citizens of the world that justified mass murder and genocide admitted much of their shame and regret only after the nuclear dust settled. In this book, I will explore personal details from the lives of Freud and Lévinas that reveal their biases in their thinking on persecution. Freud's rejection by a scientific community that he held in high regard through his life will explain his borderline concept of *trieb* and awkward formulations of principle drives.[4] His tumultuous relations with colleagues also provide a background for his theory on a frustrated homosexual drive as the cause of paranoiac delusions of persecution. A similar type of personal bias about Palestinians and certain Germans resulted from Lévinas's personal traumas that place significant limits to his theory of ethical possibilities, while his theory on openness also explains the diverse range of friends he did maintain through life. My reflection on details from their lives that relate to persecuting relations must always be remembered against their worlds of highly destructive historical events. In no

---

[4] Freud's use of *Trieb* in German will be translated as drive, rather than its more common translation and use of a biological instinct. Freud's articulation of a *Geisteswissenschaften*, or science of the spirit, did not want to be limited or reduced to the mind's biology in natural science, which would transform psychoanalysis into a *Naturwissenschaften*. Drive preserves *Trieb* as a more metaphoric or borderline aspect of the mind, and its implication that psychoanalysis is a speculative field and not a positivist one. Freud's constant repetition of his use and subversion of positivistic standards for science reveals a primary concern. *Distantiation* in the spirit of Ricœur leads me to question in the final paragraphs of this section whether Freud really believed he did something different from the goals of science or still aimed to please its standards.

way is there a judgment here of their characters, only a glance at their life-world to reckon with that which made them vulnerable, and with their complex humanity.[5]

A second significant overall yield of this work is to propose three conditions for the ethical subject that persecutes itself and others. From the lives and works of Freud and Lévinas on the persecutory relation, three clusters of characteristics emerge as general axes that work through each respective chapter in each thinker. The three characteristics for the self that persecutes are that it is: unknowable, relational, and vulnerable.

The first characteristic focuses on how one is largely unknowable to oneself and incapable of reflecting on one's motives because of the ambiguous grounds of an embodied life. Freud was constantly worried about his acceptance in the positivist and scientific community, while also experiencing fraught relationships with his protégés who could not accept his axiomatic principles in psychoanalysis. Lévinas, who lived through a holocaust perpetuated against the Jewish people, had to contend with life after the wars, but also felt ambivalent about speaking against the Jewish State in its controversial infancy. In both their lives, controversial actions that seem to arise from hidden motives are explained considering their ambivalence in these important personal relationships.

My narrative about their lives and theories begins with Freud's experiences of a pre-World War I era where he witnessed a frantic excitement for the barbarisms of war, while he also wrote on the anti-moral, anti-religious, and punitive measures of the psyche. Experiences in the life of Lévinas beginning with these World Wars, as he watched the rise and fall of the fanatically excited barbarism Freud witnessed, which led to Lévinas's writing a post-phenomenological account of an ethical self who is only as real as in those moments of an ethical demand. The last section on Lévinas's intentionality of search will, therefore, contribute to the field of phenomenology that can expand toward moral sensibilities and the ethics of being in this world.

The first sections in each thinker's chapter include Freud's hermeneutic of suspicion and Lévinas's importance of the non-phenomenal "face" as *visage*. Mastering a divided and unknowable self is put in doubt. Each thinker's first sections emphasize the characteristic of unknowability, thus indicating the insufficiency of reason to approach a persecutory subjectivity that leaves only the appearance of traces, symbols, and signs in others. These do not come with a faculty to decode them. Even if early in his career Freud strived to do this with the symbolisms in dreams, by the end of it this sort of endeavor was abandoned in despair. The "face" as *visage* is how Lévinas similarly thinks the subject can relate to others that precede thoughtful knowledge. Lévinas's post-phenomenological approach illustrates a quintessential error of knowing and essentializing the qualities of a masterful individuated ego, a realization that Freud makes by the end of his career despite the ego's seeming ability to control the id's impulses through rational reflection (Freud 1923a).

---

[5] I want to thank Avital Ronell who raised the concern about reflecting on these figures given their incommensurate time.

The persecutory and ethical subject, also called the relational person, precedes all categories of self while necessitating these categories. The duality of these relations for a person that becomes ethical or persecutory illustrates the necessity of using egoical identifications while also never remaining identical to them. The central role that unconscious infantile impressions have in drives also indicates the incapacity for a positivist's approach to find an essential truth represented at the core of oneself. Reparative relations, for example those Melanie Klein finds in object-relational psychoanalysis, are then non-negotiable to the powers of reason.

My development of unknowability in these first sections is useful for finding ways to negotiate between the other who does not appear, but who can still make demands. For Freud's hermeneutics of suspicion, which requires effort to decode the objects of one's desires, awareness of an essential unknowability of the other can prevent masochistic relations and a morality driven by guilt. If unconscious phantasy plays a large part in ego formation and limits the possibility of conscious relations that exceed the narcissistic self, then acknowledging an unexpected other can diversify what Freud understood as the homosexual components of emotional life that build social bonds. I will show how economies of masochism based on a primary narcissism, for Freud, become bankrupt when an unexpected relation to the other is welcomed for a change of self. A final turn in the section on Freud will turn to intersubjective approaches in psychoanalysis that have found ways for welcoming the other to negotiate psychic guilt.

The second characteristic of the persecutory subject is its vulnerability, or fragility—its inability to be totalized by various categorizations and labels that are made by each individual. Freud comes to understand various vicissitudes and disturbances that arise in a psyche that desires objects that remain largely unknown to processes of self-reflection. The desire to preserve psychic stability against various sexual excitations will cause the latter to include aggression. These vicissitudes and processes such as sublimation, repression, and delusions of persecution are protective measures for restoring stability in the face of conflicting desires according to Freud. By reversing unacceptable objects of desire into ones that are feared (or through imaginary explanations of safety avoid acknowledging real threats in one's environment that is invested with libidinal relations), one avoids confronting internal psychic disturbances and remains vulnerable to any excitation from both imagined and real objects. The high risk then becomes persecuting the external object in relation to the internal perception of persecution that results from one's guilt.

Egoical and relational modalities of self are introduced to extend Freud's thought on the topographies of mind toward Lévinas's ethical subjectivity and to distinguish between the different types of excitement in Freud. One appears to be fixed in these desires and objects at which they compulsively aim without the possibility of apologizing, escaping, or forming new associations out of them; however, Lévinas's understanding of substitution is seen as one way of escaping the self by finding the other there. With an admission to the difficult, asymmetrical, and affective impingement that an openness in substitution for the other inflicts, the relational subject is realized. It will be argued that the persecutory subject is vulnerable in this openness to thematization and enthrallment with others, vulnerable to these necessary enthrallments that can at the same time foreclose ethical subjectivity in the interest of the egoical self.

The third characteristic of the persecutory subject is its relational aspect. Relations of proximity that do not occlude oneself or the other can preserve indeterminacy of the self. Welcoming the asymmetry in different types of moral responses that follow from contingent relations requires developing particular abilities. Attunement to the particular other is necessary and necessarily varied according to these contingencies; however, each relational person is equally formed out of these different vulnerabilities in them. An ethical relation, or more general moral injunctions, cannot then be given in advance. Instead an attunement to always particular asymmetries in power and abilities is necessary. Bearing witness, integration, and psychic reparation are ways that intersubjective psychoanalysis has approached what Lévinas wrote on an ethics of substitution, a relation that values a disruption that comes from the other. A non-erotic proximity to the other is necessary, not for fulfilling the egoical need to repair trauma in one's ego, but precisely to disrupt the ego for finding a self in the other. In addition to substitution, I tracked Lévinas's ambiguous use of "being-for-the-other" that realizes the relational subject. In injuring the egoical self, the relational subject reaches its ethical height.

In no way is my goal to simply present these authors' background as proof for the correctness of their theory. The argument is also not ad hominem—that is, my intention is not to claim their position is valid because these thinkers have automatic credibility. Neither is the claim made that their thoughts on persecution or subjectivity are correct because they came about during a historical moment that witnessed one of the world's most atrocious moral, racial, and religious persecutions. I make no presumption of knowing the personal thoughts, intentions, and motivations of these individuals beyond what can be gleaned from common anecdotal stories in their lives and their theories in conjunction with their time and place in history. Finally, these explications on their tumultuous lives in relation to their theories should not limit the validity of their claims on persecution and its implication on ethics to their specific context, nor does their context limit the general validity of their claims on the persecutory subject.

Rather, I suggest that their personal lives can illuminate conditions that made their theories possible, as much as they show how moral failure for their standards is possible. Both thinkers wrote on the phenomenon of persecution and show the difficulties of an ethical bind as they conceived. The ways I interpret the interplay between the generalizability of their claims can expose where their personal biases and vulnerability to their social norms manifest and how these men did or did not overcome their own limited perspectives. Personal examples from their lives in relation to their theoretical insights orient us toward a future horizon beyond the use of psychosis and delusions of persecution as a means for psychic repair, as Freud theorized at the height and decline of an enlightened modern era. This work is also meant to extend Lévinas's endeavor to show how an ontologically bound life of each one to its other is traumatic, but for which a salve may be offered in a mutual recognition.

Both Lévinas and Freud use the term persecution (and its associated concepts) differently, and I will trace the sources of these differences in their personal lives. Freud uses persecution in the more colloquial sense of being targeted and singled out for different aspects of one's identity or actions. Delusions of persecution are internalized feelings of guilt that are projected onto someone else. One feels paranoid and chased by another who represents one's personal feelings of guilt, judgment, and shame. In logics of contradiction, the other requires those qualities that remind an individual of their guilt. The thin border between mental ideations that drive desires in psychosis and more common forms of perception yield conclusions for more general mental functions. Some of this is compatible with the view Lévinas has of persecution where there is an inability to apologize or decline what one is in social relations of persecution. In addition to the colloquial use, Lévinas uses this term in a seemingly hyperbolical way to talk about a subject that is ontologically persecuted to become ethical.

On the one hand, biographical interpretations will attempt to describe the way these authors found themselves in the world. On the other hand, my recourse to what Paul Ricœur calls distantiation—that is, "of placing at a distance" every consciousness of meaning—leads me to constantly interrogate and construct a view of Freud and Lévinas after an amount of suspicion is cast on their self-reflections. Suspicion in this sense does not refer to deceptions that the authors are presumed to have made with the full awareness of their deceits. Frederick Crews casts suspicion on Freud, his method, and motives in his biography, *Freud: The Making of an Illusion* (2017). Crews assume that Freud is aware of his misuse of the psychoanalytic technique as it is being developed, and intentionally playing a ruse at the expense of his patients. Freud appears anxious about his legitimacy from the many self-deprecating claims he makes about himself and his method in various personal letters. Taken in the larger context of his overall pessimism about the worth and integrity of the individual psyche, and the exacerbating condition of guilt that results from cultural production, however, I find that his ruses are barely intentional in the way that Crews argues.

In several places, Freud makes the general claim that all egos know at bottom their worthlessness, but that they need to deceive themselves about this in order to survive. He argues for this in *Mourning and Melancholia* (1917) and in a private correspondence with his friend Arnold Zweig in order to dissuade him from writing Freud's biography. Instead of deeming Freud unusual or intentionally malicious, I move forward with the admittedly psychoanalytic assumption that one's motives are largely unknowable to one's self. An incorrect interpretation of his dream may not have been an intentional ruse, but a way of protecting his ego from realizing a painful truth. As such, even acts of self-deception are meaningful for what they reveal about their author's worldview, priorities, shortcomings, and values.

In this hermeneutics of suspicion and process of distantiation, we would ask to whom Freud revealed these self-deprecating admissions, when, and what may have shifted in his life to allow him to realize an error in interpreting the dream of Irma's injection, one example where his personal desires betrayed his analytic rigor.

Distantiation at once also requires remembering that no one can ever inhabit or belong to any author's world; thus, this method simultaneously questions the generalizability and objectivity of the claims explicated here about these individual persons. The attempt is to unearth those aspects in their lives that caused trauma and need for a psychic defense. In this way, their possible moral shortcomings are more fully articulated, not excused or justified. The vicissitudes of desire and its effects that Freud articulated lead to Lévinas's adoption of a "hermeneutics of suspicion," but to him it presupposes a trust that any fissure of a fragmented self still expresses an identity that is truthfully building a substantive (albeit fragmented) and always particular person. Every moment in life, Lévinas reassures his reader, is accompanied by an event, the event of birth (Lévinas 2001, pg. 22). In these moments, one can foreclose their unsettling relation to the other or coordinate themselves in a relationship. More than just looking at Lévinas's theoretical works, I want to trace the difficulty implicit in his ethic that leaves none to be free of the psychological and ontological trauma that these relations imply. Lévinas as a person was born into social norms and is no exception to what is often considered his hyperbolic ethical demand, but who I find is realistic of its violence to individual notions of self.

My method can be broadly defined as hermeneutic and phenomenological, or what Paul Ricœur calls a hermeneutical phenomenology. Both methods according to Ricœur find fulfillment in interpretation, *Auslegung*, as explication and exegesis of these lives and objectifying attitudes that enable constructing meanings. Ricœur instructs us "that it may be that extreme iconoclasm belongs to the restoration of meaning" (1970, pg. 27). The following explications aim to elaborate the meanings in Freud's and Lévinas's unsaid expressions, omissions, and the non-ostensive references from their texts and lives. An example of the attempt to restore meaning using non-ostensive references from a personal life is to look at Lévinas's traditional Jewish learning that influences his personal life and career, though the extent is arguable. Similarly, Freud's use of fiction for gleaning general psychoanalytic insights is the basis for my argument that his interpretation of E.T.A. Hoffman's "The Sandman" reveals Freud's own repressed acknowledgment of the possibility that moral norms can contradict each other. The knowledge is seen as repressed in Freud's text because his hostile era began to confirm the uncanny truth at the expense of Jewish bodies, which was too unsettling for Freud to believe about his beloved society in Vienna. In this willingness to listen to the historical signs and symbols of their personal lives, I develop a creative engagement with their theories, and a sort of re-telling of their lives.

As much as these forays into the details of their lives open new registers and horizons of interpretation, these strings of interpretation simultaneously close others. To find strict causal relations between the events of their lives and theories is not the purpose of these explications. In Lévinas's terms, this would totalize their identity in ways that could never be done. None of the traces left from their lives can inhabit the worlds under each of their skin. Details will be given, some connections and associations bundled into specific themes, and some details will not be reconciled with the rest.

In terms of the phenomenological method, the transcendental reduction to a subjective idealism is avoided by interpreting each author's lived experiences. More than just their writing or words, I attempt to go back to the world that constituted their meanings. Along with understanding history as an unfolding of objective and successive events in a single law of causality, the multifarious possibilities of meaning, the finitude of their knowledge, and the transmission of their traditions can strengthen our link to them through their historical context.

In particular, the purpose of understanding Freud and Lévinas in their life's context is to answer a series of hermeneutical questions about the persecutory subject: For what and who were these texts written, and is it possible to read the author as vulnerable to those same reasons they articulate in their work that lead one to persecute another? What do their personal failings, read alongside failings of the persecutory subject as such, reveal about the general ways in which one can fail to be, or become, ethically responsible? To investigate these questions, I go back to the reservoir of the meaning of their life's experiences and traumas that at times injected vital emotional layers in their theories.

In sections on the personal lives of Freud and Lévinas, I choose specific scenarios and details to capture the contexts from which each author wrote, such as Lévinas's surviving a war camp. Their hyperbolic and different conclusions about the prospect of ethical relations—for Freud, its impossibility; for Lévinas, its necessity—are preceded by experiences in their lives of persecution as Jewish people and intellectuals. Their conclusions may seem antithetical to one another; however, the comparisons between their lives and theories move between the subject who is put in question and a world to which each is responding.

By positing these authors next to their theories to show how personal prejudices, or forceful imaginations, are created, I illustrate how these writers are a happening of their own limited truth. More than showing their intellectual limits, by reflecting on the historical conditions that gave rise to these inquiries we may indirectly develop theories of self and other. As a historical object, the necessity of being exposed to others constitutes the social and ethical relation for both their lives and ours.

The final sections examine how those experiences in Lévinas's life lead to his theoretical shift from the isolated subject to the relational inter-subject. Freud's presence in this work takes seriously the difficulty, or even impossibility, of ever leading a moral life given the changes and amplification of aggressive drives in psychological concealment. I will also take seriously the similarities and differences that hyperbolic reactions, such as the hysteric's psychosis in paranoid delusions of persecution, have to more stable psychic processes. Paranoiac delusions are an extreme position that exhibits the mind's desire-not-to-know and easily confounds its *Enstellung*, a distortion, in place of a presentation for one's wish, desire, or *Darstellung* that happens to lesser degrees in regular psychic processes. Like in Lévinas, these wishes and desires prevent a unified self that can be moral in the traditional sense. As I engage in the proto-typical ways that Freud found that the psyche transforms and substitutes its drives and desired objects, I also interpret when this confusion happened for Freud and Lévinas in their embodied lives, assuming their thought results from the reflections of particular bodies.

Friedrich Nietzsche wrote in *Beyond Good and Evil* that to him it is clear that "every great philosophy so far has been: namely, the personal confession of its author and a kind of involuntary and unconscious memoir; also that the moral (or immoral) intentions in every philosophy constituted the real germ of life from which the whole plant had grown" (Nietzsche 1886/1966, pg. 13). As much as there is a psychoanalytic approach here, I employ phenomenological hermeneutics to find Freud's and Lévinas's personal confessions.

In *Institution and Interpretation*, Samuel Weber writes that "[w]hat psychoanalysis suggests – and this may be its most telling contribution and challenge, to hermeneutics – is that the rules of this game are made not merely to be discovered and enforced, but also, and above all, to be broken and transformed" (1987, pg. 84). The closeness of the themes in their theories and the proximity between the *Lebenswelt*, or lived world, of Lévinas and Freud demand not only a critical consideration of their writing, but also questioning how their writing is a serious re-consideration of our lives as persecutory, always also hopelessly grasping for its moral viability; the terms that each used to reflect on the self's agency parallel how they conducted themselves in personal relationships.

The following work will adopt their different terms; for example, "ethical subjectivity" as one that is formed through our subjection to the other is used for consistency with the relational views of self that Lévinas argues for in chapter 4 of *Otherwise Than Being or Beyond Essence* (1998), which contrast individuated notions of self and moral values that idealize a "subject's" personal desire for self-mastery. The terms ego and egoical reflect the psychic apparatus according to Freud's understanding that led him to moral skepticism. The notion of a "masterful self" includes philosophical discussions of agency and the capacity for reflecting on one's values, freedoms, and vulnerabilities to choose and act for that which is perceived as good. In other words, the self is one that doubts whether it can become an ethical subjectivity considering the impinging egoical relations through which the individuated subject is forged.

Both sections, the first on Freud and the second on Lévinas, begin with their general historical circumstances. As the sections develop, each chapter focuses on particular details and scenarios from their personal lives that are related to their theories for showing limits in the consistency of their theories. The second chapter on persecution in Freud's life uses Peter Gay's biography *Freud: A Life of Our Times* to show how he coped with an unrequited love for a positivist scientific community and for his homeland in Vienna. The main texts used are Freud's *Interpretation of Dreams*, *An Infantile Neurosis*, and *The Ego and the Id*. As the chronology of his life develops toward the two World Wars, the third chapter on the uncanniness of moral ambivalence illustrates Freud's difficult realization of the ambiguous grounds of morality, and how moral standards can reach conflicting claims from his work "The Uncanny" in *Civilization and Its Discontents*. Chapter 4 on Freud's life from his *Autobiographical Study* traces how disappointing libidinal attachments in his personal life created a psychic vulnerability to ignore the atrocities developing in his hometown and shows how his work on suspecting one's proclaimed motives in *The Case of Schreber* contributed to mistrusting his own judgments for emigrating from Vienna. The chapter culminates to show Freud's moral skepticism late in life through works such as *The Economic Problems of Masochism, Civilization and Its Discontents*, and his personal correspondence with Einstein on the possibility of eliminating war. On display is his limited hope for finding a sense of morality that could decrease individual aggressions that were amplifying in social reality before his death. Chapter 5 explores object relations that begin with Sándor Ferenczi's work and Donna Orange's intersubjective approaches to psychoanalysis that have found empathy and other reparative psychic measures for renewed ethical possibilities where Freud did not find any.

After reaching a height in the psychoanalytic literature that culminates in an ethical subject, in spite of Freud's skepticism, my intermission looks closer at intersubjective approaches in psychoanalysis that lead into answering whether Lévinas's insistence on ethics as first philosophy considered the moral skepticism Freud problematized. After setting up the general circumstances of Lévinas's personal life through Malka Salomon's biography *Emmanuel Levinas: His Life and Legacy* in relation to his ethics in *Otherwise Than Being or Beyond Essence* that conceives of an individuated subject that is pre-ontologically persecuted to find itself in another in Chap. 6, new concepts of freedom that result from gaps in epistemic knowledge are yielded and demonstrated in Chap. 7 through Lévinas's works *Otherwise Than Being* and *Existence and Existents*, and in light of Freud's work in *A Difficulty in the Path of Psychoanalysis*. Chapter 8 looks further through Lévinas's *Reflections on the Philosophy of Hitlerism, Difficult Freedom*, and *Entre Nous* at the relation between Lévinas's notion of freedom for dis-identifying oneself in proximity to another and the existential vulnerability to foreclose the infinitude in ethical subjectivity, valuing totalized qualities, and risking ontic forms of persecution. Lévinas is considered to have hermeneutics of trust upon which a hermeneutics of suspicion is also possible, whereas for Freud and psychoanalysis there is only the latter. More than just looking at Lévinas's theoretical works, I want to trace the difficulty implicit in his ethic that leaves none to be free of the trauma that these relations imply or the inevitable disconnect between language and meaning. Lévinas as a person was born into social norms and is no exception to what is often considered his hyperbolic ethical demand, but who I find is realistic of its violence to individual notions of self.

On the back of a hermeneutic of trust, an intentionality of search is offered in the final chapter. Going beyond Lévinas, there is the beginning effort to think about an ethic that does not require a fully rational agency but instead values a form of intentionality that constitutes subjectivity through a mutual apprehension of the other. The work ends with a final request, an appeal, or maybe even a plea, for each reader to wonder when they may have used persecutory means to achieve moral ends.

References

Arendt, H. (1970) *On violence*. New York: Harcourt, Brace, Jovanovich.
Bernasconi, R. (1995). "Only the persecuted…": Language of the oppressor, language of the oppressed. In A. T. Peperzak (Ed.), *Ethics as first philosophy: The significance of Emmanuel Lévinas for philosophy, literature and religion* (pp. 77–86). New York: Routledge.
Buckle, H. T. (1878). *History of civilization in England*. Book 1 of 3. Toronto: Rose-Belford Publishing Company.
Butler, J. (2004). *Precarious life: The powers of mourning and violence*. London: Verso.
Butler, J. (2005). *Giving and account of oneself*. New York: Fordham University Press.
Christenson, R. (1968). The political theory of persecution: Augustine and Hobbes. *Midwest Journal of Political Science, 12*(3), 419–438.
Craig, E. (1998). Vulnerability. In *Routledge encyclopedia of philosophy*. New York: Routledge.
Crews, F. (2017). *Freud: The making of an illusion*. New York: Metropolitan Books.
Doukhan, A. (2012). *Emmanuel Lévinas: A philosophy of exile*. United Kingdom: Bloomsbury Studies in Continental Philosophy.
Freud, S. (1917). The Standard Edition of the Complete Psychological Works of Sigmund Freud. In J. Strachey (Ed.), *Volume XIV Mourning and Melancholia*. London: The Hogarth Press and the Institute of Psycho-analysis, 1957.
Freud, S. (1953). The standard edition of the complete psychological works of Sigmund Freud. In J. Strachey (Ed.), *The interpretation of dreams (second part) and on dreams, i–iv* (Vol. V, 1900). London: The Hogarth Press and the Institute of Psycho-analysis.
Freud, S. (1955). The standard edition of the complete psychological works of Sigmund Freud. In J. Strachey (Ed.), *An infantile neurosis and other works* (Vol. XVII, 1918). London: The Hogarth Press and the Institute of Psycho-analysis.
Freud, S. (1961a). The standard edition of the complete psychological works of Sigmund Freud. In J. Strachey (Ed.), *The ego and the id* (Vol. XIX, 1923a). London: The Hogarth Press and the Institute of Psycho-analysis.
Freud, S. (1961b). The standard edition of the complete psychological works of Sigmund Freud. In J. Strachey (Ed.), *The economic problem of masochism* (Vol. XIX, 1923b). London: The Hogarth Press and the Institute of Psycho-analysis.
Freud, S. (1961c). The standard edition of the complete psychological works of Sigmund Freud. In J. Strachey (Ed.), *Civilization and its discontents, and other works* (Vol. XXI, 1930). London: The Hogarth Press and the Institute of Psycho-analysis.
Fiske, J. (1881). The philosophy of persecution. *The North American Review, 132*(290), 1–17.
Lévinas, E. (1998). *Otherwise than being: Beyond essence* (trans: Lingis, A.). New York: Duquesne University Press.
Lévinas, E. (2001). *Existence and existents* (trans: Lingis, A.). New York: Duquesne University Press.
Mackenzie, C. (2013). *Vulnerability: New essays in ethics and feminist philosophy*. New York: Oxford University Press.
Nietzsche, F. (1886 [1966]). *Beyond good and evil: Prelude to a philosophy of the future* (trans: Kaufmann, W.). New York: Vintage Books.
Ricœur, P. (1970). *Freud and philosophy: An essay on interpretation*. New Haven/London: Yale University Press.
Weber, S. (1987). *Institution and interpretation: Theory and history of literature*. Minneapolis: University of Minnesota Press.

Part I
Sigmund Freud

Chapter 2
Freud's Life and Work: A Historical Horizon

Abstract In this chapter, I illustrate through the details of Freud's life that his theoretical work on a fragmented subjectivity shows it as vulnerable to the affective force of cultural norms, and as such, limits the capacity for self-reflection. I list the psychic mechanisms that he found prevent one from knowing themselves in order to present challenges to traditional moral accounts of a self-mastering identity.

Keywords Freud's life · Schreber's paranoid delusions · Libidinal desires · Desire to persecute · Aggressive impulse · Libidinal homosexuality · *Kristallnacht* · Idealized social bonds · Persecuting the other · Hermeneutics of suspicion

Freud's work on his case study of Daniel Paul Schreber's delusions of persecution begins with a quote: "I have suffered twice from nervous disorders" (1911, pg. 12). Through the words and memoirs of another, Freud begins to expose and evaluate the mechanism of forming delusions of persecution. According to his observations as a therapist, it is impossible for one to perceive the motives of one's own mental life while having delusions. Another person must approach paranoid expressions "with a suspicion" by listening for examples, quotes, and negative claims (Freud 1911, pg. 35). If examples are cited, they then take the place of an original event. If a quote is given, then it expresses a sentiment of the speaker, and if a negative statement is given, then it needs to be reversed to reveal the cause of an illness. Even if Freud's work on delusions proceeds through Daniel Schreber, the work opens with an implication about himself.

It is interesting then that the whole work on paranoid delusions of persecution is based on the memoirs of another man. Later, when Freud begins his section on the mechanisms of paranoia, he admits to his reader that he could not trust his "own experience on the subject" (1911, pg. 59). Only with the help of Carl Jung and Sándor Ferenczi was he able to attribute all observed cases of paranoid disorders "as a means of warding off a homosexual wishful phantasy."[1] Does the quote reveal that Freud originally suffered nervous disorders of paranoia and so was only capable of studying them with the help of others?

More details about Schreber's case study and its relation to Freud's personal life will come later, but it is telling that Freud's conclusion is that frustrated sexual desires aiming at another who is similar to oneself destroy the other, as much as the internal love of oneself. In the second edition of *Three Essays on the Theory of Sexuality* (1953), Freud included a footnote that bisexuality and homoeroticism constitute the first stages of development for all human beings. Many correspondences with colleagues such as Wilhelm Fleiss and Carl Jung include admissions of his own homosexual feelings (Herzog 2017).[2] His admissions reveal that his personal homosexual feelings were more of an intellectual than physical nature, but I wonder how much of their nature he could readily admit because of social restrictions on homosexual relations. Feminist critiques later question Freud's idea that a homoerotic narcissism is the foundation for development of self that must be overcome for building social relations with others (Dean and Lane 2001). At his time, however, when heterosexual norms dictated social norms and excluded others as criminal, then any deviance could lead to neurotic disorders according to Freud's own lights.

Neurotic and psychotic symptoms can be found in Freud's personal life, though he would not be able to reflect on them without the help of colleagues. Like concealed motives, the behavior that arises from delusions of persecution cannot sufficiently indicate the source of the delusion. Once paranoid delusions emerge, ideas transform into fantastic illusions and can only be deciphered by another, preferably a psychoanalyst. Freud's development of the hidden processes of the unconscious that form contradictions in conscious paranoia (Dean and Lane 2001) occurs while Freud must realize that his behaviors cannot reveal his own impulses.

One of the strengths of Freud's work in psychology was showing the unbridgeable disjunction between those outward signs, representations, and meanings that make up one's understanding of oneself and their motivating causes. Authors have tried to do away with the insight of a disjunctive mind by accusing Freud of generalizing his own paranoia to their general intellectual and rhetorical structures. In addi-

---

[1] Ibid. In Freud's early works "Creative Writers and Day-Dreaming" and "Hysterical Phantasies and their Relation to Bisexuality" (1908), he uses *phantasy* to denote instinctual excitations from the earliest libidinal phases. These early sexual drives are not tested by the reality principle that comes in later developmental stages. As such, these early phantasies do not include representational objects. In the early stages of autoeroticism, for example, phantasy does not depend on real objects for its satisfaction. Only experiences of trauma that breach the psychical libido bring this desire to conscious awareness. Symptoms include compulsion repetitions. See also *An Infantile Neurosis*, 103, ftnt. 1. Melanie Klein will later make a similar distinction between conscious fantasy and unconscious phantasy, but she subordinates unconscious phantasy to the equally strong destructive drive that accompanies the pleasure principle. See Melanie Klein and Joan Reviere, *Love, Hate and Reparation: Two Lectures* (London: Hogarth, 1937).

[2] See Chap. 2.

tion to Frederick Crews, another such author is John Farrell who writes in *Freud's Paranoid Quest: Psychoanalysis and Modern Suspicion*,

> At every level Freud's evidence was contaminated with his own interpretative activity. We can see with hindsight that his great persuasiveness lay in providing a new, hidden locus of meaning, the unconscious, and using it as a Cartesian starting point from which the psychological world could be systematically rebuilt after the demolition of the pre-existing cultural order. The potency of this maneuver lies not in explanation but in interpretation, in an interpretation grounded in suspicion. (Farrell 1996, pg. 208)

Freud's arguments about an ego separated from an id and super-ego can be seen in a negative way as in Farrell's charge where representations cannot reveal a true self that resides in the unconscious mind. "Paranoid" Freud himself cannot evade the changes and vicissitudes that his truest, but unconscious, desires undergo. These are kept unconscious from his awareness. The general claim Farrell presumes Freud makes from his own paranoia is that mere interpretation can offer coherence of one's past experiences, rather than provide an explanation based on real events that lurk only as a Cartesian "hidden locus of meaning."

Another way to approach Freud's position on the self's motivations, however, is to see these activities of the mind as the only self. There is no coherence of meaning or a singular self who is built out of the bundle of objectively experienced memories that is lurking in the unconscious as a hidden locus of meaning.[3] There is neither a Cartesian starting point nor the possibility for a systematic rebuilding of what remains only riveted and fragmented knots of psychological drives. The second interpretation more easily corresponds with a sentiment Freud expressed in a letter to Arnold Zweig during their correspondence between 1927 and 1939 (Freud et al. 1987). Zweig was an admired writer, psychoanalyst, and personal friend of Freud's who expressed interest in writing his biography. Freud sought to deter him from engaging in such work and told Zweig that any attempt at a biographical retelling commits itself to "lies, concealments, hypocrisy, flattery and even to hiding his own lack of understanding, for biographical trust does not exist, and even if it did we could not use it" (Freud et al. 1987, pg. 127). In this same letter, Freud moves from the general claim about reconstructing one's biography to a statement about its truth as such. Biographical truth "is unobtainable, (and) mankind does not deserve it" because, as we read in *Mourning and Melancholia*, the acute melancholic perspective sees the psyche as "petty, egoistic, dishonest, lacking in independence, one whose sole aim has been to hide the weaknesses of his own nature" (1917, pg. 246). In 1923, Freud further develops in *The Ego and the Id* the stronger claim that the super-ego maintains an admonishing and destructive attitude toward the ego.

Freud's insight was not just that his work was contaminated with his personal life. Freud's insight was that everyone's ego is contaminated by a personal life that must to a large extent be self-deceptive about its worth in order to avoid its self-destruction. Freud's understanding of this conflict between an aggressive drive that

---

[3] The term "individuated self" is used for the reader's ease since the concept of the ego underwent many changes in its definition. Freud (1923a), *The Ego and the Id*, 56.

finds one's sense of self worthless and a libidinal drive that aims at the same object, an individuated self to preserve its worth, creates a psychic apparatus that is split. A psychological structure that is in permanent conflict with itself, which does not have a Cartesian locus of meaning, might be the only generalizable point.

The picture Freud provides of the individuated self is as an entity that, at its most fundamental level, is a fissure driven by conflicting desires, rather than a holistic framework that works coherently to conceal truth about itself. In Freud's work, I find at least three forms of psychic conflict that contribute to the psyche's fragmentation and the inability to fully reflect on its motives. The first most general form of conflict is between the psyche's three component parts that can produce a feeling of ambivalence which he named the id, the ego, and the super-ego. The psychic organism as a whole can be characterized as in conflict since it contends with these different topographies in one organic object. The second form of psychic conflict is created between libidinal drives that aim to create social ties and an aggressive drive that seeks to dissolve libidinal ties, which can further be directed either at individual ego desires or sexual-social desires. Individual desires can also both love and hate the object at which they are directed, which creates a third form of conflict in psychic processes. For example, in Schreber's delusions he both desires a loving relationship with his doctor, Dr. Flechsig, and also hates Dr. Flechsig for inspiring a homoerotic desire. The same object, Dr. Flechsig, is both loved and hated by Schreber, which leads to his development of delusions of persecution that project his inward hate as coming from his love object. The projection and reversal of desire, according to Freud, are defense mechanisms that help reconcile the ambivalence Schreber experiences from his conflicting desires but who is himself unaware of this tension.

Given these different ways the psyche Freud articulates is in conflict with itself, Farrell falsely introduces a coherent self in the Freudian id. One's ego can be seen as driven by a death (or constancy) principle that will form relations that aim to eventually destitute it. Every relation is hostile; only through the principle for pleasures can its relations become tolerated by the self. Vulnerability is not something that only plagues those who come from lower economic classes, minority populations, or are abused by a civil or federal system that revokes basic rights for these parts of the population. If we generalize the ability to become vulnerable to others by hidden desires, and if we avoid the false pretense that Freud was deceitful and scientifically inept in his work, then an understanding can be gained from Freud of how those who are considered intelligent are also vulnerable to the experiences of judgment in their own lives. The inability to develop outside of cultural and social influence points to the necessity of developing an identity through those social norms in which each is born. Each is vulnerable to the internalized moral norms that demand conformity, including Freud in his life. Repetition of certain injuries can bring masochistic pleasure when social norms are internalized for an individual that derives pleasure from conforming to those measures.

An individuated self that has no locus of meaning, fixed values, and is not grounded in truth leads to Freud's concern with morality. Freud wonders if a moral possibility exists, defined as a concern with how one should live with others, which does not come from a harsh admonishment from the primary masochism of the super-ego. He goes on to wonder whether a ubiquitous concern for others is even desirable, a question that I will focus on in upcoming chapters (1923b pg. 170). More than what occurs for the individuated self, processes of introjection can bring genuine pleasure from imposing misery on those groups that society deems subhuman. Violent acts perpetuated against these certain groups that need to be avoided are justified by whatever reasons, which for Freud could help explain the social persecutions he witnessed during his lifetime.

Throughout Freud's life in his hometown of Vienna, synagogues were frequently burnt down with fervent pleasure. In Alon Confino's book, *A World Without the Jews: From Persecution to Genocide* (2014), he traces the atmosphere of German culture that lead up to *Kristallnacht*, when the Hebrew Bible was burnt in a public square along with rampant looting and the destruction of Jewish businesses. Rather than focus on the particular ways the Jews were persecuted and murdered in concentration camps, Confino looked at the stories told in German culture that led up to and could justify smaller acts of persecution by the common citizens. These arguably created a condition in imagination that ushered in larger scales of genocide.

Confino documented what he calls the sensibilities that were expressed in public spaces that did not welcome Jews. For example, he found pictures of street signs and town signs that listed private Jewish households for easy targeting. Pictures of public carnivals showed various types of floats with portrayals of "the Jew." Representations included contradictory images such as a greedy bank teller, a communist Bolshevik, a big-nosed Rabbi, or a secular intellectual. Women's and school organizations voluntarily initiated their own forms of exclusion and discriminatory practices against the Jews, despite having never received an order from the regime to do so. All these were utilized not only by political powers, but also by civilians as an expression of a beloved new Aryan social society (Confino 2014, pg. 71). In particular, Confino finds that the:

> burning of the books on May 10 represented a wider agenda about remaking German identity because it was initiated by students and academics, whose professions are based on the reading and writing of books, and because it took place as a public ritual in citadels of learning. [...] Even though the public burning could not have happened without the regime's approval, participants were not coerced from above but acted enthusiastically from below. (2014, pg. 79)

These acts were inspired by a long medieval tradition that initiated the Protestant Reformation, namely, burning books of an outdated God and culture. An individual that is vulnerable to cultural norms runs the risk of persecuting others based on these idealized standards, with a limited capacity to reflect and prevent these relations.

Confino imagines how anti-Jewish persecutions during the pre-war era could eventually lead to a sustained attempt at complete annihilation of the Jewish people during the war (2014, pg. 33). He argues that in a sensibility linked to the Medieval Ages, it only takes re-creating an imaginary world without Jews in order to produce genocidal complicity. Even those who explicitly did not agree with the persecutions could still imagine a future without Jews. The ability to imagine a reality without a Jewish population made each an accomplice to the genocide of these particular peoples. It is worth adding that if a horizon without Jews were imagined, then it would not take much more effort of the imagination to eradicate others who were targeted, such as the Romani peoples, homosexuals, the mentally ill, political dissidents, and the disabled.

Compliance either out of fear or out of the imaginary of a world without Jews produced implicit support for the heightening degrees of brutality leading to the genocide of a population. Still, the responsibility of those who may have eventually helped people of Jewish descent is not of the same sort that we attribute to those who intentionally committed acts of violence. We are left to ask what part of the subject bears this responsibility, what can be done otherwise to avoid such violent thoughts or, eventually, actions?

Assuming that those who lived in Nazi Germany were not fundamentally different in their ability to imagine ideals and social norms from anyone else, then it would seem that, with enough pressure, anyone who is capable of forming similar types of psychic images can be manipulated. According to Confino, one of the ideals that made those who lived in Germany vulnerable to manipulation was by an appeal to the Aryan *heimat* or homeland. Many enjoyed the abuses they inflicted by believing these were required to develop their *heimat* (2014, pg. 37). Patterns of meaning that appealed to a German homeland created "a world of fantasies that made the extermination possible precisely because it was imaginable and representable" (Confino 2014, pg. 30). So long as one can represent and imagine, then they are vulnerable to manipulation. Referring to those who supported the Nazi regime as vulnerable is not meant to regard lightly the heinousness of their acts. The emphasis is placed here on the ubiquitous possibility to be manipulated to justify such acts.

A mutual type of existential vulnerability to these types of influences explains how it is possible for a whole nation to take pleasure in such disturbing forms of persecution. Confino cites Freud as a contemporary thinker of those events who understood "the cultural importance of the presence of the past, of the idea of historical origins, and the fabled stories nations tell themselves to make sense of their history" (2014, pg. 49). It is not solely those who lived at that time, or particular place, that are vulnerable to how the past influences the idea of one's future. The unceasing practice of persecuting others indicates a constitutive element to identity itself in this practice. All are vulnerable to the ways in which images, stories, and fears constitute identity. One cannot help but be interpolated by institutional norms and the enjoyment in excluding those who threaten those favored relations. When the individual sensibility identifies and internalizes social norms, the need to repress individuated ego-drives increases for the good of social stability. In turn, these internalized norms can also be utilized to incite violence, a violence that becomes pleasurable for the fulfillment of a moral ideal. Furthermore, when the imperialism of an egoical aspect of self is prioritized, and when acts of will and self-mastery are valued as the highest normative standard (which is the Western tradition Freud articulates in *The Ego and the Id* and which Lévinas aimed to overturn), then sensing the other's suffering becomes increasingly difficult. Freud's psycho-biography of Schreber's neurosis reveals the strength of patriarchal moral norms at the time, such that Schreber would have to repress desires that condemned him as "effeminate." The study also reveals Freud's own prescriptive judgment by reading delusions as a beneficial psychic mechanism that helps to master and control excessive psychic excitement, possibly even confirming the attempt to control his own uncivilized desires.

One study on persecution and conflicts between European Jewish people coming to Israel at the beginning of the twentieth century also revealed an unconscious repetition of holding European standards against prominently Ethiopian, Sephardic, and Mizrachi Jews, as much as Arab Non-Jews. All these factions were persecuted and prevented from having the same resources that Jewish people who came from European countries enjoyed. In order to maintain psychic stability in the face of new local "others," familiar persecuting standards were repeated while the possibility for an ethical relation between these groups diminished. The "Orientals" were perceived as dark, working class, shameless, uncultured, and simpleminded. Reiterated processes of discrimination and exclusion that most Jewish people felt in the diaspora of Europe against their own "orientalism" were used to form their new ideal image of "western civilization" in their new place (2003, pg. 184–510). In "The Great Chain of Orientalism: Jewish Identity, Stigma Management, and Ethnic Exclusion in Israel," Aziza Khazzoom writes on processes of ethnic exclusion used by European Jews that resembled their own experiences of exclusion. They degraded others for those same aspects of themselves that were most despised while living among European nations. These processes also shaped their new identity of an enlightened ideal in their new place, only in their new place they were the privileged ones. Khazzoom writes:

> It is not because people apply previously established semiotic structures to new sites as the need arises, but because those "stigma symbols" that had been used to cast Jews as backward-religiousness, traditional dress, street size, peddlers, and so on resonated with Jewish selves in deep, even unconscious ways. The presence of stigma is always frightening and always generates the impulse to distance oneself; Goffman (1963) himself notes that normals fear stigma by proxy. But for those who were once stigmatized, the discomfort is stronger and more threatening. (2003, pg. 503)

Stigmas create identity and therefore these stigmas were naturally duplicated in a new dwelling. People who arrived in Israel sought refuge and safety from the discriminatory practices they experienced before and during the war. The main argument for constructing Israel as a distinct ethnic nation-state was for protection against discriminatory practices experienced all over the world. The discriminating practices they experienced, however, were the same ways they discriminated against their other, darker counterparts that they found after arriving in Israel. Because they were discriminated against for being dark and primitive, these same persecuting practices took ontic forms in their new place.

European identity was not used as a means, "as the need arose," but reflected the identity of Jewish people in Europe. Using Freud's language, Kazzhoom concludes that dominating others was a reaction to being dominated oneself. Those who have been stigmatized are more threatening when normalized because their guilt and aggressive drives increase in the wake of failing to meet their social ego ideal. The failure one feels relative to those ideals is then projected onto another. For the individuated self, inter-psychic guilt is mastered by penalizing another who represents their private transgression.

European Jewry's persecution of Jewish and non-Jewish people who were from Middle-Eastern or African countries can be read as a psychic strategy for managing their internal guilt for never living up to their ideal self. Loving the enlightened social norm, but never satisfying it, inverted their love to hate. Their self-admonishment and persecuting guilt were then projected on these "darker" people in society who resembled the source of their guilt. European Jewry retaliated against these "persecuting populations" for not living up to an internalized cultural ideal forged in the crucible of their own persecution.

Unconsciously, recovering from their guilt meant dominating the other who represented their failed attempts at European integration. Their experiences of being dominated were inverted and projected back from the other. The cultural ideals held elsewhere came with them in the super-ego to a new region. Old persecutions were pursued in new places and projected onto new people. Neither could the "persecuting" European Jewry make sense of the inverted neurosis, nor did the groups they discriminated against understand why they were hated and persecuted. Ethiopian, Mizrachi, and Sephardic Jews, and Arab Non-Jews were socially persecuted against for failing to measure up to an idealized image that did not relate to them. These relations persist in the region today. Without realizing the particular demands these ideals make and how they may not be shared among all inhabitants of that region, the possibility for a real relation grows dimmer.

Considering the capacity to take pleasure in persecuting others, on a psychic level as Freud analyzes and on a social level as Confino documents, the idea is not to excuse these types of abusive and persecuting relations. Ethics does not get thrown out the window, but just the opposite. Now there is a more demanding burden to evaluate a vulnerability to moral ideals, to evaluate who is left out from the ideal standard, and how the pursuit of these ideals can inflict violence on others. Major events, such as the military aim of the Crusades in the tenth century to defeat Turkish expansion, the Turkish genocide against its Armenian population that still remains unacknowledged, or the Inquisition in the twelfth century to defeat heretics, are made possible because of individual soldiers. Even today we see frenzied support for political leaders who wish to destroy social bonds with others, such as Muslims who are indiscriminately grouped together under one label: "terrorist." These are only a few of many historical cases that condemn parts of the population as scapegoats to unify bonds among others. Although none of these cases should be overlooked in their historical specificity, there are simply too many to cite and more that remain unrepresented.

While it may be the political powers and rulers of any time that sanction these acts, there has to be an understandable endeavor, imaginable for all those soldiers who risked their lives to attain those goals. For this reason, it is important in the discourse on the persecutory relation not to limit the conversation to only those forms of vulnerability that can be rectified, or be given reparation, through rational acknowledgment. While there are types of vulnerability to which we can all respond, there is still the possibility of different forms of responsiveness to unnoticed or unacknowledged vulnerability. It is also important to address those forms of persecution that are perpetuated without the kind of agency we typically attribute to a character who must act, as Aristotle declares, *for the good with knowledge of the good*.[4] These are necessary conditions for developing moral character, according to Aristotle and most traditional moral theories in virtue ethics. The more deliberate acts that aim at a mean between desired excesses, the more one's character becomes virtuous. The inability to be transparent in self-volition in both Freud's map of the psyche, and as will be shown in Lévinas's construction of the subject that is always impinged on by the other, is a problem for traditional approaches in moral philosophy. Both authors pick up on this difficulty.

What happens when we presuppose that we do not have full knowledge of our motives and therefore lack an amount of freedom to direct and be responsible for them? Choice, moreover *the freedom* to choose, is traditionally thought of as the factor for moral virtue. When someone on trial is found to be criminally insane while committing a murder, then they cannot be held responsible for their act. They cannot own the murder if they did not choose to do it. It is just as difficult to calculate consequences from one's actions, which leads me to wonder how it can reflect moral character. The full range of consequences is even more difficult to predict, and calculate, which further leads to wondering about their implications on character. Furthermore, consequentialist theories rely on those goods produced in each scenario, which also in turn makes us wonder whose goods are more important than others.

Without the freedom to choose, how is it possible to judge moral character? Similar to what I will show is Lévinas's version of passivity, Freud finds that an individual is shaped by the changes and developments of a psychic apparatus that is split between aggressive and libidinal drives. Perennially in conflict with itself, the psychic apparatus is always vulnerable to cultural standards, as well as personal desires that conflict with the former. Freud bites the bullet to show how moral freedom is limited by unknown psychic drives that expose an inherent helplessness and defenselessness to "a neighbor" and an other who is both a source of love and aggression. An additional complication is the ambivalent status of the neighbor as both loved for its source of individuated identities and feared for its differences that are threatening, which requires a renewed thinking about the constitutive relationship between an other, the neighbor, and oneself created through specific social bonds.

---

[4] For example, Aristotle emphasizes in his Virtue ethics that "[t]he doer at the time of performing a moral good must satisfy certain conditions: in the first place, he must *know* what he is doing; secondly, he must *deliberately choose* to do it and do it for its own sake; and thirdly, he must do it as part of his own firm and immutable character" (Aristotle, *Nicomachean Ethics*, Book II) (italics added). If you choose to give a homeless man your leftovers out of convenience, for example, then it is not considered a moral act because it is done out of utility and not done for the good itself.

References

Confino, A. (2014). *A world without Jews: The Nazi imagination from persecution to genocide*. New Haven: Yale University Press.

Dean, T., & Lane, C. (2001). *Homosexuality & psychoanalysis*. Chicago: University of Chicago Press.

Herzog, D. (2017). *Cold War Freud: Psychoanalysis in an age of catastrophes*. Cambridge: Cambridge University Press.

Farrell, J. (1996). *Freud's paranoid quest: Psychoanalysis and modern suspicion*. New York: New York University Press.

Freud, S. (1953). The standard edition of the complete psychological works of Sigmund Freud. In J. Strachey (Ed.), *Three essays on sexuality and other works, i–iv* (Vol. VII, 1901–1905). London: The Hogarth Press and the Institute of Psycho-analysis.

Freud, S. (1953b). The standard edition of the complete psychological works of Sigmund Freud. In J. Strachey (Ed.), *Jensen's 'Gradiva' and other works* (Vol. ix, 1908). London: The Hogarth Press and the Institute of Psycho-analysis.

Freud, S. (1957). The standard edition of the complete psychological works of Sigmund Freud. In J. Strachey (Ed.), *Mourning and melancholia* (Vol. XIV, 1917). London: The Hogarth Press and the Institute of Psycho-analysis.

Freud, S. (1958). The standard edition of the complete psychological works of Sigmund Freud. In J. Strachey (Ed.), *The case of Schreber, papers on technique and other works, ii–vii* (Vol. XII, 1911). London: The Hogarth Press and the Institute of Psycho-analysis.

Freud, S. (1961a). The standard edition of the complete psychological works of Sigmund Freud. In J. Strachey (Ed.), *The ego and the id* (Vol. XIX, 1923a). London: The Hogarth Press and the Institute of Psycho-analysis.

Freud, S. (1961b). The standard edition of the complete psychological works of Sigmund Freud. In J. Strachey (Ed.), *The economic problem of masochism* (Vol. XIX, 1923b). London: The Hogarth Press and the Institute of Psycho-analysis.

Freud, S., Zweig, A., & Freud, E. L. (1987). *The letters of Sigmund Freud and Arnold Zweig*. New York: New York University Press.

Goffman, E. (1963). *Stigma: Notes on the Management of Spoiled Identity*. Englewood Cliffs, NJ: Prentice Hall.

Khazzoom, A. (2003). The great chain of orientalism: Jewish identity, stigma management, and ethnic exclusion in Israel. *American Sociological Review, 68*(4), 481–510.

Chapter 3
Getting Personal: Persecution in Freud's Personal Life

Abstract In this chapter, details from the second chapter of Freud's *Autobiographical Study* shift to a narrower focus on persecuting relations in Freud's personal life. I argue that Freud's growing paranoic suspicion about the reliable status of knowledge and his perceived social alienation influenced his hermeneutic of suspicion. In addition, I use his understanding of an ego's desire to know and not know its own motives to explore the complicated implications of upholding social and moral norms.

Keywords Positivism in Vienna · Freud's positivism · Subjectivity in positivist method · Freud's Autobiographical study · Irma's injection · Homosexuality in Freud · Daniel Schreber's delusions · Delusions of persecution · Homosexuality in libido theory · Paranoid delusions · Freud's Schreber case · Ambivalent drives · Freud's Trieb · Freud and Einstein correspondence · Why War?

As much as Freud desired to be a positivist scientist early in his career, his simultaneous desire to understand the inner workings of the subjective mind would complicate his earlier, more empirical method. Despite his attraction to the ideals of a positivist method, his controversial introspective methods would prevent his ability to use them. Freud remained alienated from the scientific community and the methods that bourgeoned out of Vienna's positivist circles during his formative years and continued through his life. As we will see, the ambivalence Freud experienced for the scientific community would appear through all his work in the need to cite empirical studies that were loosely connected to his theses. He also strove for clarity using terms usually applied to processes of physical energy, such as the positive and attractive force of the libido and the aggressive force of a death drive that represents entropy in physical nature (Tauber 2009, pg. 34). If we take seriously Freud's claim that no individuated self could be transparent to themselves, then we may pursue one possible interpretation of Freud's ambivalent desires for a loved but unaccepting scientific community. Their unacceptance leads to his expressed animosity toward them. The methods he developed had to stand in relation to his super-egoical demands, an imposition introjected from that same community.

Growing up as a Jewish student in Vienna, a desire for objectivity and a reduction to materialism provided Freud solace from a fickle social and anti-Semitic world. Vienna in the 1870s was a cultural center for natural philosophers that began to call themselves scientists. Positivists lauded objectivism and impartiality for understanding a natural and valueless world. Materialistic and empirical approaches to understanding the world were a welcome method for Freud who could not understand the grip religion held on so many. Though young, Freud's interests led him to pursue a dual doctorate in medicine and philosophy. Eventually, however, he would deliberately turn away from more speculative fields early in his career (Gay 1988, pg. 26).

After he finished his studies in 1881, Freud enrolled in the university as a medical student. His interest in psychology led him to enroll in Franz Brentano's lectures. In 1874, Brentano published *Psychology from an Empirical Standpoint* that showed his commitment to empiricism, logic, and natural scientific approaches in psychology. Freud began his academic career with a string of apprenticeships under positivist scientists. His first work was in Carl Claus's laboratory, a devout Darwinist. Claus's work in biology and experimentation in marine biology brought him to teach in Vienna, where he eventually recruited Freud to work in his laboratory. A pressing issue that directly influenced Freud's work and self-image was this relation to the positivist tradition that the empirical sciences were steadfast in keeping.

An additional influence that was decisive in Freud's approach to science was Master Ernst Brücke (Gay 1988, pg. 32–4). Freud's next apprenticeship with Brücke, another Darwinist, worked on connections between the mind and nervous systems. In the laboratory, Freud was able to experiment on the nervous system of fish that led to his first publications. Brücke's methodology was medical-positivism, which aimed to "import the program of the natural sciences, their findings and methods, into the investigation of all human thought and action, both private and public. ... Brücke was its most eminent representative in Vienna" (Gay 1988, pg. 34). This method was incompatible with any form of knowledge that did not submit to common physical-chemical force, finding at bottom components reducible to forces of attraction, repulsion, and motion (Gay 1988, pg. 34). Early in his career, Freud fancied his work as contributing to the study and truth of human evolution as left in traces of human emotion (Gay 1988, pg. 36).

Freud's biographer relates the results of the scientific work Freud completed on evolutionary processes in the nervous structures of fish to "these papers (that) form the first link in the chain of ideas leading to the draft of a scientific psychology he would attempt in 1895" (Gay 1988, pg. 36). Darwinism undeniably made a very strong impression on Freud and would inform his own desire to critique and disillusion the sources of human culture, which led him to find naturalistic sources of religion and morality later in life.

Tauber continues to write in "Freud's Philosophical Path: From a science of mind to a philosophy of human being" that a complex history formed in Freud's work incorporating his speculative approaches in the material life of the mind that would ultimately lead to the hermeneutical challenge (Tauber 2009, pg. 32). "Freud struggled between the demands of a reductive science and an introspection that taxed the limits of that science," wrote Tauber. This struggle leads to what Tauber described as Freud's "physics envy," a play on Freud's theory of penis envy.[1] Formed out of a scientific community in Berlin that only used terms common to physical forces of attraction and repulsion active in matter, Freud's work is pregnant with positivism but ultimately miscarries. Empirical and logical modes of knowledge are not enough to understand the subjective psyche.

Freud struggled with these objective, scientific terms when it came time to speak about subjectivity. He would consistently develop the pleasure principle, for binding processes in human activity, and would only conceptualize its opposite force in 1920 as the death drive that causes a psychic form of entropy. Arguably these were his attempts to recapitulate the positivists' method using empirical, or physical, forces of attraction and repulsion. With every use, however, Freud admits in the text that he hesitates to use these speculative terms to describe phenomena that work beyond phenomenal appearances in the unconscious or id. His repetition of these warning remarks seems like compulsions that carry into the last version of his *Autobiographical Study* (1925), until 1935 only 4 years before his death. These drives that work in quiet ways, such as the homosexual components of libidinal life, are in his own admissions limited and difficult to empirically survey (Freud 1905, pg. 11). Positivism's most fundamental principle is that only what can be empirically verified and quantified can be considered real. Freud's work consistently found that these pairs of drives were too ambivalently related for empirical mastery. Furthermore, his work found the real effects of subjective emotions that, when repressed, would cause their eternal return in the psychic life of an individual mind.

Early in Freud's career, he also strove for scientific clarity, as Darwin, Claus, and Brücke did in their pursuit of truth. He did not care if illusions needed to be unmasked for this purpose. As his research developed, however, he could not help but find that the "mind obeys a fundamental hidden order" (Freud 1905, pg. 42). In his clinical experience and work with Jean Martin Charcot on hypnosis, Freud found intriguing a "mystical element" in hypnosis. Upon Freud's return from studying hypnosis with Charcot in Paris, he would propose a methodology where laws governed mental life in most healthy people. Freud's ambivalence about describing an objective science for understanding the trickery of psychic mechanisms finds traces in both Brücke's work, the positivist, and Charcot, who worked on neurosis. These men were made into "intellectual fathers" that he looked up to and tried to emulate (1905, pg. 52).

Freud's conclusions made him suspect of the same empirical method he desired to use. Several additional specific examples are his fluctuating use of the word *Trieb*, his developing theory of infantile sexuality, the development of this second topology that divides the psychic life into domains that are opaque to each other (such as the id and super-ego), and his need to rely on clinical techniques that constantly changed. These are some ways Freud's method was at odds with the positivists' method. These same insights about a mind so fraught with its own imaginings, impenetrable by rational or reflective measures, contributed to his mental struggle

---

[1] See Tauber's book *Freud, the Reluctant Philosopher* (2010).

for acceptance within a scientific community that his work ultimately subverted. According to Freud's method that is suspicious of explicit declarations, his own declarations in most introductions to his work about not caring what others think since psychoanalysis is "not to produce conviction" become suspicious.[2] Why must Freud make this declaration in what are otherwise case studies, or medical notes? His relationship to the scientific community changed throughout his life and work, but it was up until his death that he wished to win a Nobel Prize in Medicine. The prize, however, was never awarded to Freud.

One glaring example of Freud's desire for acceptance from the scientific community while also working against it is *Trieb*, the German word Freud frequently used to describe psychic impulses translated either as a biological instinct or mental drive. Vacillations in his work and the interpretive work by others that followed about whether it was a biological instinct or subjective drive acutely show the difficulty to understand through empirical means what he found to be a natural phenomenon. A drive is not strictly biological; it is what Freud calls a border concept occupying "the frontier-line between the somatic and the mental … (as) the psychical representative of organic forces" (1925, pg. 74). *Trieb*, impulse, instinct, or drive negotiates between the somatic body and its psychic ideations. The border concept ultimately relates those biological processes of the body to a mind that is vulnerable to its imaginings.

A border concept complicates the empirical method for understanding these mechanisms that hide shameful desires from empirical sight. Some of the psychic mechanisms that duplicate cultural ideals in an individual psyche are processes of identification, introjection, sublimation, and transference. Freud's work on the subjective mind uncovered drives that were ambivalently related to each other and connected to ideational or representational objects in discrete categories that, as such, prevent empirical mastery.

In *Beyond the Pleasure Principle* (1920), Freud cites Gustav Theodor Fechner, a psycho-physicist who describes psychology in natural terms. Freud draws a surprising comparison between the biological life of gametes and the necessity for all living organisms to develop toward their death (pg. 39). As usual, Freud ends up departing from these naturalistic approaches to pursue his own interpretive ones. He pays more attention to that which remains unsaid, hidden, or obscured; his interpretive lens focuses on those meanings that only leave traces in language, mental representations, and empirical phenomenon. Frequently, Freud also uses literature to reveal the subjective psychic processes that he desired to systematize. Literature revealed more for Freud than any natural scientist would feel comfortable using in the empirical method. In the next chapter, I will turn to "The Uncanny" that includes Freud's interpretative work on E.T.A. Hoffman's short story *The Sandman* for what it reveals to Freud on the precarious origins of meaning and moral norms.

Often in Freud's biography, he defends his work against those who constantly aimed to discredit it. One traumatic break that was caused by the disagreement on

---

[2] See Freud's introduction section to *Introductory Lectures on Psycho-Analysis* (1936). More difficult than finding this claim at the beginning of his work is trying to find a work by Freud that does not contain an apology for his method that does not fit the standards of empirical science.

his method was from Wilhelm Fleiss. Fleiss found more interest in the biological origins of neurosis than Freud thought appropriate for a "scientific psychology." Freud on the other hand would emphasize "the amounts of energy and their distribution in the mental apparatus" that were caused by the repression of infantile sexuality (Gay 1988, pg. 79). Freud's unique emphasis was to examine the content of dreams and memories, on the production of symbols, slips, jokes, and repressions that leave interpretive content hidden from the analyst-doctor as well as the patient.

On this reading, social standards as well as personal experiences have serious consequences on the mental apparatus as a physical object.[3] His patients showed how "humans can know and not know at the same time, understand intellectually what they emotionally refuse to accept" (Gay 1988, pg. 86). Freud repeatedly encountered the power of mental operations to disclose, while also keep hidden, one's constantly forming and deepest wishes. At the same time, in Freud's personal life he was experiencing the same psychic struggle to keep hidden his homosexual attraction to colleagues and friends like Wilhelm Fleiss who was fitted to help Freud develop a theory of the scientific truth of the mental apparatus. Much of Fleiss's work in biology and the connections he found between the nose and stages of sexual development have since been discredited by the scientific community. Still, for Freud he was an important interlocutor and friend; despite what Freud felt comfortable revealing, Fleiss was also much more. A clear example of Freud keeping from himself a truth about his emotional life can be seen in the importance dreams have for revealing unconscious desires, and the wrong interpretation he offers of his own dream to conceal his desires, famously known as the dream of Irma's injection.

As early in his career as 1895, Freud used symbols in dreams to interpret and reveal wishes one would have difficulty admitting. He writes, "attention is without hesitation displaced from what is actually intended on to some neighboring association" (1900, pg. 295). Excitement that arises from the dream in the life of one's mind is enough to fulfill the private wish. For example, in order to preserve his self-image and an important friendship, Freud could not explicitly accuse himself and his friend Fleiss of what was clearly medical negligence. In his interpretative work of Irma's injection, most obvious are themes of her symptoms, treatment, and Freud's guilt for his faulty medical practices. In the dream, Freud is confronted with a patient who appears familiar enough. She suffers from various symptoms in her nose, throat, and stomach, some of which Freud was familiar with in her treatment.

---

[3] In her work on *The Matrixial Borderspace* (2006), Bracha Ettinger proposes that one is affected already in the womb by external sources impinging on it before birth. Before one can respond to a threatening object with flight, there is the presence of an instinctual life that is impinged from within. Freud writes in *Instincts and their Vicissitudes* that, unable to flee from its internal pressure, "an 'instinct' appears to us as a concept on the frontier between the mental and the somatic, as the psychical representative of the stimuli originating from within the organism and reaching the mind, as a measure of the demand made upon the mind for work in consequence of its connection with the body" (122). Here again is the significant difference between an *instinct* and a drive, which more appropriately translates from the German word *Trieb* and works as the border concept between mental representation and the physical instinct. What impinges on the physical space of a sensible body creates a corresponding impression on the mind.

One friend appears in the dream by name—Otto Rank—while another appears as nameless at first but who is later described as familiar with Freud's work on sexuality (Freud 1900, pg. 116). Later in his interpretative work, Freud names Fleiss as this friend, who was a biologist that specialized on the throat and nose. Their early work together found origins of "the chemistry of the sexual process" in the nose, which was later disregarded in Freud's theory.

Freud experiences frustration in the dream at the approach of this patient because she rejected his treatment, which made it easy for him to blame her for her symptoms. Freud also concludes that the process of what he called "condensation" created two figures who also appear in the dream. Each represents bundled feelings of blame or agreeable understanding. The first is Otto Rank, with whom Freud had many recent disagreements, and the other was noted only as "the doctor from Berlin." It was Fleiss who did understand Freud, who took his side, and to whom he owed "much valuable information" (Freud 1900, pg. 294).

According to his own admission, Freud misinterpreted this dream that gave clues to malpractice in areas of the throat and nose. Although he uncovered dreams as "wish fulfillments," Freud did not acknowledge his own wish of acceptance from Fleiss. The dream acts as a defense, if the dream is driven by a wish that needs to be hidden (Freud 1900, pg. 146). Much scholarship has noted that Freud's interpretation of himself in this dream work did not venture into its complete truth. Different from Crews's evaluation of Freud as an intentionally deceptive charlatan, my argument is that this illustrates how Freud attempted to both reveal and hide his desire for Fleiss's acceptance. His mind was attempting to both reveal and hide this knowledge of his desire from itself.

Freud often took himself as his own patient all the while constructing general principles of the mind. Many years after the incident, "Freud bluntly told several of his closest disciples that his attachment to Fleiss had contained a homosexual element" (Gay 1988, pg. 87). For Peter Gay who wrote *Freud: A Life for Our Time*, the case of "Irma's injection" discloses "Freud's anxiety to conceal his doubts about Fleiss not just from Fleiss but from himself. It is a paradox" (1988, pg. 86). It is indeed a paradox, but the kind that Freud developed though his psychoanalytic method. Experiences of these types of paradoxes would lead to Freud's view of a mind driven by inescapable, inconsistent tensions that are constantly in conflict (Gay 1988, pg. 87). Gay observes that Freud's typical fashion is to translate "private turmoil into analytic theory" (Gay 1988, pg. 275).

Freud's readers are prevented from reducing Freud's findings narrowly to his own neurosis since he documented similar patterns in many other patients. However, it is the task of his readers to see what general claims about neurotic drives of the mind can arise from experiences that also afflicted Freud's mind given his particular life. Even though he was considered liberal-minded in his time because of his theories of sexuality, Freud led a conservative life that was typical of polite, middle-class Viennese society. Freud's ambivalent feelings were created from the presence of a libidinal drive aimed at Fleiss who was also representative of a scientific community, while simultaneously feeling aggression toward the positivists' method and his own homosexual feelings for the same object, Fleiss. His interpretation of Irma's injection is paradigmatic of the deceptions of the mind, and Freud's mind in particular, while conducting his research on subjective experiences. Freud's private desires can be seen here to conflict with his social norms, which renders him incapable of interpreting his dream. Freud continues to write on the inheritance of moral sensibility and its place in the unconscious psyche by developing the second topology in *The Ego and the Id* (1923). The ego was conceived as a bodily ego that stands in closest relation to consciousness and represents reason and common sense. He contrasted the ego with the id that contained the passions and, in this work, Freud argues the id also contains the highest, most moral ambitions. Freud writes on the preconscious operation of moral sensibility,

> On the one hand, we have evidence that even subtle and difficult intellect operations which ordinarily require strenuous reflection can equally be carried out preconsciously and without coming into consciousness (such as in sleep). There is another phenomenon, however, which is far stranger. In our analysis we discover that there are people in whom the faculties of self-criticism and conscience-mental activities, that is, that rank as extremely high ones – are unconscious and unconsciously produce effects of the greatest importance […] and compels us, in spite of our better critical judgment, to speak of an "unconscious sense of guilt" […] If we come back once more to our scale of values, we shall have to say that not only what is lowest but also what is highest in the ego can be unconscious. (1923, pg. 27)

In my reading of Freud's work, the inability to interpret the desires and motives of one's own mind, including what drives moral behavior, shows a constitutional unknowability in those moral pursuits that can become zealous and persecuting. Pursuing moral ends cannot always be known by calculated measures of the mind. Freud's personal life reflected this with the returning iterations and repetitions of this paradigmatic relationship with Fleiss that his conscience would not accept. The relationship returns in Freud's life with the figure of Carl Jung, for example, for whom he felt as strongly and similarly conflicted about as he did with Fleiss.

From this early work on Irma's injection and its implications on Freud's desire for and against Fleiss, Freud later develops a similar analysis in a case study of paranoia. A psyche that is in permanent conflict with itself returns in Freud's theoretical analysis of paranoiac delusions of persecution in Dr. Daniel Schreber. While Freud's work on the mechanism of paranoia is still helpful today, the causal relation he found between homosexuality and paranoia is not as useful (Gottlieb 2006, pg. 427–428). The connection he found between homosexuality and paranoia may have more to do with experiences in Freud's particular life, rather than making a general claim about all mental processes.

Freud's work on a psychological biography on neurotic paranoia in delusions of persecution (1911) helped him understand the general patterns of a psyche in permanent conflict that is capable of deceiving itself, and contributed to his work on conditions in the mind of unknowability. Freud's writing about the autobiographical account written by Daniel Paul Schreber has the double effect of revealing not only Schreber's paranoia but also Freud's own projected concerns and interests, which are thus freed from the contingencies of an actual patient's life, and possible resistance. In other words, by turning to this "psycho-biography," I can parse general concerns during the time of Freud's life, and find how Freud expressed his own concealed desires by finding them in his "patient" instead. In *The Case of Schreber, Papers on Technique and Other Works* (1911), Freud problematizes the ambivalent relation between libidinal and destructive drives by making a distinction "between ego-instincts (drives) and a sexual instinct (drives); for such a distinction seems to agree with the biological conception that the individual has a double orientation, aiming on the one hand at self-preservation and on the other at the preservation of the species" (Freud, pg. 74). Drives that serve individual desires that come into conflict with the desire to preserve their social life have an influence on the health of mind (Freud 1923, pg. 56). In developing types of therapy, Freud can also be seen to investigate how one should negotiate personal desires against social expectations, which is explicitly a moral question. More than just looking at what kinds of behavior count as moral, psychoanalysis aims to understand how broader sexual bonds, also called libidinal attachments, influence individual mental functioning.

Freud's case study of Schreber describes delusions of persecution as one means of warding off ego-driven desires that are not culturally accepted. Freud's details in the case show that Schreber began developing neurotic symptoms after admitting in his sleep that he would like to be passive like a woman during intercourse. After a "nervous collapse," Schreber pulled away from his wife and saw a doctor for his symptoms (Freud 1911, pg. 45). Upon hearing that his anxiety was incurable, necessitating that he would be handed over to a beloved former doctor, Dr. Flechsig, Schreber became convinced that Dr. Flechsig was trying to injure and persecute him.

Schreber also lost interest in his life, often imagining himself dead and dismembered. After 9 months in an asylum, Schreber's delusions transformed into a mission received from God. In these delusions, Schreber imagined that he was called upon to become God's wife and bear a new race of men through his body. In this second permutation of the delusion, he was able to accept this "passive" and emasculated sensual pleasure as a direct mission from God and return to functioning in a community. Yet Schreber's paranoid delusions about Dr. Flechsig continued as he slowly returned to a functioning life.

Freud's hypothesis in Schreber's case is that an intense resistance to the fantasy of being emasculated like a woman arose in him and caused his psychosis. In psychosis, an ego becomes detached from external reality due to frustrated desires. A defensive struggle in Schreber's psyche ensued, which resulted in the repression of his libidinal homosexual desires. The repressed content of his desire to become like a woman created a libidinal disturbance, and the conflict between his ego and sexual instincts shot back the desire in a pathological form (Freud 1911, pg. 62, 79). Dr. Flechsig, the object of Schreber's desire, became his persecutor. The content of his homoerotic fantasy became the very object that abused him. His feelings of love turned to hate, and that hate was projected onto Dr. Flechsig who was perceived as aiming to injure Schreber.

Delusions of persecution justify emotional changes between competing individual desires and the desire to meet social expectations (Freud 1911, pg. 41). Later in *An Infantile Neurosis*, Freud writes that ambivalent feelings develop from "contrary component instincts" that are incompatible with acquiring a stable character (1918, pg. 26–27). Contradicting drives characterize the unconscious and persist into consciousness in paranoia (1918, pg. 118–119). Freud lists several symptoms that lead to delusions of persecution, which begin with an internal perception of a desired object. If the desire cannot be satisfied according to one's own psychic ideal, then suppression of the internal perception ensues before repression. The "internal catastrophe" begins to heal only after a distortion of content, namely, the desired object becomes hated for creating an unacceptable desire (Freud 1918, pg. 66–68). By projecting onto the other an internal perception, what was abolished internally returns from the external other. In other words, Schreber returned to living a social life with the help of his delusions.

An important consequence of the ego's detachment from the external world in psychosis is that sensory knowledge of the external world is categorically denied.[4] Schreber's delusions of external persecutions formed after suppressing an internal perception of emasculation. In order to make Schreber's internal perception bearable for returning to an active life, a transformation of affect that changed his love to hate was affixed to an external perception of Dr. Flechsig (Freud 1911, pg. 66). An "unconscious contradiction" becomes a conscious paranoia that replaces one's internal perceptions, ideas, and feelings with external perceptions (Freud 1911, pg. 63). In addition to inflicting injury on oneself, on one's desires by suppression, there is also the possibility of inflicting injury on those who are the object of delusion. Freud would eventually give up looking at problems of psychoses—those of a detached ego—because he found no curative hope.

Psychic repair occurs when one's "persecutor" reconciles an emotional change between desires that are contradictory to each other, an ambivalent relation that sits at the heart of all psychic activity in a developing culture. Feelings of persecution are the way in which the psyche justifies emotional ambivalence in extreme cases, but conflicting desires for Freud characterize all relations to objects as a universal fact of psychic life, and for most are negotiated without the help of delusions of persecution. As civilization grows, however, the possibility of feeling hatred and fear for what is loved and honored will become more common. Neuroses, such as compulsive repetitions, are judged by Freud as more common mechanisms that repress libidinal disturbances. Morality is another means for mastering aggression internal to the ego that can lead to living a stable life with others.

Freud writes that in psychosis, there is an "external perception" of the other that persecutes oneself, but if we assume that perception is always internal, then the paranoiac perception is in error thinking it originates from the external object rather than from an internal source (Freud 1911, pg. 66, 69). Persecution *seems* to originate from the other. Thinking to oneself, "I do not *love* him – I *hate* him because HE PERSECUTES ME," the other is completely occluded (Freud 1911, pg. 66). In delusions of persecution, the distortion consists of a transformation of affect; "what should be felt internally as love is perceived externally as hate" (Freud 1911, pg. 66). We may wonder here how the lines of love turned to hate in Freud's life and

---

[4] Schreber was unique, as Freud noted, because of his capacity to eventually distinguish between the persecuting doctor of his delusions, from the real and harmless Dr. Flechsig.

what psychic distortions they underwent, since he is the one that developed an insight about them.

Comparisons between Freud's theoretical understanding of Schreber's paranoid delusions of persecution and the biographical details of Freud's life reveal resonating similarities on the root cause of psychosis and its symptoms. The theoretical yield of the following analysis is for tracking the theme of unknowability in desires that are ambivalently related, and how these affect interactions with others in external social reality. James Strachey, the editor of Freud's work on *The Wolfman*, notes that the chief clinical finding was evidence for the "determining part played in the patient's neurosis by his *primary* feminine impulses. The very marked degree of his bisexuality was only a confirmation of views (the fact of the *universal* occurrence of bisexuality) which had long been held by Freud and which dated back to the time of his friendship with Fleiss" (Freud 1918, pg. 6). In pioneering a scientific account of psychological events that are of "undreamt-of novelty and complexity," it stands to reason that Freud would have his own experiences on which to reflect, along with his clients' for building this science.

Freud engaged in the cultural milieu of his time by developing psychoanalysis, travelling all over the world for establishing his psychoanalytic method. Investigating the historical-temporal past, Freud sought an understanding of the deep recesses of the mind. At the same time, he constantly faced a critical scientific community committed to positivists' standards. In Freud's terms, his scientific pursuits indicate large libidinal investments of a sexualized social instinct. Already fulfilling one component of frustrated libidinal investments that sit at the root of paranoid delusions, Freud also admitted that he had homosexual feelings for Fleiss.

Freud's exchanges with Fleiss were of professional and personal observations whose nature was of the "most intimate you can imagine" (Gay 1988, pg. 613). Thinking again about his personal ambitions and considering his cultural milieu, Freud also exhibited the modesty and privacy typical of a nineteenth-century bourgeois man (Gay 1988, pg. 614). His relationship with Fleiss may have come too close to reveal homosexual desires with significant effects on his later theory of delusions of persecution that are also, according to Freud, rooted in homosexual impulses. It is worth noting that Freud's later relationship with Jung was colored by similar (emotionally) homosexual—but unacceptable—desires, resulting in an intense fracture. During the years 1912-1913, around the same time that Freud was theorizing and making explicit the relation between frustrated libidinal interests to paranoia he also broke from Jung. The guilt Freud felt in these intimate relationships with colleagues also explains why these tensions often resulted in a definitive end. Freud repeats that these breaks resulted from theoretical disagreements; however, his oft-misplaced defenses about these breaks indicate a motive hidden from Freud's own conscious awareness that begins in his interpretation of Irma's injection. His misplaced defensive claims beg asking what his ego desired to know and not know by repeating these explanations, shown here as a conflict between individual desires and moral norms.

Along with everyone else wondering how close Freud's personal biography influenced his theories, it also stands to reason that Freud had more cause to worry about how much of himself he injected into his general theories. He was at the forefront of systematically navigating the borders between the vicissitudes of contradicting desires and their effects on an individual mind. Freud continually claimed that his clinical results were partial. He even accused scientists that were averse to his work as driven by a general fear of diminishing the value of a rational mind and privileged ego (Freud 1918, pg. 137–144). Despite these repeated claims, he later admitted that he was "anxious not to be misunderstood" (Freud 1918, pg. 51). These admissions may not only reassure his reader to continue reading his work charitably, but also reassures him on the purpose and quality of his work.

These claims act as disclaimers, but in this meta-reading of Freud living alongside his work they also reveal his own hesitations. As a pioneer into the intricacies of personal desires, social expectations, and moral possibilities, his hesitation is surely justified. I continue to read Freud by taking him at his word. When he interrupts his clinical observations on the effects of an unconscious primal scene, for example, he makes a confession: "I can assure the reader that I am no less critically inclined than he [the reader] towards an acceptance of this observation of the child's, and I will only ask him to join me in adopting a *provisional* belief in the reality of the scene" (Freud 1918, pg. 39) (brackets added for clarity). Freud makes the same request about accepting a *naif* faith that infantile phantasies are true since they are taken as such in the adult life of the patient (Freud 1918, pg. 50). In other words, even if claims about a primal scene do not correspond to anything real, the psychic products of the mind are true enough for their author. Maybe this is what motivates Freud, who explicitly claims to forge forward into the deep stratus of the mental life, rather than be held back by a sense of his own inferiority (Freud 1918, pg. 104). Explicit statements made in his *Autobiographical Study* further illustrate those issues in the experiences of Freud's particular life that made him doubt his perceptions in a similar fashion that he doubted the perceptions of a delusional Schreber. After all, already in his interpretation of Irma's injection he proved himself capable of self-deception in this interpretive process that he claimed was scientific.

While his work in *An Autobiographical Study* (1925) was to account for "the internal growth of psychoanalysis and turn to its external history," as stated in its first pages, Freud frequently interrupts this task. Freud collapses his self with his work throughout the text. Only through the literary genre of the autobiography, which is a story of the self, does Freud embark on the story of psychoanalysis. In chapter five of his autobiography, couched in his defense of the scientific rigor of psychoanalysis, he distinguishes two phases in the history of psychoanalysis. The first was when he "stood alone and had to do all the work" from approximately 1895 to 1907 (Freud 1925, pg. 55). The second phase was when he started to work with collaborators and pupils. He had come to disagree with many of his pupils in the latter phase, such as Carl Jung and Alfred Adler. Disagreements ranged from the importance of infantile sexuality (Freud 1925, pg. 52–3), to the fundamental role of aggression, to the Oedipus complex as the nucleus of neurosis.

Freud defends the position that all psychoanalysts must accept his views on these cardinal points of infantile sexuality and the centrality of the Oedipus complex for neurosis if a theoretical approach is to be considered psychoanalytical. In his defensive claims, Freud judges that for this reason, Carl Jung and Alfred Adler should not be considered practitioners of the psychoanalytic method. Jung wanted to reduce all drives to the libido, while Adler placed more emphasis on aggression. Even if Freud's initial argument with Adler on an aggressive principle that accompanies a libidinal one was to be included in his later work *Beyond the Pleasure Principle*, the presence of Freud's personal relationships to protégés in an autobiography is not odd if it is meant to soothe his own psychic feelings and repetitions of guilt. Even while he did not understand his own motives, these explanations contribute to his understanding of his own identity rather than explicate the history of a psychological method.

Freud continues, "the secession of former pupils has often been brought up against me as sign of my intolerance or has been regarded as evidence of some special fatality that hangs over me" (Freud 1925, pg. 53). First, I wonder who has brought these charges against him. If I follow his own psychoanalytic principles that are born of his life and understanding that are ultimately meaningful for him, then I surmise that Freud is quoting his super-ego. A "fatality that hangs" over one also sounds like a neurosis that can lead to repetitive and compulsive behaviors. In this case, it would be to compulsively detach from pupils for whom he felt a strong, but ultimately frustrated, libidinal bond.

Freud goes on so that he "can say in his defense that an intolerant man, dominated by an arrogant belief in his own infallibility, would never have been able to maintain his hold upon so large a number of intelligent people, especially if he had at his command as few practical attractions as I had" (Freud 1925, pg. 53). Against what anyone else might say, the severing of relationships is due to disagreements in those cardinal psychoanalytic principles, not personal character, according to the admission of Freud's understanding of the events in his life. Different schools in psychoanalysis understand these cardinal points in various diverging ways even until today, as we will see later in the work of Donna Orange. Freud had a difficult time accepting dissenting opinions. His readers may have a harder time understanding why these opinions were so offensive to him despite writing about the highly speculative nature of his work.

In these autobiographical confessions, we find clues about his self-diagnosed neurosis. Freud admits the doubt he felt about the whole enterprise of psychoanalysis. When he arrived in America to deliver his five lectures at Clark University in Worcester, Massachusetts, he had a feeling of acceptance, which he interpreted as confirming the reality of his feelings of persecution in Europe. In spite of constantly ridiculing American readers of his work and ultimately rejecting American interpretations, and their uses and abuses of psychoanalytic theory, he records his *feeling* of acceptance in this autobiography.[5] The hostility he felt from the analytic and scien-

---

[5] See the edited collection, *After Freud Left* (2012) edited by John Burnham for more on Freud's criticism of psychoanalysis in America.

3 Getting Personal: Persecution in Freud's Personal Life   49

tific communities in Germany would be confirmed only years later when he was denied a Nobel Prize and forced to flee German Austria (Freud 1925, pg. 49). Meanwhile, Freud felt in Europe,

> as though I were despised; but over there (America) I found myself received by the foremost men as an equal. As I stepped on to the platform at Worcester to deliver my "Five Lectures upon Psychoanalysis," it seemed like the realization of some incredible daydream: psychoanalysis was no longer a product of delusion, it had become a valuable part of reality. (Freud 1925, pg. 52)

If we take Freud at his word here, then he believed psychoanalysis was the product of a delusion. Schreber's delusion resulted from an unacceptable desire and initial break from reality. The delusion of persecution was the noisy recovery of this break. Freud's break from reality started from a similar frustrated homosexual desire. Through building a psychoanalytic community, Freud returned to social reality; it was his way of recovering from a loved but reprimanding scientific community. A daydream is associated with giving pleasure to the dreamer. In this experience, Freud's doubt about his unconscious phantasy of wish fulfillment was verified in reality. His rejection by the scientific community was a conscious reality. The acceptance he experienced in America showed this truth in its contrast to his perceived reality in Vienna.

Psychoanalysis did enjoy a fast-growing audience and established many training institutes during Freud's lifetime in Budapest, Vienna, Berlin, London, and beyond. Despite the growing movement psychoanalysis enjoyed during his lifetime, these objective facts can have had little influence on Freud's psychic life, who always sought acceptance from a scientific community that in principle could not accept his work. Furthermore, his personal desires that conflicted with prevalent social norms would also cause psychic tensions, according to his own method and theoretical understanding of an individuated self who struggles against restrictive moral norms.

Still defending himself, Freud begins chapter six of his autobiography with a clear reference to a possible repetition in his observation of France's reluctant acceptance of psychoanalysis. Freud chalks up their sensitivity to what appears as the "pedantry and crudity of psychoanalytic terminology" (1925, pg. 62). Their objections, however, "seem like a reproduction of something I have lived through before, and yet it has peculiarities of its own" (Freud 1925, pg. 62). Again, Freud wonders whether the hostile feelings he perceived in France may be a repetition of his own neurotic insecurities originating in Vienna or persecutions experienced in his youth and professional life.

In the 1935 postscript of *An Autobiographical Study*, Freud listed his work in psychoanalysis with those in the natural sciences and medicine as detours to his original, youthful fascination for understanding cultural problems (Freud 1925, pg. 72). Aware that his personal life influenced his scientific work, we are left with a revealing line at the end of his postscript. Where Freud lists the honors received for his work, he concludes "[n]evertheless, the impression is a satisfactory one – of serious scientific work carried on at a high level" (Freud 1925, pg. 74). Freud's use of the term *impression* is interesting since it keeps the encouraging statement enclosed as a psychic representation—that is, possibly a conscious fantasy—in the mind in place of a factual claim about the scientific value of his work.

Even in the retelling of his life and work, it is not revealed whether his estimations about his own life, as a bold sojourner on the frontier of mental life, are based ultimately in reality. Here is an admission of his fear that, like his patients, his desires color the impressions of his life and his impressions of psychic life in general. Farrell's criticism was anticipated in Freud's thoughts and writing, only he never kept a "Cartesian starting point" from which a real self could be understood or constructed, as Farrell wrongly argues of Freud (see Chap. 1). If we take seriously Freud's claim that no subject can be transparent to itself because its self-loathing would undo itself, then we find one possible interpretation of Freud's fears as a super-egoical persecution, an imposition introjected from that unaccepting but loved scientific community.

Despite Freud, it is here that I find a generalizable point in his work on the possibility of feeling hate toward that which is libidinally invested or loved the most, which results in an amount of unknowability. Freud's revised interpretation of Irma's injection and theoretical work on Schreber's delusions of persecution exhibit an inability to reflect on one's self and motives where there is a tension between drives that are ambivalently related. Delusion is admitted by Freud to be an extreme form of repairing a psyche torn by desires that are ambivalently related. However, the presence of individuated desires that are ambivalently related to social norms creates a degree of psychic tension for all. Crews's depiction of a conniving doctor in Freud is also only partially true. Through and through Freud accepted this possibility, but continued to work despite his flaws, as only a man who loved the deep mysteries of human life can.

Given all the ways Freud finds that drives can assume other symbolic forms, through repression, sublimation, or the reversal of their content or their aim, suspicion is cast on the possibility of a growing intellect or cultural life to make itself immune to the constitutive desire to persecute that which is found hateful. During increasingly hostile times in 1932, Einstein corresponded with Freud to consider the possibility of eliminating hate and destructiveness from human instincts. Freud responded that it only seems as if aggression is mastered with the growth of culture and intellect. Instead aggressive impulses become introverted (Freud and Einstein 1933, pg. 195–216). The pacifism Albert Einstein feels as an affective repulsion and constitutional intolerance to war is what Freud calls the most drastic form of an idiosyncrasy, an exception, to the majority who act on their aggression when social life permits (Freud 1933, pg. 214).

Drives that cannot be directly perceived depict for us a subject who cannot be straightforwardly understood. Inherent in the method Freud aimed to make scientific was the need to interpret and improvise psychoanalytic therapy in order to reveal a subject to itself. Even if the particular economies and analytic methods that Freud introduced became obsolete in certain regards, he made clear that all subjective minds are vulnerable in the mere contact between their mental and somatic life. Any method of interpretation touches the interpreted, creating an endless loop of undetectability.

Ambiguity in the term *Trieb*, which is often translated to either *instinct* or *drive*—that "frontier-concept between the physical and the mental"—takes us to the root of Freud's problem. In *Three Essays on the Theory of Sexuality*, Written in 1905, Freud did not draw a distinction between a drive and its psychical representative. Here the drive is straightforwardly linked to a psychical representative of somatic impulses; however, later in his work "Repression" (1915), a drive is said to lack representational content.[6] So long as the physical stimulus of a drive is only indirectly connected to a mental representation, it cannot be directly understood given the various vicissitudes that can mask the object a drive aims toward. The mechanisms of psychosis and neurosis, as well as how these were experienced in Freud's life, illustrate this undetectability in the most extreme fashion.

Additionally, if behavior and character are determined by experiences in early infancy, as Freud argues, and these memories are not directly representable in adulthood, then Freud must acknowledge that the mental economy only has use of a decoder that works with indirect representations. Only with the help of another can one's delusions be analyzed, which makes the opening statement to Schreber's case study so telling. Freud knew that the representation of desired or hated objects also continues to alter as an understanding of them is approached. The objects one desires may not be directly related to what one will seek for its satisfaction. Freud, who fathered generations of insight and future research into types of trickery that make up the mental economy, could not evade the vicissitudes and trickery of his own impulses during his "scientific studies." He paid the price for what he desired to understand in his guilt, constant self-doubt, and suspicion of the methodology he developed.

From a discussion in this section on the ways Freud's life and theory illustrate the ways an individuated self cannot know its desires and the ways these desires can be masked by conscious reflection in Freud's theory of paranoiac delusions of persecution, I move in the next chapter to implications on social and moral norms. More than just an individuated psyche that is forged out of conflicting desires, social and moral norms can reflect ambivalent standards and similarly emerge from unreflective process of thought. I will show how the circumstances of Freud's life lead him to approach theorizing this unstable ground of moral norms, but ultimately repress this realization in his text "The Uncanny." The general yield of the following section *The Uncanniness of Conflicting Moral Norms* shows how Freud continued to, for example, make moral judgments about inhabitants in Palestine, based on cultural norms that implicitly he could no longer accept.

---

[6] See chapter 5 of *Psychoanalysis in a New Light* (2010) by Gunnar Karlsson for a fuller discussion on changes to Freud's theory of drives.

References

Burnham, J. (ed.) (2012). *After Freud Left: A Century of Psychoanalysis in America*. Chicago: The University of Chicago Press.

Ettinger, B. (2006). In B. Massumi & J. Butler (Eds.), *The matrixial borderspace*. Minneapolis: University of Minnesota Press.

Freud, S. (1953a). The standard edition of the complete psychological works of Sigmund Freud. In J. Strachey (Ed.), *The interpretation of dreams (second part) and on dreams, i–iv* (Vol. V, 1900). London: The Hogarth Press and the Institute of Psycho-analysis.

Freud, S. (1953b). The standard edition of the complete psychological works of Sigmund Freud. In J. Strachey (Ed.), *Three essays on sexuality and other works, i–iv* (Vol. V11, 1901–1905). London: The Hogarth Press and the Institute of Psycho-analysis.

Freud, S. (1955a). The standard edition of the complete psychological works of Sigmund Freud. In J. Strachey (Ed.), *An infantile neurosis and other works* (Vol. XVII, 1918). London: The Hogarth Press and the Institute of Psycho-analysis.

Freud, S. (1955b). The standard edition of the complete psychological works of Sigmund Freud. In J. Strachey (Ed.), *Beyond the pleasure principle* (Vol. XVIII, 1920). London: The Hogarth Press and the Institute of Psycho-analysis.

Freud, S. (1957). The standard edition of the complete psychological works of Sigmund Freud. In J. Strachey (Ed.), *Repression* (Vol. XIV, 1915). London: The Hogarth Press and the Institute of Psycho-analysis.

Freud, S. (1958). The standard edition of the complete psychological works of Sigmund Freud. In J. Strachey (Ed.), *The case of Schreber, papers on technique and other works, ii–vii* (Vol. XII, 1911). London: The Hogarth Press and the Institute of Psycho-analysis.

Freud, S. (1959). The standard edition of the complete psychological works of Sigmund Freud. In J. Strachey (Ed.), *An autobiographical study* (Vol. XX, 1925). London: The Hogarth Press and the Institute of Psycho-analysis.

Freud, S. (1961). The standard edition of the complete psychological works of Sigmund Freud. In J. Strachey (Ed.), *The ego and the id* (Vol. XIX, 1923). London: The Hogarth Press and the Institute of Psycho-analysis.

Freud, S. (1964a). The standard edition of the complete psychological works of Sigmund Freud. In J. Strachey (Ed.), *Why war?* (Einstein and Freud) (Vol. XXII, 1933 [1932]). London: The Hogarth Press and the Institute of Psycho-analysis.

Freud, S. (1964b). The standard edition of the complete psychological works of Sigmund Freud. In J. Strachey (Ed.), *New introductory lectures on psycho-analysis and other works* (Vol. XXII, 1936, pp. 1–267). London: The Hogarth Press and the Institute of Psycho-analysis.

Gay, P. (1988). *Freud: A life of our times*. New York/London: W.W. Norton & Company.

Gottlieb, S. (2006). Some thoughts on Schreber (and Freud): Depression, paranoia and a delusional system. *British Journal of Psychotherapy, 22*, 427–428.

Karlsson, G. (2010). *Psychoanalysis in a New Light*. New York: Cambridge University Press.

Tauber, A. I. (2009). Freud's philosophical path: From a science of mind to a philosophy of human being. *The Scandinavian Psychoanalytic Review, 32*, 32–43.

Tauber, A. I. (2010). *Freud, the reluctant philosopher*. Princeton University Press.

Chapter 4
The Uncanniness of Conflicting Moral Norms

Abstract In this chapter, I use Helen Cixous' text on Freud's repression of repression in "The Uncanny" to guide my argument that moral instability is a repressed knowledge that is further repressed in its acknowledgment. I find traces in Freud's text of his uncomfortable but growing realization that cultural and moral norms are not objective.

Keywords Freud's The Uncanny · Helen Cixous Uncanny · Moral ambivalence · Reality principle · The Sandman · E.T.A. Hoffman · Un/heimliche · Freud's Moses · Friend-emy · Moral ambiguity · Delusions of persecution

In addition to observing and trying to work out the growing tension Freud sees between libidinal and aggressive drives, and the personal ambivalence he felt toward Fleiss that became apparent in his interpretation of Irma's injection, social and political norms were found to frustrate individual desires in his understanding of paranoiac delusions of persecution. It is the last set of conflicting desires, between individual ones and their social implications that help understand Freud's approach to moral theories. Through all three sets of conflicting relations, however, runs the common theme of the incapacity to reflect on all of one's desires. Freud enjoyed a particularly productive period before the break of the First World War on the development of an individual psyche. Before 1914, he developed the pleasure and reality principles, ideas on the Oedipus complex, and on childhood sexuality. His analyses and case studies were published on the transition from early stages of narcissism to how the psychic apparatus relates to others. By looking at cases where these processes develop into neurosis/psychosis, such as in Schreber's case written in 1911, Freud could empirically gather data on otherwise general, stabile functions. As his personal experiences and clinical data included more reflections on war, Freud's interests also increasingly became critical of moral and socials bonds that conflicted with individual desires.

The historical timeline "disrupted Freud's thoughts in the most spectacular, most brutal way" (Gay 1998, pg. 342). Leading up to the Great War in 1914 and equipped with clinical observations of traumas incurred by soldiers during the war, Freud reached the conclusion that he must revise his theory of drives. The pleasure and reality principles did not sufficiently account for those patients who would seek injurious relationships considering a past trauma.

Already before the Great War, Freud had looming feelings of unease mostly as a result of the Kaiser's division between races. These were vulgar forms of Darwinism, a racism used to promote national health (Gay 1998, pg. 344). Freud initially supported a confrontation between Austria and Sarajevo in the months leading up to the war. He finally "felt like an Austrian" and held that Germany should courageously go on the offense against Serbia on the side of Austria (Gay 1998, pg. 346). Freud supported going to war with an admittedly religious fervor that was driven by nationalism at its "highest pitch of hysteria" (Gay 1998, pg. 346). Later in his correspondence with his friend Zweig, they would eventually reflect together on the shame and guilt they felt for supporting the war, a war that eventually turned both authors into pacifists.

Attributing moral worth based on genetic or cultural types was an unsettling idea for Freud. He understood it as a misappropriation of value onto a Darwinian insight. Darwinism explained the need for a biological organism to adjust for its material survival, but how does this carry into judging the values of different people or cultures? However delusional justifications for the war felt to Freud, he also felt comfort knowing he was on the "civilized" side of the fight with Germany and not on the Balkan's "enemy's side." The division became more uneasy for Freud, however, when England eventually joined the war but against Germany. England, which was once an ally, now became the enemy. Speaking about the war as "ours," Ernst Jones, Freud's British colleague, asked Freud whether it was a strange feeling for him, too, to regard an old friend as newly an enemy. An "enemy" now was a term that could also encompass a "friend," definitions of which are dual and contradictory but found in this one person. Ernst Jones might be more appropriately called a "frenemy."

Gay writes that Freud felt this "strangeness keenly"; however, "uncannily" may be the more appropriate word. Without recourse to any obvious reason, and despite Freud's nationalism, Freud responded to his old friend Jones simply: "It has been decided not to regard you as an enemy!" (Gay 1998, pg. 350). Freud kept his correspondence throughout the war with Jones who was both an enemy but also no enemy at all. We may, however, track in this incident the fact of an ambivalent feeling from changing moral norms that resulted from the sudden shift in social norms, which Freud also discloses in his work "The Uncanny."

Jones was deemed a friend and enemy at a time when the good or bad could not clearly be determined. These seemingly fixed norms changed into their opposites during this time in Freud's life. The strict demands of a super-ego and its moral standards became questionable in Freud's personal life and clearer in his theoretical work. Adding to his first-hand experience with Jones of holding conflicting moral judgments, his reflections on those who returned from war also show a development in his theories on war neuroses, repression, and the mechanism of compulsive repetition as curative measures for an injured psyche.

Freud's essay "The Uncanny," though published after the war in 1919, was admittedly a final draft to a work dug up out of a drawer (pg. 218). Not much is known about when the first drafts of the essay were begun, but Freud cites his

4 The Uncanniness of Conflicting Moral Norms

thought on the uncanny impression as far back as *Totem and Taboo*, which was published before the war in 1912–1913. He writes in *Totem and Taboo*, "[w]e appear to attribute an 'uncanny' quality to impressions that seek to confirm the omnipotence of thoughts and the animistic mode of thinking in general, after we have reached a stage at which, in our *judgment*, we have abandoned such beliefs" (Freud 1913, pg. 241). The uncanny experience arises, in other words, when mere thought seems to have the power to control or shape reality after belief in this omnipotent power has been abandoned as childish.

In his more complete work dedicated to the experience of "The Uncanny," he similarly writes, "an uncanny experience occurs either when infantile complexes which have been repressed are once more revived by some impression, or when the primitive beliefs we have surmounted seem once more confirmed" (Freud 1913, pg. 249). Freud's text shows how the "primitive" belief in the psyche's omnipotent power to shape moral reality is confirmed in E.T.A. Hoffman's short story *The Sandman*. The omnipotent power of the mind to shape moral reality is also made apparent in Freud's personal life during the rise of Nazi power.

An uncanny feeling arises when reality justifies the belief that moral and cultural norms are not rooted in an objective source of meaning and truth beyond human subjectivity, but in human power. His unstated conclusion on the ambiguous moral status of social norms is that this fact should remain hidden from oneself. When the ambiguous nature of moral value is remembered, and the meaning of what one *should do* can be dual and contradictory, the uncanny experience arises. Freud seems to repress the uncomfortable discovery from his etymological work on the German words for uncanny and in his accompanying reflection on E.T.A. Hoffman's short story written in 1816, "The Sandman." Hélène Cixous' article "Fiction and Phantoms" (1976) further illustrates Freud's repression of the unknown aspects of the short story so that I may add Freud's repression of the contradictory meanings of social and moral norms to her observation that Freud uses literature to reflect on the repression of a general unknowability in representational consciousness. Cixous presents Freud's repression of the uncanny experience of death that I will review shortly. How can Freud express his realization that morality sits on non-objective grounds while also suppressing such a realization?

At the beginning of his account, Freud moves away from studying the objects that give an uncanny feeling, which he recounts in the only other study on the uncanny experience conducted by Dr. Ernst Jentsch's medico-psychological study. Jentsch was cited by Freud as the only psychology study to examine the feeling of uncanniness and ultimately rejected his hypothesis since the uncanny feeling rests merely on a state of uncertainty. Freud also decidedly moves away from actual objects as lacking certain criteria, such as definitiveness, to the objects in experience, representations and fantasies, that are more important for him. For the investigation, he will not attempt to recreate the experience. Instead, it is important for him to submit uncanny impressions in the content of the experience to form a concept of the uncanny. Whether any of the objects encountered in these experiences are themselves uncanny is not as significant as seeing how certain representational content gives rise to an impression that is described as such.

He calls this a whole translation of "himself into that state of feeling" even though he claims not to have experienced it recently. In contrast to this claim, Freud does share numerous uncanny experiences of his own after exploring the etymological meanings of the German words "'*unheimlich*' (which) is obviously the opposite of '*heimlich*' [homely], '*heimisch*' [native]– the opposite of what is familiar; and we are tempted to conclude that what is 'uncanny' is frightening precisely because it is not known and familiar" (1913, pg. 220). Freud resists the temptation to conclude that *unheimlich* simply represents unfamiliarity or strangeness. He proposes instead that the uncanny experience is frightening because it indexes the repression of that which is *most* familiar.

Through his presentation of the lexical definitions and meanings of *Heimliche* and *Unheimliche*, Freud reaches a theoretical insight on meaning itself. Meaning is not only ambiguous, but the meanings of a word can be dual and contradictory. An uncanny sensation arises when something is both familiar, comfortable, proverbially speaking at home with oneself, but also makes one uncomfortable. He writes, "In general we are reminded that the word '*heimliche*' is not unambiguous, but belongs to two sets of ideas, which, without being contradictory, are yet very different: on the one hand, it means that which is familiar and agreeable, and on the other, that which is concealed and kept out of sight" (Freud 1913, pg. 224). Cixous writes that the unclear domain that Freud assigns this phenomenon within human experience has to do with the sensation of ambiguity itself. She finds that Freud's use of the poet Schelling provides a new understanding of this difficulty to understand concept, domain, and sense (1976, pg. 528). I will return later to her argument that Freud himself represses several of his own realizations in the performance of this very text.

Just as Freud could only reflect on delusions of persecution with the aid of colleagues, and through another person's memoirs, it is through Schelling that Freud comes to understand that "everything is *unheimlich* that ought to have remained hidden and secret but has come to light" (1919, pg. 225). Pausing at the word "ought" can help understand the moral implications of the uncanny feeling. The *ought* signifies a moral domain, for example, that one ought not fling food across the table in polite society. An uneasy and precarious relation is revealed about cultural and ethical injunctions when "a word the meaning of which develops towards ambivalence […] finally coincides with its opposite" (Freud 1919, pg. 225). The uncanny feeling results from a vulnerability to what should remain hidden and to what is only shared with those closest to oneself that can be exposed.

Freud writes next, "Thus *Heimliche* is a word the meaning of which develops in the direction of ambivalence, until it finally coincides with its opposite, *unheimliche*. Let us bear this discovery in mind, though we cannot yet rightly understand it, alongside of Schelling's definition of the *Unheimlich*" (1919, pg. 226). Development of the word *Heimliche* into its opposite *Unheimliche* indicates an obscurity in the development of meaning, as such. In the development of meaning, its evolutionary stages based on contingent history are inaccessible to the logical processes of knowledge. Deep down it is known that the origin of moral norms is unstable.

Furthermore, Freud uses Schelling to show that the possibility for reaching moral injunctions that contradict each other should remain hidden.

Freud presents from Grimm's dictionary, "*Heimliche* in a different sense, as withdrawn from knowledge, unconscious … *Heimliche* also has the meaning of that which is obscure, inaccessible to knowledge" (1919, pg. 226). In relation to morality, do we not fear losing the correct and absolute norms of our society, ones that help appropriately judge right from wrong, good from bad, real from false? Might it be feared so much that this indeterminacy in meaning and morality never ought to be thought aloud, that it should be kept hidden in the "home," or recesses of one's mind?

The exposure of contradicting moral norms in the short story by Hoffman makes it obvious that social norms are ambiguous, possibly unknown, or worse: nonexistent. If commandments, social norms, and religious norms are rendered essentially ambiguous and based on meanings that can become their opposite, then a time is possible when flinging food across the table could become what one ought to do in polite society. Freud's work poses for his reader that this drastic change in norms is known all along but is a knowledge that is repressed. Would this explain the ability to constantly vacillate between the incompatible claims that one should never murder but that in certain cases murder may be justified? Murder that is justified seems like an impossibility since, by definition, murder always lacks justification. An uncanny experience that arises from conflicting social norms leaves open the possibility that the non-justifiable act of murder can also be the most justified. Indeed, it is only after reflecting on the possibility of a justified murder that distinctions, such as senseless murder from killing in self-defense, can lead to more strict and explicit prohibitions. Unjustified murder, thus, becomes a justified act in the distinctions it provides.

The presentation of Schelling's definition introduces a moral aspect that Freud himself never properly addresses, or represses, in the rest of his article. Ambiguity in meaning regarding moral claims, what one *ought* to keep hidden, may be related to Freud's own inability to decide whether he was really persecuted or if his experience of persecution was a delusion. Despite the rising hostility he felt, he did not flee and did not reflect on why he needed to stay in Vienna at any cost. In the latter part of Freud's life, he did not know how to approach, rely on, or even live in a social reality that developed Nazi ideals that found his life morally reprehensible. Given his theoretical understanding of the power of delusional psychosis, Freud hesitated about the possible delusional nature of the hostility he felt from the changing norms of his society. Freud admittedly could never understand why his Jewish origins need be so morally repulsive. It was a difference, but he did not understand why it was a difference that should make him inferior. Freud's inability to leave Vienna is arguably also due to his rightist politics that sympathized with a movement that hated Bolsheviks as much as he sympathized with a dislike for lower class Shtetl Jews who came to Vienna after his own family immigrated there. Freud had a difficult time understanding that he might share their same fate, in spite of warnings from close friends about the increasing risk.

For example, in a quick note in his *Autobiographical Study*, Freud refers to his early years at the University of Vienna. It was expected that Freud "should feel ashamed of [his] descent or, as people were beginning to say, of [his] race" (1925, pg. 8). Before describing his own feelings of being ostracized, Freud brings up his parents' persecution that forced them to flee eastwards to Cologne.[1] His father who was famously scorned by Freud for being weak in the face of anti-Semitism came from a family who fled eastwards during Jewish persecution in the fourteenth and fifteenth century (Freud 1925, pg. 1). The family migrated back from Lithuania back to German Austria in the nineteenth century, as Freud retells the story. To his reader, this quick note indicates Freud's awareness of repetition in experiences of Jewish persecution in Europe. Although he refused to feel inferior during his life, he did personally feel alien and fated to be in opposition against the majority in other ways, such as in his work.

If the moral dimension of uncanniness relates to losing the correctness of social norms, and the ability to know how, for what, and from where these norms are constituted, then Freud is reflecting on an amount of possible arbitrariness and meaninglessness to his and his family's persecutions. These questions relate to the origins of ethical life, which Freud admittedly was concerned with finding already in *Totem and Taboo* (1913, pg. 46). Is this not the preoccupation echoing through many of Freud's texts, most memorably in *Civilization and Its Discontents* (1930) when he admits at this late stage of his career, "But we are unable to understand what the necessity is which forces civilization along this path and which causes its antagonism to sexuality. There must be some disturbing factor which we have not yet discovered?" (pg. 91). The origins of moral life are as unknown as those standards that are upheld. While moral demands create the possibility for a social life, they also repress individual drives that make living with others a precarious balance between individual and social demands.

After his etymological work, and after summarizing the plot of Hoffman's short story *The Sandman*, Freud writes that anyone is capable of seeing through the eyes of someone with delusional neurosis, similar to the way he reads through delusional Nathanael, the main character of E.T.A. Hoffman's "The Sandman" (1919, pg. 230). In the short story, Nathanael has several psychotic breaks after an uncanny experience with a barometer salesman and with a woman who becomes the object of his love interest. Both these figures stir an emotional trauma from childhood and reveal the instability of norms in Nathanael's social reality. In being able to see the menacing character of the Sandman through Nathanael's delusional eyes, the reader's eyes are distorted, indeed, castrated from its rational mind. The reader perceives that Nathanael cannot escape images of the Sandman, just as Freud cannot escape images of his rejections from the scientific community and in his personal relationships. Even if Freud was justified in his worry because of his persecution as

---

[1] I will address his vacillation between his own ambivalent feelings regarding his status as a Jew and the hostile environment of his beloved Vienna in his correspondence with Zweig later.

a scholar who was Jewish, the degree to which he felt persecuted may have been amplified by externalizing his own internal desire to be accepted.

It is worth recounting Hoffman's story to see its parallels to Freud's life and its use by Freud for developing the uncanny feeling that arises from conflicting moralities. "The Sandman" was originally published in 1816, and in what seems like a predecessor to Kafkaesque themes in storytelling, the narrative places the reader in a bewildering perspective whose psychological state is questioned throughout. The short story begins with the first person perspective of our protagonist Nathanael who recounts a fairytale told to him and his siblings as children. If they did not go to bed, the Sandman would come and blow sand in their eyes, making them heavy with sleep.

Even as he grew old and came to recognize that the fairytale could not be real, Nathanael nevertheless wrote to his friend, "the Sandman was still a frightful phantom to me, and I was seized with terror and horror when I heard him not merely mounting the stairs, but tearing the door of my father's room violently open and going in" (Hoffman 1963, pg. 23). After some snooping around, Nathanael discovered that the dreadful stomping came from his father's frequent visitor, Coppelius, an old lawyer who was a friend of the family. It would be his father's alchemic experiments with Coppelius that would eventually cause an explosion that killed his father.

This childhood "experience" of a frightening fairytale, the death of his father, and the recurring presence of the villainous character of the Sandman are retold coherently and with vivid recall in letters written by Nathanael. Nathanael seems to know that his fear of the eye-stealing Sandman is irrational and rooted in a personal childhood experience. This knowledge does not remove the horror that enters his life as "Dark premonitions of an atrocious fate loom over me like the shadows of black clouds, impervious to every ray of sunshine" (Hoffman 1963, pg. 1). The letter written by Nathanael never reaches its intended audience and instead reaches his love Klara.

Like those figures in Freud's life to whom he could turn for help with analysis, Klara is sympathetic to the trauma of Nathanael's childhood experience and the emotional effects it has had on his mind. She is also hopeful that with her and her brother, Lothar's, interpretive help, Nathanael can be cured of these recurring visions of the Sandman. They will help clear his mind of the false belief that the Sandman appears as different figures that threaten to steal his eyes, most recently as a barometer salesman. As much as they try to persuade him of the connection between the Sandman and his childhood, Nathanael's capacity to reason is not strong enough for him to internalize this connection in the face of a repressed memory. His fearful delusions of persecution from the Sandman are too strong. During one last correspondence from Nathanael to Lothar about the unfortunate mix-up with the letters, Nathanael includes an uncanny vision he recently had of a lovely girl named Olympia.

As delusions take a stronger hold of Nathanael's psychic life, an omniscient narrator occasionally describes Nathanael's lived experiences where he envisions the fairytale character of the Sandman as the barometer seller Coppola and the lawyer

Coppelius. The shift in narrative from Nathanael's first person to an omniscient narrative indicates that the light of his reason and sight is put out in the face of his traumatic memory. Nathanael can no longer reliably recount his experiences since they are not rooted in objects outside his delusions. The Sandman as castrating site, a metaphor for knowledge, has done its work. The story develops between Nathanael's delusional eyes and the occasional omniscient narrative.

Nathanael's general mood is described as sinking into a foreboding gloom, as if cruel powers decided every one of his actions, emotions, and thoughts. The omniscient author explains how his relationships were effected, especially with Klara who would often try to convince Nathanael that the dark powers of the characters he perceives are in his mind. She tries to convince him that the character's power is granted more strength by his growing belief in them. Nathanael, on the other hand, "knows" that these dark forces and powers come from forces outside his mind. These conversations between Nathanael and his rational friends resemble Freud's own early struggle to find the ways in which rational knowledge and empirical data in therapy may possibly cure the powerful psychic forces of experiences rooted in childhood. By the end of his career, like the end of Nathanael's life taken by a delusional force, Freud abandoned finding cures for a mind wrought out of its representations.

At the height of Nathanael's gloomy and foreboding mood, Nathanael found a new companion in Olympia that seemed to him to understand his soul's troubles. Unlike anyone before, especially the rational-minded Klara, Olympia understands "his whole poetic talent, and from the depths of his own soul, as though the voice had come from within himself" (Hoffman 1963, pg. 28). The narrative suggests at times that Nathanael knows the truth that the uncanny figure of Olympia is only a mechanically constructed mannequin who is animated by his delusions.

At this point in the story, the reader is only left with an omniscient narrator who occasionally hints that Olympia is animated by Nathanael's mind. At other times, the narrator justifies the harmony between their minds by referring to their compatibility as lovers. The reader, along with Nathanael, is never sure about the woman with whom he has fallen madly in love. Hoffman almost forces the reader into Nathanael's delusion, as if anyone could experience a rational blindness that arises from a childhood trauma. Freud commends this fictional writer for creating such an environment, where "uncertainty disappears in the course of Hoffman's story, and we perceive that he means to make us, too, look through the demon optician's spectacles or spy-glass – perhaps, indeed, that the author in his very own person once peered through such an instrument" (1919, pg. 230). This passage is Freud's most telling line in his analysis of uncanniness. To which author is Freud referring—to Hoffman who peered through delusional eyes, or to himself? Has Freud similarly possessed a distorted gaze for understanding the uncertainty that accompanies delusions? Freud admitted as much at the beginning of his account of Schreber, and the need for his friend's aid to interpret the data. Freud continues to wonder if we can sympathize with Nathanael's delusion because of delusions from our own particular and personal repressed memories.

As the story develops, the reader is just as influenced by Nathanael's delusions as he seems to be. While the reader moves forward in the plot of his love affair with Olympia, Nathanael complains about Klara's love that cannot understand the deepest effects of his experiences with the Sandman on his present state of mind. Several more characters through the story attempt to clarify Olympia's nature without success. One friendly character in the story, Siegmund, describes Olympia's perfections, her measured movements, accurate rhythm, and symmetrical face. He notes, however, that the face has no vision, no *visage*, no life. Like the psychoanalytic work Sigmund Freud develops for understanding neurotic and psychotic breaks, Siegmund attempts to reveal to Nathanael his delusions but fails. In an almost ironic foreshadowing of Freud's fears about his own psychoanalytic efforts, Siegmund is not heard of much in the rest of the story.

Despite these hints about Olympia's true nature as an automaton, the reader (like Nathanael) is never sure of this until his psychotic break. Only when Olympia is dismembered in a physical fight between Nathanael, the feared Coppola who had come to take her, and her creator Spallanzani, does it become clear that she is in fact a wooden doll. After Olympia fraudulently attended parties that were hosted by polite society, a general claim in the story is made about lovers who insist from then on that their mistresses sing out of tune, or dance out of time, to prove that they were not automatons. Norms of Nathanael's day changed into their opposite for remembering the messy business of human nature. Instead of holding the ideal of self-mastered dance and holding accurate time, inaccuracy was valued. Instead of undivided attention paid to one's spouse, one was expected to knit while the other spoke in order to show the imperfections of an emotional nature. In these moments of Hoffman's story, the possibility of reaching a dual and contradictory meaning of words and social norms becomes explicit. The moral dimension in uncanniness becomes explicit when these idealized social norms change into their opposites due to the contingent events that surrounded Nathanael and Olympia's relationship.

Neither reason nor light can penetrate the dark clouds childhood experiences create for Nathanael in his individual private life or anybody under Freud's estimation. After Nathanael's psychic break, the reader wakes with him recovering in his home. His beloved Klara is back at his side, nursing him to health. Waves of reassurance wash over Nathanael, his loved ones, and the readers. The conclusion of the narrative gives relief from a delusional world where things like impolite society can appear as polite, and where norms once doubted are secured.

Before the end of Hoffman's short story, however, Nathanael has one final psychotic break. Nathanael leaps to his death from a tower, after which Coppelius lives on, laughs, and admits to expecting this ending. He vanishes into the crowd as a symbolic gesture that anyone can suffer from blinding delusions. The question left open at the end of "The Sandman" is whether all these characters that repeat in Nathanael's life, such as Coppola the optician or the lawyer Coppelius, were The Sandman. Freud definitively asserts, there is "no question" and "no doubt," that "the conclusion of the story makes it quite clear that Coppola the optician really *is* the lawyer Coppelius and also, therefore, the Sand-Man" (Freud 1919, pg. 230). For Freud, delusions of Nathanael's mind made The Sandman real, for him. Whether there is a real object and person of The Sandman that corresponds to the belief that he exists does not matter to the psyche. Hélène Cixous, in "Fiction and Its Phantoms," writes that Freud is committing here a repression of repression, a desire not to think about that which one wants to avoid acknowledging, namely, the indeterminate nature of knowledge of the neuroses.

In finding cause and effect, Freud makes an analytic argument to declare certitude in his conclusions of the story (Cixous 1976, pg. 533). There remains no *Unheimliche* in Freud's retelling of the story. In his act of sidestepping the imaginary axis of the story, or incomplete perceptions of identities, the uncertainty implied in Nathanael's neurosis is left out. Freud recounts the fictional character's experiences as a case study for the general feeling of uncanniness, rather than confront it as the uncanny ability to deceive oneself, or the unreflective ability to adopt any moral standard. More interesting is what Freud never explicitly states in his analysis on the uncanny experience, namely, the sexual character of morality, and the possibility that moral standards rest on ambivalent meanings.

Morality is sexual in nature by enabling one to form enlarging social bonds, beginning with those who are like one's self. Freud found that the homosexual component of emotional life moves one from the autoerotic position to forming relations with those who are dissimilar from oneself. The omnipotence a child initially feels in controlling autoerotic feelings of love eventually becomes frustrated by meeting others that are different and possibly hurtful. Freud developed what he understood as the reality principle that acknowledges confrontation with a harsh reality outside of individuated desires. The omnipotent control enjoyed in earlier stages of autoeroticism is repressed as the reality principle develops. At this time in history, however, it is becoming apparent that social norms can transform into their opposite. Minds do have the power to create social and moral norms, but also have the power to change them into their opposites. Many in liberal Austria, for example, wished to be annexed by a fascistic Nazi Germany. Freud's personal experience with his frenemy Jones, for example, also signaled a moral dimension to the uncanniness of social norms that can change based on contingent facts. Jones was both friend and enemy, based on fluctuating cultural standards from which Freud had to personally choose.

Freud shows his desire-not-to-know the amorphous root of moral and social norms. Cixous calls attention to Freud's attempt to fill in gaps, identifying it with his own fear of castration, the castration of reason. As Cixous argues, "[t]he hypothesis aimed at filling the gaps (these 'become filled with meaning') derives from a refusal to admit the insignificance of certain characteristics" (Cixous 1976, pg. 536). In her meta-reading, Freud is the one that avoids an uncanny absence, or loss, of meaning by using the tools of psychoanalysis. His repetitive use of claims, such as "it has become certain," or "no doubt," shows all the different ways Freud wants to claim mastery in his knowledge, which is the aim of positivism. By only accepting empirical or verifiable knowledge, meaning is confined to that which appears and can be verified. Substitutions made for the repressed fear of castrated knowledge—that is, of sight, of light, of the light of reason, and of the power of experience—echo through Freud's text to illuminate the uncanny origin of meaning that cannot be grasped or fixed.

Freud challenges the positivist method by emphasizing the power of repressed memories that come to light only through substituted objects, or a reversal of desire from love to hate. Against himself, Freud continues to fill the gaps of his knowledge on delusions by repeating certitude that he does not have because, first, Nathanael is a fictional character. Positivist methods would not accept medical data that were based on a literary figure since the story is an invention of a singular author. A single fictional character born of an author's imagination cannot be used as verifiable data to find a real general principle. Freud's repression of the uncanny in Hoffman's story can also be found in his ignoring that it was written in such a way as to keep these ambiguities open, as Cixous observes.

At the end of his article on "The Uncanny," Freud turns to the experience of the uncanny in relation to death. Death is the clearest example where ideas and experiences attempt to explain that which cannot be known. Death represents the unknowable, as such, since where death is life is not, and where there is life death is not. There is an inability to master knowledge about death and yet the sheer volume of work produced on the matter is enormous. Freud realizes this, and yet continues to theorize about death, such as in this essay and later speculating on its biological origin in *Beyond the Pleasure Principle*. In these instances, he commits a similar repression of the uncanny experience of death that arises from unknowable conditions, as he does on the underdetermined source of morality.

Death holds the highest degree of *Unheimliche* (Cixous 1976, pg. 542). Therefore, as Cixous finds, there can be no representation for death, "As an impossible representation, death is that which mimes, by this very impossibility, the reality of death. It goes even further. That which signifies without that which is signified" (Cixous 1976, pg. 543). Freud's defense against death's invasion is a response through fabricated stories for consolation. He explains, for example, how religious, political, and social orders utilize the unknowability of death for population control. Cixous sees, however, something much more pernicious in Freud's inability to draw sharp distinctions between the real and the fantastic, between what is imagined and what is really experienced (Cixous 1976, pg. 545).

What can be surmounted or overcome in reality by a reality principle is not to remove an experience and the feeling of omnipotence that comes from "something contained in representations which is repressed, that is to say a *psychic* reality" (Cixous 1976, pg. 545). That which is surmounted is not expelled from the psyche but kept in its most archaic beliefs. A real fact, or extraordinary coincidence, can make these surmounted beliefs "return," and literature has the unique ability of removing rigidity in real objects to show the truly uncanny. Freud's use of common tropes in literature and analyzing recurring symbols in dreams is his testimony that positivist science cannot capture the unreal and the phantastic truth contained in one's psyche. In "A Difficulty in the Path of Psycho-Analysis," Freud claims that the "ego is not master in its own house," a consequence that follows from the inability to distinguish one's conscious (or internal) perception of self from what one wills and desires (1918, pg. 143). Drives that cannot be discerned are what Freud calls "alien guests" hosted in the ego that cannot be driven away (1918, pg. 141). Freud leaves the door open for us to wonder about these aliens that are in the house of the ego and sheds a proverbial black light on the condition of unknowability in the formation of self. It is a black light because Freud sought those non-phenomenological conditions that make any phenomenon possible, including moral standards.

Cixous concludes that fictional reality is a vibration of the real, turning Freud's own writing on the castration complex and the myth of Oedipus into his own creative fictions. Freud develops this approach at grasping the illusory, contradicting, and elusive meaning of the uncanny despite his own inability to fully realize it. As Cixous writes, "Freud's adventure in this text is consecrated to the very paradox of writing which stretches its signs in order to 'manifest' the secret that it 'contains'" (Cixous 1976, pg. 547). The *unheimliche* refers to the secret it possesses on death. The use of *Unheimliche,* for Freud, also serves to redouble the discomfort of never knowing the certainty of moral claims, while the use of fiction attempts to characterize and represent that which is presented with much difficulty.

Just as the character of Nathanael cannot escape images of the Sandman, I argue that Freud cannot escape images of what he perceives to be his own rejection by a loved scientific community and the rejection of his theoretical work. All the success he had in establishing a psychoanalytic method could not remove the view of his shortcomings relative to positivism and the method of scientific investigation. The proximity of his insight on neurosis and psychosis when social instability increased from wars fought on ideological grounds could only contribute to his uncanny sense of the unstable origins of morality and knowledge based on reality. Additionally, his childhood love for an enlightened culture contributed to his inability to fully acknowledge the threatening truth of a corrosive Viennese culture.

If I return to Freud commending Hoffman for creating a story through which delusions are experienced by any healthy-minded reader, he wonders whether the author was once delusional enough to recreate this environment where the light of reason is impenetrable next to the density of a repressed memory that creates a delusional reality in its defense. For Nathanael's character, a live girl is seen where there is only an inanimate object. Did Hoffman once possess the gaze of a psyche wrought with repressed memories, seeing the delusions of his neurosis in reality? Might any reader be able to sympathize with Hoffman and Freud's writing on delusions because the line between reality and fantasy is blurrier than is comfortably admitted to oneself? We must answer in the affirmative if we can sympathize with those who are laughing in the cover picture of this very book.

When I ask the same about Freud, I wonder whether he has looked through repressed eyes to see a live girl where there is only an inanimate object or, more relevantly, whether he doubted seeing persecuting relations where they may have actually existed. Under the horizon of meaning in Freud's life and theoretical work on the illusory nature of paranoiac delusions, what becomes of real persecutions that are feared as only representative of a delusion? The ambiguous line between imaginings based on real events in memory and imaginings that result from a paranoiac delusion is thin and requires constant verification. But how do we undergo this process of verification? Before Freud started his interpretative work on Schreber, he admits a mistrust of his own experiences on the root of paranoiac disorders in a frustrated homosexual wishful phantasy. His work, therefore, on Schreber can only proceed with the help of his "friends" Sándor Ferenczi and C.G. Jung (Freud 1918 pg. 59). I must ask what other methods are available since these same mechanisms also lead to persecuting and harming those who are perceived to threaten one's perceived worldview.

Given the events of Freud's life and time, including the history of his parents and the Jewry of Europe, much of his feelings of persecution may have been warranted. A homosexual desire for Fleiss and the proximity Fleiss had to bio-medical research lead to Freud's misinterpretation of the dream of Irma's injection. Only years later could he admit the inability to face these repressed desires associated with Fleiss. Freud's sour break with a close colleague continues to happen repeatedly through the rest of his career. What first happens with Fleiss similarly happens later with Adler, then with Jung. These relationships ended in the same catastrophic way as with Fleiss. Freud admits in his autobiography that his relationships seem to follow an unknown but determined pattern. The same patterns seem to follow his mere impression of acceptance in the U.S.A. as opposed to his rejection in Europe from the science communities. Freud used Schreber's biography to understand paranoiac delusions of persecution and commended him on the difficult ability to distinguish between a real and an imagined-persecuting Dr. Flechsig. In this exposition of certain biographical details from Freud's life, alongside his essay "The Uncanny," I have shown several places where he comes close to regarding himself and his findings as the product of his own neuroses.

With all this research and insight into the imaginings of a psyche that deceives itself, he may have asked through to the end of his life how much of his own unconscious phantasms, repressed fantasies, and conscious imaginings made up his representation of reality. In addition to the fearful, but strong, attempt to approach the intimate but unknown experience of death, he also confronts the instability of social norms. Freud's enacting the very castration of a fearful but familiar knowledge of the antagonisms morality possesses to oneself and oneself in a community also strengthens the relation between phantasy, imagination, fiction, and knowledge.

The time and place of his life confirm the real persecution his family and ancestors felt in Europe; however, through his writing there is a consistent presentation and representation of these persecutions, the latter opening the door for his wondering: are these impressions of persecution real or delusions and is it possible that these persecuting acts are moral? The differences between representations and fantasy for Freud matter little to the life of the psyche, which also could have made him reluctant to ultimately abandon an increasingly hostile but loved community.

In the trajectory of his own work, unconscious phantasy plays an increasingly important role in the ego's formation. Distinguishing between persecutions that are experienced by psychic mechanisms and social persecutions rooted in a hostile other becomes further complicated. Freud's work "On Narcissism" (1914a) and "Instincts and their Vicissitudes" (1914b) shows an individuated self who is always vulnerable to the persecutory relation, either by the harshness of an impinging and external reality, or by other objects and people that have to be integrated with the images of oneself, such as in processes of introjection.

The worry that unconscious processes of moral thought effect super-egoical demands is also expressed in *The Ego and the Id* (1923). Freud writes,

> [t]he ego ideal is therefore the heir of the Oedipus Complex, and thus, it is also the expression of the most powerful impulses and most important libidinal vicissitudes of the id. By setting up this ego ideal, the ego has mastered the Oedipus Complex and at the same time in subjection of the id. Conflicts between the ego and the ideal will, as we are now prepared to find, ultimately reflect the contrast between what is real and what is psychical, between the external world and the internal world. (pg. 36)

As the ego represents common sense and reason, it is affected by an id that contains elemental aggression as well as the "higher nature of man" (Freud 1923, pg. 37). The ego exercises standards inherited to it from former religious values and standards for self-judgment in the form of its conscience, but a conscience that is not reflective only of standards in one's life. Moral censorship can also be experienced when there is "tension between the demands of conscience and the actual performance of the ego [that] is experienced as a sense of guilt" (Freud 1923, pg. 37). Having theorized about the real effects that the inherited aspect of psychic life has on a sense of morality and guilt leads to questioning whether moral standards are merely inherited and contingently stable, and which are worth upholding as if they are rooted in an external world with objective validity.

Freud's method documented psychic development at a unique time such as his. The historical time that experienced two World Wars provided material for interrogating psychic forms of persecution in a culture where the ambiguous nature of morals became explicit. The ability and even joy exhibited in persecuting others moved the scenes for Freud between psychic, historic, and cultural material for investigating this phenomenon. He began with clinical research on individual patients that were dealing with personal childhood traumas. The wars enabled understanding individual traumas that resulted from the imposition of social norms on the individual and the effects of extra-psychic dynamics on individual patients.

It will finally be useful to place Freud in the context of his own history to understand how personal desires and drives that are ambivalent to each other relate to social, extra-psychic conditions. Returning to Alon Confino who traced German culture when it tried to create itself anew without reference to Jewish morality, he writes, "The main issue with explaining the Holocaust is not about what happened in Auschwitz, but it's about the imagination that made Auschwitz possible to begin with."[2] Confino traces the role imagination plays in those that made Auschwitz possible, which also allows the listener to acknowledge the humanity of both victims and perpetrators. Whether imaginings of the Jew were based in reality or whether they were based on illusions is of no importance to the life of the psyche. Imagination has a persuasive effect on the individual person. Freud experienced

---

[2] Quoted from an interview with Confino Alon, author of *A World Without Jews: The Nazi Imagination from Persecution to Genocide*. Hear a blurb about the book here: https://youtu.be/C1BwavNXK-k

first-hand the persuasive effects imaginings have for an individual psyche in himself and his analysands.

The increasing mental and physical weakness Freud felt late in life may be due to the dissolution of the bonds he found significant during his life. As early as 1926, he is quoted as saying in an interview, "My language is German. My culture, my attainments are German. I consider myself German intellectually, until I noticed the growth of anti-Semitic prejudice in Germany and German Austria. Since that time, I prefer to call myself a Jew" (Gay 1998, pg. 448). Later in life, he would correspond with Arnold Zweig who wrote a book titled *Insulted and Exiled* in 1937 on the psychological impact of feeling exiled from one's land or nation. Whether the reflection contained there was true to historic, psychoanalytic, or social fact is not as important as the preoccupation with the internal perception of exile. Freud and Zweig's mutual feelings of exile from their secular communities in Austria for being Jewish added to their feeling of exile as Austrian Jews who could no longer apply the nation's symbols to them. By the end of his life, Freud's identity was in exile from all he held dear.

Before finally settling in London, Freud discussed moving to Palestine with his friend Zweig who immigrated there in 1933 after his books were publicly burnt. Palestine was not a real option for Freud to make a new home and identity. Many reasons can be found in his letters for not moving there, such as the lack of material provisions and cultural resources there. Furthermore, beneficiaries such as Ernst Jones and Princess Bonaparte helped secure material resources for his move to London. What becomes abundantly clear through his personal letters is that he would not move there also because of his own racialization of Palestine. Referring to inhabitants in Palestine as "savagery" (Freud et al. 1987, pg. 36, 40) he would not even consider immigrating there. Even as he describes in December 1937 that the noose around the necks of Viennese Jews was tightening, he remained in Vienna (Freud et al. 1987, pg. 154). Freud's correspondence with Arnold Zweig also reveals his motives for writing *Moses and Monotheism*, where many of his conclusions are reached about a moral civilization and the damning effects of such tight bonds.

In this historical novel, Freud represents Moses as a sun-worshipping Egyptian. As the one who brought the Hebrews out of Egypt, Moses is credited with turning this wandering group of Hebrews into a Jewish community entering the promised land of Israel. The commandments at Mount Sinai gave these people an identity in their morality and obligation to the one God of their forefathers, Abraham, Isaac, and Jacob. Freud writes to Zweig in September of 1934, "faced with the new persecutions, one asks oneself again how the Jews have come to be what they are and why they have attracted this undying hatred. So I gave my work the title: *The Man Moses, a historical novel*" (Freud et al. 1987, pg. 91). As he repressed the severity of changing moral and social norms in his time and confronting the possibility that a move would be unjustified, Freud instead attempted to dissolve the difference between the Jew and Egyptian gentile as a solution to this undying animosity. Though the novel began its life as a historical work, it started taking the shape of a psychoanalytic reflection on the origins of moral and Jewish life.

Significantly, it seems as if Freud himself did not remember that he began this work as a historical novel and was discontent with the lack of precision and accuracy of the facts he presented after it was published. Freud sent many laments about his historical inaccuracies to Zweig. The historical novel as he intended to write it, however, does not require an accurate historical account. The historical discrepancies in a fictional novel are not as significant as when their true historical origins are attempting to be traced. These laments reveal frustration at his attempt to undo his Jewish identity and to reconcile it with the Gentile. Freud was forced to withdraw libidinal interest in his society and lost sight of the reality of his claims. When the relationships around him were literally in flames, and his siblings were sent to gas chambers after he fled to London, and the work of his colleagues burning in public squares, Freud's own attempts at their undoing can be seen as coherent with the attempts of his Austrian neighbors. Like the attempt at burning others, Freud similarly burnt his libidinal ties and attachments. Near the end of his life, after most of his assets were seized, and after the Gestapo interrogated his daughter Anna Freud, Freud finally agreed to move to London in 1938, where he died approximately 1 year later of cancer.

Confino's remarks about acknowledging the story and imagination of German culture that led up to these events are relevant for the lives of both Freud and Lévinas, and their insight on a kind of person that persecutes others. According to the second topology Freud developed in *Beyond the Pleasure Principle*, the super-ego, and any moral sentiment, is a violent force formed to find pleasure in denouncing aggression and guilt that cultural norms demand and will be addressed in the next section on vulnerability. Some moral sentiments that produced pleasure and guilt in Freud's own life centered on his feelings of homosexuality (see: Chap. 2) and in feeling inadequate relative to a positivist's scientific community that sought empirical clarity. The part of Freud's life that had an explicit effect on his theories in the ways he predicted can be seen in his interpretation of Irma's injection, and the parallel details between his life and analysis of delusions of persecution. The uncanny showed his repression of unstable moral norms and the conditions of unknowability when one's individual desires clash with moral sentiments that seem to be socially fixed. In the battle to aggressively silence one's aggression for appeasing its sociality, the desire also ambivalently serves the pleasure principle. Libidinal excitement comes from violently silencing troubling desires. Troubling desires, however, are always lurking at the bottom of a psyche that on the one hand aims to preserve unity and harmony in the face of an unexpected world and, on the other, will zealously pursue imagined desires even at the expense of others—and especially at the expense of others who presumably threaten such harmony.

Cultural progress through the scientific means of gaining self-knowledge and control was surmised as good enough to reduce a persecutory spirit in the early 1800s; however, Freud shows how these aggressive impulses multiplied its force. The duplicities inherent to the psyche and its knowledge are palpable and make their way into Freud's theoretical reflections. The highest goal presumed in the scientific model is total self-knowledge and, as such, an omniscient ability for self-control. Imagine all the accounts of joy that were felt when one completed an art piece, musical score, writing a book, or working out a scientific theorem. The same amount of force that is sustained in this pleasure is the same force used to repress aggression toward those who would prevent the goal of omniscience and for the ego's oldest wish for omnipotence (Freud 1930, pg. 121). Freud's life illustrates his desire for scientific clarity while his work suspects the possibility of objective knowledge and confirms the absolute reality psychic representations hold for the mind. Calls to persecute those who risk this self-mastery were prevalent in modern civilization and were convincing enough for the individual to zealously pursue them.

On the basis of my thesis that subjectivity is always negotiating between persecutory relations and ethical demands, I want to further understand the extent that Freud participated in this culture of persecution toward other Jews, and himself, in what he developed elsewhere as moral masochism. In Freud's correspondence with Arnold Zweig, it is apparent that Freud was not free from the kind of thinking and imagination rampant in Viennese culture at the time. He desired to be a positivist scientist yet was incapable of using its method for investigating psychic drives. In *Moses and Monotheism,* he attempted to occlude his otherness and to make the Jew the same as the Gentile by unraveling the origin of otherness in the Jew. Perhaps most damning was his obvious reluctance to admit the severity of German culture's own barbarism. Taken together, all of this traces Freud's participation in the imagination of his time and place. These also illustrate some ways of dealing with the fact of inheriting cultural and moral norms that leave reason incapable of finding a stable truth or a set of true relations between others; each becomes existentially vulnerable to social norms that are largely accepted unreflectively. Despite his keen awareness of this fact, vulnerability to the norms of social life can be seen in Freud behaviors and the theories he developed.

References

Cixous, H., & Dennomé, R. (1976). Fiction and its phantoms: A reading of Freud's Das Unheimliche (The 'uncanny'). *New Literary History, 7*(3), 525–548. (528).
Confino, A. (2014). *A world without Jews: The Nazi imagination from persecution to genocide.* New Haven: Yale University Press.
Freud, S. (1955a). The standard edition of the complete psychological works of Sigmund Freud. In J. Strachey (Ed.), *Totem and taboo* (Vol. XIII, 1913). London: The Hogarth Press and the Institute of Psycho-analysis.
Freud, S. (1955b). The standard edition of the complete psychological works of Sigmund Freud. In J. Strachey (Ed.), *An infantile neurosis and other works* (Vol. XVII, 1918). London: The Hogarth Press and the Institute of Psycho-analysis.
Freud, S. (1955c). The standard edition of the complete psychological works of Sigmund Freud. In J. Strachey (Ed.), *The uncanny* (Vol. XVII, 1919). London: The Hogarth Press and the Institute of Psycho-analysis.
Freud, S. (1955d). The standard edition of the complete psychological works of Sigmund Freud. In J. Strachey (Ed.), *A difficulty in the path of psycho-analysis* (Vol. XVII, 1918). London: The Hogarth Press and the Institute of Psycho-analysis.
Freud, S. (1957a). The standard edition of the complete psychological works of Sigmund Freud. In J. Strachey (Ed.), *On narcissism* (Vol. XIV, 1914). London: The Hogarth Press and the Institute of Psycho-analysis.

Freud, S. (1957b). The standard edition of the complete psychological works of Sigmund Freud. In J. Strachey (Ed.), *Instincts and their vicissitudes* (Vol. XIV, 1914). London: The Hogarth Press and the Institute of Psycho-analysis.

Freud, S. (1959). The standard edition of the complete psychological works of Sigmund Freud. In J. Strachey (Ed.), *An autobiographical study* (Vol. XX, 1925). London: The Hogarth Press and the Institute of Psycho-analysis.

Freud, S. (1961a). The standard edition of the complete psychological works of Sigmund Freud. In J. Strachey (Ed.), *The ego and the id* (Vol. XIX, 1923). London: The Hogarth Press and the Institute of Psycho-analysis.

Freud, S. (1961b). The standard edition of the complete psychological works of Sigmund Freud. In J. Strachey (Ed.), *Civilization and its discontents, and other works* (Vol. XXI, 1930). London: The Hogarth Press and the Institute of Psycho-analysis.

Freud, S., Zweig, A., & Freud, E. L. (1987). *The letters of Sigmund Freud and Arnold Zweig*. New York: New York University Press.

Gay, P. (1998). *Freud: A life of our times*. New York/London: W.W. Norton & Company.

Hoffman, E.T.A. (1816/1963). *The tales of Hoffman* (trans: Bullock, M.). New York: Frederick Ungar Publishing Co.

Chapter 5
Freud's Vulnerability to the Social Ideals of His Time and Moral Skepticism

Abstract This chapter explores how cultural bonds and experiences unknowingly affect personal judgment and so lead to Freud's moral skepticism. I recount Freud's inability to reflect on risks to his life—despite theorizing about the opacity of knowledge—to show how more generally one is always unknowably affected by social and personal expectations. Freud's vulnerability coupled with his astute observation about the opacity of knowledge demonstrates the human subject's existential vulnerability to suffer from, and enjoy the use, of persecuting violence to attain moral ideals. Finally, I present and respond to Freud's hyperbolic conclusion on the impossibility of living an ethical life. I expose his moral skepticism as representative of a tradition that values an individualized self and that culminates in the erosion of moral responsibility for the other.

Keywords Freud's vulnerability · Existential vulnerability · Jewish Persecution · Arnold Zweig · European Jewry · Persecution to genocide · Freud's Autobiographical study · Nazi persecutions · Freud in Kristallnacht · Paul Ricouer on evil · Distantiation · Hermeneutics of suspicion · Moral skepticism · Natural morality · Sadistic super-ego · Primary masochism · Sense of guilt · Moral masochism · Ego ideal · Narcissistic identifications · Love they neighbor · Freud's correspondence Einstein · Why War? · Cultural normativity · Aggressive super-ego

Freud's self-image was vulnerable to the social ideals of his time, one that he loved but that excluded his Jewish heritage. He was also vulnerable to a scientific community whose standards were appreciated but could not be met by his own psychoanalytic method. Each of these vulnerabilities that caused Freud to question morality and the possibility of ethics generally in relation to the particular experiences of his personal life is treated in this chapter.

After the legal destruction of the Weimar Republic in 1933, violent hostilities steadily increased in Germany and Freud's hometown of Vienna. The routine persecution of Adolf Hitler's political opponents began in 1925. The Fuhrer's bodyguard unit, the *Schutzstaffel*, was responsible for conducting routine forms of violence. Dressed in brown, they conducted mass arrests *en force* and perpetrated brutal killings of political opponents. Concentration camps such as Dachau started appearing on the German landscape.

During these years, when Viennese culture became increasingly hostile to Jewish citizens, Freud found a friend and pen-pal in the historical-fiction author Arnold Zweig. In their correspondences, Zweig provides a friend to Freud who answers several of his main concerns. They both come from Viennese culture, wonder about the role fantasy plays in creative writing, and appreciate psychoanalysis's insights about society's ills. Both also thoughtfully engage the other in regard to the question of Palestine and their European identity as Jews.

For most of Freud's life, he fancied himself a product of European culture and assumed the values of this place as his own. Confino describes more fully what these ideals during Freud's most productive years included. Returning to Confino's re-imagining of an origin story for the German people and culture, he finds a similarity between their desire and Freud's expressed desires at that time (2014, pg 37–38). Confino found that for German culture, "[i]n the mind of the Nazis, this was a war about identity. Nazi anti-Semitism was all fantasy: nothing about it was driven by a desire to provide a truthful account of reality. Yet it was nonetheless believed by many Germans and therefore was for them real and truthful" (2014, pg. 23). Freud's abandonment of real infantile sexual abuse for the equal trauma caused by an infantile childhood fantasy is similarly concerned with the horizon of meaning and truth created by the individual psychic mechanism rather than a version of truth justified by objective fact.

Confino's survey of popular cultural items like street signs, travelogues, and parade floats shows how anti-Jewish thoughts were manipulated by the images found in public. People's imaginations mimed and circulated these images, informing their thoughts. Confino argues that burning the Bible enlivened the imagination toward a future that did not include Jewish morality (2014, pg. 39, 71). This aim—which was imagined with increasing frequency in the years leading up to the *Anschluss*—fueled the persecution and eventual genocide of an imaginary enemy. In reality, however, Jewish people possessed no self-aware intention to threaten the political or social fabric of German society in the ways inflicted upon them, at least in no greater degree than any other minority group in that society.

Confino's thesis develops with the view that anti-Jewish sentiments were not a private and unknown affair that suddenly became known to the world and German citizens. With the erection of Dachau, he argues that already in 1933 "[p]ublicity about the camps served as a Nazi warning for loyalty and conformism. Many Germans were horrified by the violence, but many others greeted it with a sense of anti-leftists and antidemocratic relief and support" (Confino 2014, pg. 68). Freud, who was writing to Zweig during these years, noticed the "tightening noose" around the necks of Jews and other political dissenters in Germany, a pain that was often perpetrated with more ruthlessness in Vienna. In 1933, Freud's books were burnt in public squares along with other books written by Jewish authors.

In a moment of self-reflection, Freud wrote to Zweig on December 6, 1934—from his *Bergasse* apartment in Vienna. Not long after concentration camps began appearing on the German landscape, Freud writes that the mounting crisis in 1930s Europe must feel like the following,

> In one of Caesar's battles in Gaul it happened that the besieged (was it Alesia) and Vercingetorix had nothing more to eat. They then drove out their wretched women and children into the no-man's-land between the fortress and the besieging Roman army, and there the poor creatures starved miserably to death between their own people who could not give them anything to eat and the enemy who would not, or who perhaps had not much to eat either. It would have been more merciful to kill them in the town. Faced with such decisions one recoils in horror without taking sides. It's like shipwrecked mariners deciding to slaughter one of their own comrades. (Freud and Zweig 1987, pg 96)

This passage where Freud describes these "wretched," "poor creatures" bears a frightful resemblance to what we can understand is happening to Freud between his two identities, as an Austrian-German and as a Jewish man. Neither can feed him nor offer a sense of identity within which he can rest. He condemns neither side for their relation to the wretchedly vulnerable population. Food is deprived from the wretched in their hometown because of scarce resources. Do the austere conditions in Vienna justify pushing out the Jews by locals, for Freud? He adds that it would have been more merciful to kill them in town, rather than to force their exile. Based on his analogy, if these people must be dealt with, is it more merciful to kill the Jews in their German homeland, rather than push them to exile anywhere, from London to Israel? As someone who was reluctant to leave his hometown until very late in Jewish persecutions, maybe this is the horrific fate he personally preferred. Confino agrees with Freud's testimony to:

> the basic elements of Europeans' view of national identity at the time, evident also in Freud's description of the Jewish nation in *Moses and Monotheism* and in the Nazis' view of the German nation: the search for origins; the nation as an organic entity endowed with soul or psyche or racial attributes; the parallel between the life of the individual and that of the collectivity; and the importance of memory and the transmission of legacy over many centuries. (2014, pg. 50)

Immersed in a culture that was desperate to find the origins of Jewish life as different from the Gentile for constructing a new Aryan race, Freud, whose life was threatened by this search, was desperate to conduct his own study. Freud sought to find the Gentile in the origins of the Jew for dissolving their hostile relationship. Both conducted their study on historical fact, but also in their collective legacies and memories. As much as Freud also engaged the origins of his identity, personal and national, understandably these two were at odds within him. The fraught relationship between a loved Viennese culture and an unavoidable Jewish heritage compelled him to create a story that would disintegrate the strict binary between them.

Many Jews who may or may not have been observant resented Freud for writing *Moses and Monotheism* (Gay 1988, pg. 604, 646–647). Published in 1939, his attempt to take away their origin was perceived as particularly cruel. At the same time, European as much as Arab nations desired the same: to dissolve the Jewish people. His Jewish kin did not realize that this text was Freud's attempt to complicate their identity in the eyes of their persecuting neighbors. If the Hebrews shared an Egyptian origin, then these two groups were not as different as was commonly perceived. He was vulnerable to his Jewish nature as much as his German one, a conflict that put him and his family at risk until the end of his life. As the vulnerable wretched and poor creature in the story of Cesar's battle, Freud can only see a morality in the merciful killing of those caught between two cinctures.

In the final version of his *Autobiographical Study*, published in 1935, after preliminary remarks about the purpose of the autobiography, Freud begins his life's story with his birth in Freiberg, Moravia. He writes this strong declaration on what is essentially the first page of his final autobiography, "I was born on May 6th 1856, at Freiberg in Moravia, a small town in what is now Czechoslovakia. My parents were Jews, and I have remained a Jew myself" (Freud 1925, pg. 7). Significantly, next he remarks on the profession he chose: that is, a preoccupation with human concerns over natural ones, which he remained faithful to throughout his life. Interestingly, Freud links this professional pursuit to his first reading of the Bible, which had an enduring effect on the direction his interests took. Could this lingering effect of the power of biblical story refer to his hermeneutical approach, which asks about the development of meaning, heritage, and memory that accompanies the natural life of a human being? Freud's commitment to his profession in human concerns created a second, deep vulnerability in his identity as a natural scientist that cannot use empirical means championed by positivists to observe the subjective human mind.

In the twentieth century, many Jews converted (or considered converting) to Christianity to avoid persecution. Through his studies of the representational and biologically driven psyche, Freud would come to understand the social, political, and psychological forms of persecution. It is worth repeating Freud's exact sentiment on the expectation that he should feel inferior because of his Jewishness, he had

> never been able to see why I should feel ashamed of my descent, or as people were beginning to say, of my "race." ... These first impressions at the University, however, had one consequence, which was afterward to prove important; for at an early age I was made familiar with the fate of being in the Opposition and of being put under the ban of the "compact majority." The foundations were thus laid for a certain degree of independence of judgment. (1925, pg. 9)

Freud's experiences in academia support Confino's argument that the persecution of Jews was not a surprise event initiated in Dachau or Auschwitz, but that its realization in systematic murder was the result of a long history of persecution. Though Freud recognized the expectation that he should feel inferior, he did not do so. Instead he found strength in the outsider position that the Viennese community, whether as Jew or subversive of the positivists' method, maliciously granted him. He found strength in being the other.

Identified as Jewish, which made Freud "the other" from a young age, he seems to have molded his defensive character already as a young student. Not accepting the demoted position, but still gaining some prestige within broader Viennese culture, granted Freud strength. Still, his origins did not prevent Freud from the attempt to change its meaning. Freud's appreciation of the Jewish religion and culture was infrequently positive. Writing to Zweig, who immigrated from Berlin to

Palestine soon after his books were burnt, Freud describes the "tragically mad land" of Palestine,

> this strip of our mother earth is connected with no other progress, no discovery or invention – the Phoenicians are said to have invented glass and the alphabet (both doubtful!), the island of Crete gave us Minoan art, Pergamon reminds us of parchment, Magnesia of the magnet and so on ad infinitum – but Palestine has never produced anything but religions, sacred frenzies, presumptuous attempts to overcome the outer world of appearance by means of the inner world of wishful thinking. And we hail from there (though one of us considers himself a German as well [Freud]; the other does not); our forebears lived there for perhaps half or perhaps a whole millennium (but this too is just a perhaps) and it is impossible to say what heritage from this land we have taken over into our blood and nerves (as is mistakenly said). (Freud and Zweig 1987, pg. 40)

The mistaken assumption is placed in hesitating parenthesis marks. Perhaps cultural heritage *can* be carried in one's blood, as the norm contemporary to Freud's life insisted? Written in a letter dated May 8, 1932, Freud's attempt to find what it means to be Jewish in relation to his German upbringing is clear. He asks explicitly about what Palestinian "heritage" infuses his "blood." This vision of racialized biologistic origins contributed to the frenzied beliefs that developed across centuries and continents, as well as to Freud's personal individual beliefs.

Freud's description of the presumptuous desire to impose order on the outer world of appearance through wish fulfillment comes frightfully close to his description of psychotic delusions of persecution and the uncanny feeling of omnipotence in creating moral norms. The presumption, however, is not unique to the inhabitants of this "mad land" but an organizing principle of an individual developing in an unpredictable reality in the rest of Freud's writing. As developed earlier, an uncanny feeling arises when one understands what is most familiar, but usually repressed. For morality, this is the source of contradictory norms that do not remain stable. Norms during Nathanael's life in "The Sandman" illustrated an implicit but repressed realization for Freud. Norms fluctuate and can turn in their opposite, such as the requirement for disharmony and rude interruptions in polite society. Additionally, in his own writing on Schreber Freud finds reparative value in objects of delusions of persecution that are personally desired, but socially unacceptable. An unconscious wish is fulfilled by engaging an object of desire, while also returning to invest libidinal interest in social reality.

Zweig's response to Freud is no less interesting. He also points out that Freud, despite his own objections, is similar to these delusional and frenzied Jews in more ways than he is willing to admit.

> Is not the frightful struggle you have been waging for about forty years (or more?) against the fallacies, taboos and repressions of our contemporaries comparable with the one the prophets waged against the recalcitrant nation of their day? Your radiantly clear intelligence shifts the nature of man and the purpose of his development on to an incomparably more realistic plane than did the people of those days, who could only murmur the word "God" – but apart from this, I see much in common between you two. And we certainly have our Germanness in common – only it's a Germanness of the past, it seems to me. (1925, pg. 43)

Zweig accuses Freud of repeating the same presumption as his bloodline. Both Freud as the father of psychoanalysis and historical Jewish prophets introduced a new nature for man, rife with conflicting desires and unclear motivations that were largely hidden from view. Although Zweig is consistent in his representation of the image of the Jew in a new Austria-Germany, it would take years for Freud to realize that his version of Germany no longer existed.

Freud's response to Zweig shows that he took seriously the threats against Jewish life in Berlin, which was enough to cause many to leave during these years, including Albert Einstein who left in 1933. In recognition of the dire times, he muses to Zweig, "Should we not leave this God-forsaken nation to themselves?" At other times, Freud remains cautious about jumping to conclusions and taking "every hint into the ultimate event. And then I wanted to say to you: send as much as you like [to Vienna] and come yourself whenever you want to" (Freud and Zweig 1987, pg. 44). Freud's fixation on an idealized Austria-Germany had not receded into the past enough for him to seriously consider moving. The caution he felt about the delusional nature of persecutions he experienced was apparent in the open invitation he extended to Zweig to return to Vienna anytime and stay with them, even in such a dangerous year.

Zweig points out Freud's unrelenting Germanness in the summer of 1932. For a broader view of this year, it is the same summer "the statistician Emil Gumbel, a pacifist and a Jew, was hounded from the university by his intolerant nationalist colleagues and their supporting students (he ended up at Columbia University)" (Confino 2014, pg. 72). Even with the community at large finding much that was offensive about Freud, beginning with a Judaism he hardly engaged, we find in the following story one that is consistent with his general love for this community from whence his personal life originates. The ambivalent relation between this love for the place in which he was born and the current general atmosphere that at times inspired a fear for his life is palpable.

Peter Gay writes that few honors were as cherished by Freud as the memorial tablet unveiled in the town of his birth in 1931. Freud could not attend the ceremony in Moravia because of his declining health. However, the importance of this event is shown by the people Freud sent to attend the ceremony in his place; "the size and the quality of the Freud delegation – his children Martin and Anna, his brother Alexander, his loyal adherents Paul Federn and Max Eitingon – reflect the importance Freud ascribed to the occasion" (Gay 1988, pg. 575). Freud could not resist the small token of appreciation from European soil that was so important in forming who he was. His identity, vulnerabilities, and sense of fulfillment came no less from this than his Jewish counterparts, perhaps even more so.

Despite his declining health and spirits at the age of seventy-five, Freud wrote about receiving this honor that "[d]eep within me, covered over, there still lives that happy child from Freiberg, the first-born son of a youthful mother, who had received the first indelible impressions from this air, from this soil" (Gay 1988, pg. 575). Freud also frequently expressed to Zweig the deep connection he felt to the land, who shared the sentiment to a large extent. The deep connection both felt made their

5 Freud's Vulnerability to the Social Ideals of His Time and Moral Skepticism   77

self-image vulnerable to their conflicting assessments of home and the horror of their subsequent exiles.

In 1934, Zweig's description of a main character reveals similarities to his own and Freud's exilic positions.

> And the basic problem is such an important one – the cultured man who refuses to recognize reality and who would like to cling to his childhood in the shape of the war! He has fallen into a den of murderers which he regards and insists on regarding as a den of noble knights – *coûte que coûte*. He is then slowly molded into shape by the sheer mechanical passage of time till he is forced to concede: Yes, the world is as it is; the Germans are as they are; and my ego is as I am. Well, you will see. (1987, pg. 68)

The Nuremberg racial laws that restricted Germany's Jews followed shortly after this in 1935. Even so, Freud does not see the imminent threat to his life; it would be another five years until he finally agrees to leave for London.

Finding strength was possible for Freud before his Jewish otherness demoted him and his family to partial legal and civil rights. Working to form his own fantasies about a Jewish identity that was reconciled with the Gentile, Moses as the Egyptian Arab, Freud's German counterparts were also envisioning a present that annihilated the Jewish identity through more tangible means. In their desire for a new cultural beginning, Germans and Austrians did not wish to find the precarious balance and ambivalent relation between their identities with Jewish people, but sought only to completely remove these undesirable elements.

Even after the devastating events in 1938 that culminated in what has become known as the night of shattered windows, *Kristallnacht*, Freud remained rooted in Vienna. By that time, nearly 50,000 Jews had been deported to concentration camps, heavy racial and discriminatory laws had restricted Jewish life and businesses, and rampant vandalism and violence was perpetrated on Jewish men, women, and children in the streets. Most reporters were struck by the enthusiasm and "general mood of celebration" with which Austrians enjoyed perpetrating the violence (Gay 1988, pg. 621). Freud could not have remained ignorant of these worsening times; he was, by all accounts, glued to radio broadcasts and clearly aware of these events.

Still, Gay writes that for Freud all of this "could not wholly divert Freud's attention from the mundane business that mattered to him, psychoanalytic business. This was just another distasteful set of problems the Nazi's had visited upon his world" (Gay 1988, pg. 639). While Gay's description does justice to the fervor with which Freud pursued his work, it does not appreciate the amount of vulnerability Freud must have felt, the ambivalence tearing at his sense of identity, and arguably the fantasy engaged to remain in his Vienna home. His refusal to leave was not just because of his usual "restraint," but must have had more elements of fantasy than previously uncovered (Gay 1988, pg. 641).

As late as 1938, Zweig wonders about Freud's welfare in Vienna. "But there are now such odd things in the papers that I am first of all hastening to enquire how you are and what plans you have for the next few weeks. It is so strange to think that you are not really obliged to live in Vienna and that you are spending your peaceful old age there of your own free will" (Freud and Zweig 1987, pg. 156). Zweig would indeed find it strange that if one's motives were clear, how could Freud remain in

Vienna as persecution mounted against the Jewish community? But one of the central insights in the hermeneutics of suspicion that Freud's psychoanalysis developed is that motives are anything but clear. In delusions of persecution, Schreber was *unique* according to Freud in his ability to distinguish his delusions from reality. Even those who engaged in persecuting others are often acting in response to their personal wishes and cannot understand that this victimizes the other who is persecuted, such as in Freud's relationships with several of his closest protégés beginning with Fleiss.

Free will is no longer at play when repressed desires that can develop into delusions keep the rays of reality from penetrating through, like Nathanael's castrated eyes in "The Sandman." Freud's development of this fictional character and his incapacity to see the difference between a mechanical doll and real human reveal not only the condition of taking fantasy for reality, but also of Freud's own sensitivity to this blindness. Awareness of this blindness, or unknowability in differentiating between reality and fantasy, between one's objects of desire and those that stand external to one's mind must have an influence on Freud in relation to his own thought processes. Personally, Freud did not experience as much physical violence because physical illness kept him homebound. His offices and publishing house at his *Bergasse* apartment were searched by Hitler's SS troops, but they did not manage to inflict too much damage. To his good friend and colleague Ernst Jones, Freud responded to his argument for fleeing that he "could not leave his native land; it would be like a soldier deserting his post" (Gay 1988, pg. 624). All these vacillations between real injuries and hesitating doubts cast a shadow of doubt on Freud's ability to act out of soundness of mind and engage a truly free will. More importantly, these contradictory claims make it worth considering how Freud may have been concerned about his own objectivity and judgment to leave or stay in Vienna.

To his daughter Anna's question about whether it was better for them all to commit suicide, he kept "the defiant mood that dominated so much of Freud's life" (Gay 1988, pg. 622). But was it only defiance that kept Freud tied to Vienna, or was it a vulnerable love of the land that kept him from seeing the new reality in Austria? Much like the wretched he described to Zweig, their town included concentration camps, while the rest of the world did not care to or, as Freud explains, could not intervene on their behalf (Gay 1988, pg. 622). He was cut from every origin he had known, a Jewish one he barely accepted and the German one he loved. In *The Symbolism of Evil*, Paul Ricœur aptly writes that Freud is the modern image of the wanderer: "symbols of alienation and dereliction; the interruption of dialogue, having become a situation makes man a being alien to his ontological place" (1967, pg. 73). During this ontological place of alienation, Freud's internal world collapsed, and libidinal ties retreated. Freud experienced what he called an internal collapse, a break with reality as he also read into Schreber's psychosis.

As discussed previously in this book, prior to developing delusions of persecution, Schreber went through a period of imagining himself dead. Freud interprets Schreber's fantasies as indexing a removal of his interest from social life. In this stage of regression, Schreber underwent a general detachment of libidinal interest.

He reverted to an unthreatened psychic state that could lead Schreber to believe that the judgmental, objective world had come to its end.[1]

Before reaching a similar internal collapse near the end of Freud's life that matched an external world rife with war, the concept of internal collapse continued to develop in his theoretical work *Beyond the Pleasure Principle* (1920, pg. 63). Freud published this work shortly after his daughter Sophie died from influenza. Undergoing what could be an internal catastrophe in the time leading up to and after her death, the second version of *Beyond the Pleasure Principle* included his fullest formulation of the death drive. Although Freud would never admit the influence his daughter's death had on his theoretical work, Gay writes that "[t]he term 'death drive' — *Todestrieb* — entered his correspondence a week after Sophie Halberstadt's death" and surmises that the "loss can claim a subsidiary role ... (in) his analytic preoccupation with destructiveness" (1988, pg. 395). Near the end of his life, Freud concludes that the neurotic condition reveals what is common to all mental life. Traces of the death drive that seeks to return to a stability inherent in all organic life impels all living matter and the aggressive impulse to undermine any achievement.

By 1930, Freud comes to understand that all forms of paranoia have an element of megalomania since the ego is the object preserved, returning to its stable, or oceanic, condition of stability from injury (1911, pg. 72). Social considerations are sacrificed, which for Schreber caused him to "hate Dr. Flechsig." During this phase of the catastrophe, which according to Freud is libidinal excitement returning to itself, Schreber believed Dr. Flechsig was committing "soul murder" on him. Freud argued that the delusions eventually helped Schreber find interest again in a familiar world. In this process of recovery, partial detachment of Schreber's libido would enable him to find interest again in other aspects of his life, such as his job (1930, pg. 73) (1911, pg. 15). This repression silently detaches libido from people and things once loved; whereas, the delusion is the noisy process of recovery, according to Freud's understanding of this condition. As such, the persecuting other is none other than one's process of recovery. Considering Freud's understanding of psychic mechanisms, after experiencing an internal catastrophe from the illness and eventual death of his daughter, could Freud have returned to social life with some paranoiac doubt for the European civilization and world he once loved? He continued to write, albeit with a much more tragic and fuller understanding of what he newly termed "the death drive."

Would this return to social life also include objects that appear to him as they are not in reality, sought by desires that can switch into their opposite? More than wondering how much Freud may or may not have been delusional, or paranoid, the idea is to understand how much Freud must have worried about this after a lifelong reflec-

---

[1] "Passivity" in Freud can be understood as the inorganic state to which all life wants to return. The stability and constancy principle (known, in the "The Economic Problem of Masochism" (1924), as the Nirvana Principle) is to that which the death drive aims. The ideal of an undisturbed peace undoes the bonds created by a sublimated sex drive that finds excitement outside itself. The development of archaic and conflicting desires inflicts the ego from within, in addition to introjected social standards and confounds the goal of an undifferentiated passivity and excitement.

tion on the vicissitudes of desires and their objects with a clear understanding about how they could not be clearly understood. In other words, the condition of unknowability tied to drives that are ambivalently related could justifiably cause Freud to doubt the soundness of his own judgments. If delusions cannot be understood through one's rational faculties as illustrated in The Sandman as well as Schreber's case study, along with his own experiences interpreting Irma's injection, and as he understands moral ambivalence in the uncanny, then there is room for Freud to doubt the degree of real persecutions that he felt. Did they result from his own paranoia, or was the origin of these relations based in reality? His hesitation can explain some of the reluctance he felt to abandon the only place he felt at home.

Freud also saw this ability to distinguish the real from imagined, persecuting Flechsig as a rare accomplishment due to Schreber's intellectual ability. Freud's reading of Schreber's psychic abilities allows him to wonder about the ability to distinguish delusional feelings of persecution from those that are real. Most of those who have paranoid delusions of persecution do not distinguish their idea from a real other person who is believed to be the persecuting one. The paranoiac who is persecuted in one's own idea is often led to retaliate against an innocent other, enacting the logics of contradiction seen in Christensen's understanding of Hobbes and Augustine's political philosophies. Nathanael's attempt to kill Klara, the real "automaton" who he loved most, illustrates this possibility. The one who speaks against homosexuals, for example, finds an amount of libidinal satisfaction in doing so because often it chastens oneself for their perceived abhorrent desire that it simultaneously locates in the other. Although one can view another as a persecutor, cleanly severing agent from object, there can never be any guarantee that such a perception is free from one's own paranoiac fantasies. There is also an amount of persecution that the paranoiac is self-inflicting for living up to social expectations. For these reasons, the binary terms of persecutor and persecuted are misleading, and may be more usefully replaced with the term *persecutory*, which complicates finding absolute blame or absolution from those who commit violence for a moral ideal.

Freud argues that no rational process could prevent Schreber's projections on Dr. Flechsig. Schreber was passive to the psychic processes of repression and delusion. Freud, however, did conceive of the process, not in himself but in Schreber. Freud begins the essay with a claim that he must go through another to perceive something about one's own mechanism, for the general principles he sought. Assuming a position of distantiation in the hermeneutics of suspicion, Freud can reflect on his own delusions through Schreber's case. One can only remain passive to the internal vicissitudes that result in external perceptions projected on others. Schreber's projection of an internal catastrophe onto an external world resulted from a libido returning to the security of itself. However, it was injury from his internal desire that conflicted with a social norm that resulted in his paranoia.

To make matters worse, Freud intimately knew that these psychic defense mechanisms were active with real as well as imagined fears. For example, the psyche does not distinguish between a sense of guilt that arises in a mere wish to inflict harm from an actual wrongdoing that was actually committed, as with Schreber's mere wish for homosexual relations that caused his psychotic break from an unaccepting social reality. Freud distinguishes between *remorse* that comes after committing a misdeed and a sense of guilt that is inherent to the psyche. The psyche then has real *and* imagined scenarios against which it must psychically defend itself, as Freud continues to understand through Schreber's case. Does Freud wonder to himself whether he is projecting only a paranoid delusion on his Viennese neighbors? Freud's reluctance to leave can be explained in terms of his commitment to psychotherapy, or to the necessity of relying on his benefactors' arrangements, but the long delay can also have resulted from a suspicion of his own fears.

One consequence of this libidinal diversion is that delusions of persecution are one way for the ego to return to its cultural life, according to Freud's psychoanalysis. The return, however, is with the accompanying paranoid delusions that jeopardize and threaten those objects one loves because of phantasies that do not exist. Social bonds are then made more difficult by this psychic mechanism that is meant to restore participation with others while at the same time trying to maintain stability for itself. The formation of cultural life, therefore, is grounded on an impetus within the psyche to preserve itself but also maintain safety in one's community by destroying itself if needed. These compounding vicissitudes, sublimations, repressions, and processes for recovery make up Freud's hermeneutics of suspicion, which he has in full view as his own life becomes saturated in real persecutory relations.

The logical conclusion that can be reached from his work on Schreber and reaching all the way to Freud's work in *Civilization and Its Discontents* is that, as cultural expectations rise, there is a greater psychic need to deflect individual sexual and aggressive impulses. With every limitation, sublimation, or libidinal transference that risks the privation of a sexual or aggressive drive, the possibility increases for a masochistic or sadistic gratification attached to an imagined object. Meanwhile, the ego that mediates between these is not aware of the various vicissitudes that transform desires and their related objects during this process. In the ego's development through its cultural relations, passivity lies in its incomprehensible and increased urge to deny its own satisfactions, while at the same time maintain them (Freud 1930, pg. 87). Aggressive desires can be sublimated in the unconscious into activities that are accepted by cultural norms, such as into artwork, literature, or technological advances (Freud 1930, pg. 79–80). The rest of these drives must find other outlets and without the ego's awareness, according to Freud.

As we see with Schreber, however, repressed aggression also risks imposing delusions that divert and prevent one from making deliberate moral decisions. Freud writes that Schreber's delusions "formed a fixed complete system, inaccessible to correction by objective judgments and external facts" (1911, pg. 15). As intelligent as he was, during his therapy and eventual "recovery," delusions of persecution were the way, Freud observed, his ego renewed bonds with others

Late in Freud's life, the reality of an increasing threat from his beloved German counterparts came into a full and undoubted view only when his children were in direct danger. In 1938, Martin and Anna Freud were summoned to the Gestapo headquarters. They appeared with enough Veronal to kill themselves in case they were tortured. Freud's physician, Dr. Schur who provided the Veronal, commented that it "was Freud's worst day" (Gay 1988, pg. 625). The summons put his daughter in direct danger, a result of what can be seen as Freud's denial of the increasing threat to their lives. In this event, Freud could also no longer deny the new cultural atmosphere in Austria.

Gay continues: "this event, even more than Ernst Jones's eloquence, convinced Freud that it was time to leave" (Gay 1988, pg. 626). The administration had such a hold on all affairs by this time that Freud's belongings underwent an audit for confiscation. The Vienna Psychoanalytic Society's assets, the library, and the property of the publishing house were confiscated. The Freud family had to pay a tax for "fleeing" and all cash was confiscated (Gay 1988, pg. 626). Similar to his dealings with the scientific community, his religion gave him constant cause for anxiety and worry through his life. He was as exposed and vulnerable to the scientific community to which he strived to belong, as much to the German and Jewish communities that demanded from him different cultural sensibilities. These conflicting ties forged meaningful ties, as much as they created fracturing traumas. The idea is not to equate the immediacy of material threats that came from genocidal practices by the Nazi regime with the ideological demands of these cultural demands. Rather it is the combination of all these that made the coherence of Freud's identity vulnerable to fracturing at the end of his life, beginning with the material threats and the ideals that left him socially exiled.

His relation of love, and then later feelings of betrayal, colored Freud's representation of various friends, countrymen, colleagues, and students all through life. We can see a vulnerability to feelings of persecution on several levels. As we have seen, they begin in his identification as a Jewish person, or German, the demands of polite society and the medical community in Vienna, relations with friends, and repressed emotional homosexual tendencies by a conservative super-ego that cannot help but cherish his dwelling from infancy, beginning in the forests of Moravia.

Freud's internal catastrophe came at a time when an external projection for recovery would be met with a catastrophic reality to match. Between the years 1915 and 1939, Freud revised his view of drives that are ambivalently related. When once Freud had found sexual, pleasurable, and libidinal drives—those life-orientated *Triebe*—he increasingly found signs from an aggressive impulse. As the First World War erupted and continued, Freud's optimism about the mind's plasticity and resilience waned. A death drive that worked most quietly would impel the organism toward its own death to rejoin an ultimate form of undifferentiated, stabilized pleasure.

At this precarious time and place when racist and nationalistic powers were rising to power, and when Freud constructed an elaborate map of the psychic constitution of the ego, he asked what can stabilize social bonds whose aims are to quiet the libidinal and aggressive excitations of each individual. Before his final work *Moses and Monotheism* (1939), he most explicitly explores in *Civilization and Its Discontents* (1930) what means civilization can "employ in order to inhibit the aggressiveness which opposes it, to make it harmless, to get rid of it, perhaps?" (1930, pg. 123). Namely preoccupied with what exists as the individual psyche, Freud late in life ultimately speculated about what should or could be an appropriate ethic.

Given that individually embodied people develop in a community, ethicists ask (along with Freud) how an individual can live with others and achieve a happy and flourishing life. Different moral theories demand certain actions, thoughts, or behaviors that respectively constitute the right way to behave or even think, as for example in Aristotle. Moral theories must conceive first what type of being the human subject is, or its purpose or function, in order to then instruct how it should behave and how it can live with others. Given the mental apparatus that Freud has mapped, he eliminates common moral principles, such as universal moral commands to love one's neighbor, as possible solutions to relieve a primary aggression against others.

Even more so, Freud suggests that the structures of civilization amplify the aggressive tendency by enforcing norms that require the repression of individual desires. What he calls "natural morality" is the way for the cultured one to enjoy these restrictions imposed on aggression. At bottom, however, discontent arises every time it cannot usurp or "kill" a fellow and rival because of injunctions such as "Thou shalt not kill." At the bottom of the unconscious, the human being is always a brutish, murderous, and clever animal for Freud. External powers of authority are internalized through processes of identification into a sadistic super-ego to which the ego submits and offers libidinal-sexual excitation with each admonishment from one's conscience. If morality is one way to enjoy these restrictions, then the super-ego's function to enforce morality is a primary form of masochism, presented first in Freud's *Beyond the Pleasure Principle* (1920, pg. 54–55).

In "The Economic Problems of Masochism" (1924), Freud articulates the full severity of the sense of guilt that can come even from imagined aggressions to reinforce a moral masochism of the ego. Punishment is sought for one's individual desires, "which must then be expiated by the reproaches of the sadistic conscience" (1924, pg. 169). Freud finds that an ethical sense then develops in response to the sense of guilt that grows with every imagined ego-drive that conflicts with a social one, "which expresses itself in conscience and demands a further renunciation of instincts" (Freud 1924, pg. 170). Moral masochism of the ego is the unconscious extension of a conscience helping to form social bonds. In addition to a sense of morality that admonishes one's individuated desires unawares, I find in *The Ego and the Id* (1923) that the unconscious sense of morality aims primarily at preserving bonds with those who resemble oneself.

Along with describing the influence an unconscious sense of guilt has on the ego, Freud also states clearly that "social feelings rest on identifications with other people, on the basis of having the same ego ideal" (1923, pg. 37). Not only do aggressive and libidinal drives affect the operations of an ego caught by these contradicting impulses, but the ego is also influenced by an unconscious sense of moral obligation to those who are like oneself. Freud's personal experiences at school and his family's history both find traces of this bias that is created in the development of a moral sensibility that can turn murderous against those who are different or deemed "other" from the individuals who are alike or bonded as the same as oneself.

In addition to the insufficiency and detrimental effects of universal injunctions, such as "Thou shalt not kill" in chapter five of *Civilization and Its Discontents* (1930), Freud also rejects the universal moral injunction to love all as one's self. He insists that love should be valued highly and given only to those who are deemed worthy. Writes Freud: "He deserves it if he is so like me in important ways that I can love myself in him; and he deserves it if he is so much more perfect than myself that I can love my ideal of my own self in him" (1930, pg. 109). The one who is deemed worthy is based on narcissistic gratification since it aims where the libido can find itself. For Freud, extending moral responsibility to just any other person is not recommended and even deemed a shocking and bewildering sentiment. Even if it were possible to love others as oneself, the way in which we love ourselves can be excessive and lead to danger.

At the end of the chapter in the same discussion of moral ideals, or ethical demands, Freud at the same time goes back to discrediting ethos that are based on narcissistic identifications. The same way he understands the difficulties in emotional life to only love those who deserve it and who are like us in important ways, Freud also says that there lies a danger of psychological poverty "where the bonds of society are chiefly constituted by the identification of its members with one another" (1930, pg. 116). The risk surmised from narcissistic investment is the catastrophe that follows when individual desires fall outside these normative identifications and are then frustrated. Schreber's megalomania, for example, was illustrated when his homosexual desire fell outside his norm. An attachment to that which was like him, his love for Dr. Flechsig, led to an internal catastrophe. According to Freud's understanding, rebuilding his ego was accomplished by means of psychotic delusions. These helped Schreber emerge from an impoverished sense of self, a self that fell outside normative standards of acceptable sexual desires for acceptance into social life again.

In a quick survey of the time and place of Freud's adult life, we are also reminded of the German *folk* who were aggressive toward others who were not the same. An ethos such as this is based on sameness and ended with the murder of those with whom they did not identify. Surely these murders were justified by irreversible qualities that frustrated their own narcissistic investments. While Freud gropes for moral possibilities that exist in the cultured life of an individual ego passive to its aggression, he also rejects the categorical, spiritual, and socialist moral injunctions each for different reasons.

Freud writes near the end of *Civilization and Its Discontents* that individual happiness has become such that it can be satisfied in a communal bond (1930, pg. 140). Pleasure is achieved by sublimating individual aggression for cultural expression. Distinguishing between an "integration of separate individuals into a human group, and in the other case the creation of a unified group out of many individuals," Freud notes that the former possibility effaces the individual in the name of an abstract, universal love (1930, pg. 140). The lesson he advances is: tolerate differences, rather than homogenize all to one ideal. An analogous claim would be that it would behoove an individual to learn a multitude of languages rather than strive to make all languages conform to one ideal form of languages. The ridiculousness of trying to create one language is denounced in the earliest mythology, such as in the destruction of the tower of Babel. At the end of his correspondence with Einstein, Freud makes a similar claim about honoring differences among individuals in a community rather than to create an ideal for all to conform but relates it to the possibility of eliminating war from the human psyche.

In his exchange with Einstein about the possibility of eliminating war, Freud reflected on the psyche's origins that necessitate recourse to such social and collective forms of violence. In broad movements, Freud describes how brute force turns into intellectual violence as tools are developed for the purposes of eliminating one's enemy. The means by which individuals secure themselves against those with more might is by organizing many to fight against the one powerful despot. "Violence could be broken by union, and the power of those who were united now represented law in contrast to the violence of the single individual" (Freud 1933, pg. 205). The strongest form of security one can preserve, Freud writes, is to organize with other individuals for their mutual protection against the mightiest individual. Here begins the social and relational bond of individuals and society at large, organized through legal restrictions.

What happens when this union becomes essential for the protection of an individual? These bonds are then defended to the death as if each individual life depends on it. To a certain extent, this is true and has been normalized to solidify social and group loyalties. The vulnerability of those who are left outside and exposed to the elements makes it such that, for survival, each must distinguish who makes up their bond. This procedure is necessary not only for enemies that threaten from outside the community, but also to prevent threats of disintegration from within. Developing an idealized image is the easiest way of securing safety for the collective, but Freud understands through the events of his personal life that its risks are too great.

These bonds, which turn into law and emotional ties between members, require that:

> the community must be maintained permanently, must be organized, must draw up regulations to anticipate the risk of rebellion and must institute authorities to see that those regulations – the laws – are respected and to superintend the execution of legal acts of violence. The recognition of a community of [individual] interests such as these leads to the growth of emotional ties between the members of a united group of people – communal feelings which are the true source of its strength. (Freud 1933, pg. 205)

The stronger the bond, the better the chance of an individual's survival. This stronger bond, however, also increases the alienations of those who fall outside the stratified "communal feelings." Any violent attempt to gain strength, whether by an individual against the group or one group against another group, is a repetition of this procedure.

Building cultures out of the differences present in separate individuals, according to Freud's estimations, decreases the sadistic and masochistic economies required for lacerating one's drives and desires that fall outside communal norms. These violent economies built to satisfy social demands risk reifying any one ideal. Rather than maintaining friction between the individual that inhabits happiness and becomes vulnerable to its aggression and guilt, "the most important thing is the aim of creating a unity of the individual human beings" (Freud 1933, pg. 141). The ambivalent bind that makes one love and hate the neighbor, Freud tentatively suggests, can be reconciled by binding together individuals that maintain their differences. In this case, super-egoical guilt will suppress smaller individual desires, if these happen to fall out of the norm.

Lost in the intricate phenomenon of a psyche that negotiates drives that are in conflict with each other, Freud's growing awareness of how his own life penetrated his analysis kept his answers about the moral life in the dark. These answers impart value to the whole mechanism of human life and no longer belong to any science, but to speculative philosophies which Freud was loathed to consider his work. He believed that the non-empirical, speculative fields of philosophy, theology, and ethics are more accustomed to answering questions about the origins of moral life, which is why Freud repeatedly hesitated conjecturing about them.

Processes in psychic development for Freud, however, are unambiguous. Aims are displaced, and drives become restricted which leads to further changes in ethical ideals (Freud 1933, pg. 214). One's intellect inevitably grows with the internalization of regressive impulses that adapts to different individuals. Those like Einstein who are averse to war negotiate their strength while they may unknowingly challenge the ubiquitous control of these norms. In his final assessment, Freud justifies a future without war, if "the cultural attitude grows with the justified dread of the consequences of a future war" (Freud 1933, pg. 215). Freud's somewhat optimistic claim to Einstein can be qualified after seeing the events of the Cold War, the Korean war, the Vietnam War, and the Gulf War, to name a few. As much as large-scale war might be prevented for those who remember their atrocities, small levels of persecution, and the moral development of individuals by way of a masochistic super-ego still occur. Furthermore, other war mechanisms would emerge to perpetuate what Freud understood as the death drive.

From Freud's perspective of an ego that begins individuated and that "sacrifices" its desires for the social bond, the value of others and relations are only significant for the survival of the individual, material organism. No other value is added to moral relations or social bonds that exceed their use as a means for the individual's survival. It is unfathomable in the organic nature of life to give up one's strength for those bonds, which may explain Freud's own aversion to the possibility of a bonded moral life. It was an anachronistic and unjustifiable desire to try and pacify men, as he told Einstein. Furthermore, he only sees the utilitarian and egoistic motives as "productive" for the transition to a moral life. While the origins of morality remain elusive, they are justified by their function of survival.

Freud paints the picture of an individual who forges relations with other objects out of the necessity to survive, ultimately paying the price with an aggressive super-ego that limits the expression of individual drives. Ambivalence between the need to survive as an individual and its necessity to live in a social bond leads to Freud's position where moral masochism is a valid form of enjoyment. Moral pleasure reveals the truth of a desire that is so intertwined with a desire for its own individual destruction that moral action is a masochistic enjoyment. The super-ego enjoys repressing and as such transforming individual desires to preserve the social bond.

Whereas Freud only had view of all the ways an individual sacrifices desires for its social bond, and so the impossibility of an intrinsic value of morality, other trends in psychoanalysis disagreed with this conclusion. Disagreements about the onset of the Oedipus complex is one example that we will see where the theoretical approach shows different degrees of relationality between individuals and shows the limits of a norm that values individual self-mastery, which ultimately provides a potential change in the possibilities for living an ethical life.

References

Confino, A. (2014). *A world without Jews: The Nazi imagination from persecution to genocide*. New Haven: Yale University Press.
Freud, S. (1955). The standard edition of the complete psychological works of Sigmund Freud. In J. Strachey (Ed.), *Beyond the pleasure principle* (Vol. XVIII, 1920). London: The Hogarth Press and the Institute of Psycho-analysis.
Freud, S. (1958). The standard edition of the complete psychological works of Sigmund Freud. In J. Strachey (Ed.), *The case of Schreber, Papers on technique and other works, ii-vii* (Vol. XII, 1911). London: The Hogarth Press and the Institute of Psycho-analysis.
Freud, S. (1959). The standard edition of the complete psychological works of Sigmund Freud. In J. Strachey (Ed.), *An autobiographical study* (Vol. XX, 1925) London: The Hogarth Press and the Institute of Psycho-analysis.
Freud, S. (1961a). The standard edition of the complete psychological works of Sigmund Freud. In J. Strachey (Ed.), *The ego and the id* (Vol. XIX, 1923). London: The Hogarth Press and the Institute of Psycho-analysis.
Freud, S. (1961b). The standard edition of the complete psychological works of Sigmund Freud. In J. Strachey (Ed.), *The economic problem of Masochism* (Vol. XIX, 1924). London: The Hogarth Press and the Institute of Psycho-analysis.
Freud, S. (1961c). The standard edition of the complete psychological works of Sigmund Freud. In J. Strachey (Ed.), *Civilization and its discontents, and other works* (Vol. XXI, 1930). London: The Hogarth Press and the Institute of Psycho-analysis.
Freud, S. (1964). The standard edition of the complete psychological works of Sigmund Freud. In J. Strachey (Ed.), *Why War?* (Einstein and Freud) (Vol. XXII, 1933 [1932]) . London: The Hogarth Press and the Institute of Psycho-analysis.
Freud, S., Zweig, A., & Freud, E. L. (1987). *The letters of Sigmund Freud and Arnold Zweig*. New York: New York University Press.
Gay, P. (1988). *Freud: A life of our times*. New York/London: W.W. Norton & Company.
Ricœur, P. (1967). *The symbolism of evil* (trans: Buchanan, E.). Boston: Beacon Press.

Chapter 6
A New Kind of Psychotherapy for Ethical Subjectivity

Abstract I move from Freud's skepticism in Chapter 5 to now explore Sándor Ferenczi's emphasis on affective relations. Ferenczi developed his psychoanalytic insights by combining emergent elements of Object Relations and Intersubjective approaches, and I use Ferenczi's work to pivot the chapter toward an ethic that lies beyond horizons of self-mastery. I undo the moral binary between self-mastering reason and embodied vulnerability before proposing an intersubjective self where one is always vulnerable to aggression in oneself and from another.

Keywords New moralities · Passive ego · contextual intersubjectivity · Guilt in Melanie Klein · Reparative relations · Ambivalent love and hate · Ambivalent relations · Radical inter-dependency · Relational ethics · Intersubjective ego · Sándor Ferenczi · Empathetic ego · Empathy · Tenderness and care · Professional hypocrisy · Infantile tenderness · Coterminous self · Elemental altruism · Unbearable trauma · Psychotherapy · Object relations school · Loewald Oedipus complex · Donna Orange · Care

As a final option for showing the complicated relation between ethics and persecution, intersubjective and relational accounts of personhood in psychoanalysis, in addition to Lévinas's ethics of alterity in the next section, can develop Freud's understanding of the death drive. Mutual dis-identification with the other, or expulsion of self, rather than its mastery can contribute to future moral possibilities that according to Freud were more difficult, but realistic. Even if Freud could not find a way to negotiate the individual's psychic need for survival with the necessity of preserving social bonds, I mine Freud's text for lingering residues or traces of a principled urge, motivation, or drive that throws an ethical line for pacifying the narcissist self. If a principled desire for passivity constitutes the death drive for Freud, the drive to aggressively undo restricting libidinal constructs, then can social and moral constructions more closely accommodate this drive? I argue for this possibility, if radical differences in moral injunctions are accepted without an accompanying social need to master and repress them.

Setting aside the unrealistic moral injunctions Freud lists in *Civilization and Its Discontents*, which for similar reasons drew Lévinas's suspicion as much as they did Freud's, a few hints in the ego's cartography—like its conflicting nature—can lead to what Lévinas calls the *pneuma* of the ego, which requires another for a passivity that stuns egoical identifications. I also transition from the super-individuated ego that begins by negotiating between parents in an Oedipus complex as late as five, and toward a view of the ego as an individuated object that always stands in relation to others, in order to finally reach a view of the inter-subject that is always already immersed in contextual relations.

Even if Freud's life ended at the height of a culture that forced the annihilation of those who were deemed inferior because of some difference, psychoanalysts saw potential in the super-ego building a moral life out of what came to be seen as an infant's *persecutory* phases. Melanie Klein worked with children as a psychoanalyst to develop an alternative understanding of the super-ego and moral possibilities in her object relations theory. Before reaching Lévinas's ontological view of the ethical relation, the Kleinian approach to object relations takes us from Freud's problematic approach through Sándor Ferenczi's intersubjective approach to contemporary practitioners who explicitly use Lévinasian insights on ethical subjectivity in psychotherapy, such as in the work of Donna Orange.

Freud's depiction of a psyche that is confronted with external uncertainties that desires to preserve its stability at all costs is the self-interested and narcissistic ego that only incorporates the other for itself. Psychoanalysis saw the inability to bear this situation. In *Love, Hate and Reparation* (1937), Klein internalizes Freud's super-ego into the infant. Already differentiating and distinguishing the good breast from the bad breast—that is, the nourishing and satisfying breast from the absent and insufficient one—the infant begins to feel guilt for its desire to consume, cannibalize, and destroy its object of love. The infant's cannibalistic rage at the object on which it depends is introjected.

With the aggressive super-ego in overdrive, processes of reparation also begin in the earliest stages of infancy. In her work with children, Klein observed that infants negotiate between a death drive, a push to consume and destroy, and the desire to preserve the loved one. The rage that seeks to destroy develops a mechanism whereby the ego reproaches itself, expresses remorse, and curbs its aggression. Guilt has the active function of developing a moral sense that acts to preserve the other out of this ambivalent relation that seeks love and protection. A framework of radical inter-dependency and subject formation thus develops for the one who persecutes in a cannibalistic rage the one who is simultaneously loved and desired. The dependent and relational aspects of self can be seen then to have two modes of persecution: one that is violent against the self that is found guilty for its aggression, and another mode of violence that acts against the other on whom one is dependent. Klein developed what came to be called the objection-relation school in psychoanalysis, and it became most popular among psychoanalysts in Britain. Her work began, however, with Sándor Ferenczi whose methods can offer additional insight into the relational aspects of the individuated psyche.

Sándor Ferenczi was part of Freud's inner circle in Vienna and developed a more intersubjective theory of the ego, one that is constituted relationally. Intersubjective approaches in psychoanalysis dissolve the priority of an individuated ego. There is no individual before the primal horde, and the child who desires the mother does not contend with its needs against hers. The exposed self that is always under an accusation and vulnerable to mutually redeeming relations culminates in Ferenczi's work. There is a subsequent flourishing of an intersubjective psychotherapy that comes closer to Lévinas's view of the ethical subject, a view of which will be developed in the next section.

Freud and Ferenczi disagreed about when the commencement of the super-ego begins in infancy. According to Ferenczi, an individual psyche does not develop alone in an autoerotic position, developing into narcissism where the grounds for sexual gratification are based on similarities to oneself or in repressive cases aim at dissolving all libidinal bonds. Rather, Ferenczi points out that empathy and care toward others develop sooner than Freud acknowledges, begging the question of how strong the hold is of one's individuated ego-drives. If processes of libidinal attachment to objects come before identification and transference, then it is first another who forms the self. Ferenczi found that a considerable amount of empathy, tenderness, and care alleviate amplified aggression repressed by the super-ego. These relations that can relieve trauma seriously challenge the notion of an interiority that requires self-mastery of repressed guilt for recovery, as Freud would see in paranoid delusions, for example.

Ferenczi noticed that his patients felt condescended to in a purely analytic-patient environment where the analyst gives the impression of holding all the answers. The traditional psychoanalytic method is to make aware a patient's unconscious concerns for addressing problems in behavior. In therapy, patients were expected to confide the most intimate details of their life. Ferenczi, however, found that a strictly professional relation would further alienate or even exacerbate the very symptoms a patient came to relieve. They came to share an original trauma that they had worked hard to repress when among others. If sincere empathy and care were not exhibited, then (as with children who suffer from traumatic sexual abuse) pathological symptoms would continue to develop with the analyst. The patient would not respond to intellectual and analytic explanations. Instead, feelings of loneliness and abandonment increased. In his article "Confusion of the Tongues Between the Adults and the Child – (The Language of Tenderness and of Passion)" (1949), Ferenczi develops a view of what he called "professional hypocrisy." Through an "almost clairvoyant knowledge," the patient can intuit whether the analyst is sincerely engaging with sympathy (Ferenczi 1949, pg. 227). With the sole purpose of reaching a clear understanding of the patient's symptoms, a calm analytic therapist does not ease hysterical symptoms but actually makes them worse by contributing to feelings of shame and frustration.

An analyst's goal for the patient is to establish the "contrast between the present and the unbearable traumatogenic past, the contrast which is absolutely necessary for the patient in order to enable him to re-experience the past no longer as hallucinatory reproduction but as an objective memory" (Ferenczi 1949, pg. 227). Ferenczi draws the parallel between his patient's need for a sympathetic voice, or even intuitive knowledge of the therapist's care during hysterical outbursts, and sexual trauma in children. Rather than exacerbate the traumatic event that split an ego from its repressed experience, a therapist's goal is integration through the patient's sense of infantile tenderness.[1] A comfortable environment is required for experiencing a trauma, like a painful memory. An objective memory of another's abuse of oneself makes it possible to distinguish between their pleasure and one's own trauma. In sexual trauma, Ferenczi found that children subordinate themselves to their abusers when they are physically and morally incapable of resisting them. They will identify with the external aggressor's sense of desire and introject it as one's own primary process. The external and rigid reality becomes a controllable, intra-psychic source of pleasure. The child retreats to a dream-like state during the event, but the most important change produced in the mind of a child, "by the anxiety-fear-ridden identification with the adult partner, is the introjection of the guilt feelings of the adult" (Ferenczi 1949, pg. 228). The psychic capacity to split, particularly between the innocent child who is helpless and has no control of the situation, but who also comes to have feelings of guilt and shame is reproduced to shed light on the confusion in assuming another's—the aggressor's—guilt.

Ferenczi's observation that the child will also feel responsible because of an introjection of the aggressor's feelings indicates an empathetic relation was formed before a narcissistic identification. Only when love is excessively thwarted, or lacking, can pathologies and neuroses develop. Ferenczi replaces this with Freud's argument that there is an inherent and more dominating aggressive impulse that is ambivalently related to libidinal desires. For example, a child deprived of care is anxious at the reality of lost tenderness, even if it is only in phantasy that the desire exists. Children can become alienated and act out in defiance, but they cannot reflect on the reasons for these behaviors. One assumption that these behaviors imply is that children feel they deserve and anticipate a reality of tenderness.

Psychosis and neurosis in adult sexual life follow for the one who identifies and introjects the aggressor, dividing the psyche only into the id and the super-ego, since there is no ego to maintain its "stability in the face of unpleasure" (Ferenczi 1949, pg. 228). An individuated self is now also seen as becoming constituted through its intersubjective relations. Before identifications are made,

> there lies hidden an ardent desire to get rid of this oppressive love. If we can help the child, the patient, or the pupil to give up the reaction identification, and to ward off the over-burdening transference, then we may be said to have reached the goal of raising the personality to a higher level. (Ferenczi 1949, pg. 228)

Similar to the death drive that according to Freud, drives toward its own particular way of perishing, Ferenczi finds a similar desire to connect in a way that is free of

---

[1] There have also been recent studies that suggest the futility of compassion in psychotherapy for patients with extreme trauma, grief, and mourning from systemic political and social violence. We may wonder how much of the clinical setting was reduced for a real compassionate encounter between subjects ("patient" and "therapist") to alleviate symptoms. See David Becker et al. "Subjectivity and Politics: The Psychotherapy of Extreme Traumatization in Chile," *International Journal of Mental Health* 18.2 (1989): 80–97.

haunting traumas and identifications—free to be decided by the individual before manipulations of psyche are affected. Maybe it is this *eros* that Freud writes about at the end of *Civilization and Its Discontents*—that is, libidinal drives that are not associated with its ambivalent aggressions. It is a love that dissolves the antagonism associated with distinctions between the self and other, where the other is not a represented object for an enclosed self to master. The other also does not merely mirror an image of oneself but reflects a love of another that could have been an aspect of oneself.

Ferenczi concludes that tenderness and caring relations precede infantile love objects. A child's emotional development occurs by sharing in empathy, not as an imposition, but as a coterminous self who is elsewhere. Tenderness is enjoyed as *saturation* of one in another, rather than a primal scene of struggle between the sexes, or the internality of one subject against an external object. Like Klein who placed aggression in overdrive earlier in infancy, Ferenczi adds that development through empathy also heightens one's vulnerability to feeling an abuser's guilt and trauma by adopting the same neurosis unawares.

An elemental altruism, or what Ferenczi calls a "terrorism of suffering," can be seen in a child's assumption of full responsibility for a family's problems, and the attempt to return to a lost sense of rest, care, and maternal attention (Ferenczi 1949, pg. 228). Passionate love and hate result from a love that is lost. A feeling of guilt that accompanies a loved object marks the ambivalence on which Freud focuses. Infantile tenderness, for Ferenczi, "lacks as yet this schism. It is hatred that traumatically surprises and frightens the child while being loved by an adult changes him from a spontaneously and innocently playing being into a guilty love-automaton imitating the adult anxiously, self-effacingly" (Ferenczi 1949, pg. 230). Ferenczi assumes here, somewhat differently than Freud, that splits and fragmentation in the psyche that follow from trauma can be integrated again. One finds "threads that can link up in the various parts," a complex weave that can allay traumas or individual desires that are socially deemed perversions (Ferenczi 1949, pg. 228).

Analogously, as a therapist, Ferenczi thought it was more helpful to reflect on trauma by singing a lullaby to his hysteric patient than by preserving his austere persona as "analyst" (Ferenczi 1949, pg. 226). While Ferenczi is in agreement with Freud about the impact feelings of guilt have on the individuated psyche, his observations on the primacy of a caring infant have lead contemporary psychoanalytic theorists like George Atwood and Donna Orange to further develop the intersubjective approaches in psychotherapy for psychic integration. They also articulate moral possibilities for a psyche fraught with desires that contradict each other that Freud articulated at the end of his life, but possibilities which he could not articulate due to his time and place.

Atwood and Orange value Ferenczi's relational approach to his patients and view of psychological formation. Seeing one's patient as a person beyond contractual obligations starts to alleviate the trauma of psychic isolation. Substitution and transference become ways to offer witness and testimony (instead of detached clinical insight) for extreme forms of trauma. When understood as intersubjectively configured experiences, trauma and the accompanying shame can be alleviated by a responsible caretaker. Rather than efface, ignore, or suppress these experiences with a clinical and distancing response that keeps traumatic experiences a hidden yet open wound, exposure allows the experience to breathe with others and heal.

In Donna Orange's *Nourishing the Inner Lives of Clinicians and Humanitarians: The Ethical Turn in Psychoanalysis*, the unbearable effects of trauma are explored when one lacks "the requisite attuned responsiveness (needed) from those who surround to assist in its tolerance, containment, modulation and alleviation" (Orange 2015, pg. 2; Stolorow and Atwood 1992, pg. 52–3). To accomplish this, the therapist is urged to become another human, even to share their own experiences, to bridge over to the speaker's trauma. Understanding the effects of trauma does not only serve to regard the disruption of temporality and profound sense of personal alienation, nor only the destruction of a familiarity with the everyday. Most important is understanding the intractable suffering of trauma "in the absence of relational holding and even more so in the presence of relational contempt and devaluation" (Orange 2015, pg. 2). These therapists have begun taking a highway from one psyche to the other in order to prevent the client from feeling masochistic pleasure in repressing their trauma. Terms such as hospitality, radical passivity, vulnerability, and receptivity are developed. These describe the subject as constituted and reconstituted in curative relationships with others.

The self does not have to remain narcissistically bound in its aggressive psychic energy. The vicissitudes and feelings of persecution that arise from repressing unacceptable love objects have alternate grounds where they are not rational, but based on a sense of hospitality, and atonement from the other. Hans Loewald was another psychoanalyst who also took seriously the guilt that arises from triangulated Oedipal relations but saw these relations of primary conflict as necessary for the integration and maturation of an individual. Rather than repressing or avoiding guilt, Loewald argues that Oedipal guilt provides the opportunity to break from parents as libidinal objects for individuating oneself.

In "The Waning of the Oedipus Complex" (2000), Loewald writes:

> The Oedipus complex wanes as a crucial pathogenic focus to the extent to which its resolution – never achieved once and for all – is "more than a repression," something other than a retreat from and exclusion by what Freud called the coherent ego. Seen from the perspective of parricide, guilt, and responsibility, repression of the complex is an unconscious evasion of the emancipatory murder of the parents, and a way of preserving infantile libidinal-dependent ties with them. … Insofar as human beings strive for emancipation and individuation as well as for object love, parricide – on the plane of psychic action – is a developmental necessity. (pg. 242)

Motivation arises after the phantasy of parricide in the Oedipal conflict, rather than a need for punishment. Punishment for destroying social bonds based on sameness includes a sadomasochistic pleasure that is inexhaustible. However, in reality the destruction of these tight kin relations is essential for the development of autonomy and new social configurations.

Psychic atonement negotiates and harmonizes between its different parts, reconciling and integrating conflicting desires. However, "if atonement, reconciliation, is not eventually brought about by mourning which leads to a mature super-ego and to the possibility of non-incestuous object relations," then masochistic pleasure from similar abuses can follow (Loewald 2000, pg. 241). In Freudian psychoanalysis, the masochistic self seeks suffering for neurotic reasons. Suffering is always related to an injury that one has experienced. The goal is to resolve Oedipal guilt or for resolving guilt for some injury in one's personal history. A proper amount of mourning for the loss of parental guidance, however, enables integrating that disappointment with a greater sense of responsibility for the other now placed with each other.

Objectors to these more intersubjective and relational approaches in psychoanalysis emphasize that personal relationships between therapist and patient open the therapist to emotional injury by the patient. In other words, therapists could be required to become masochistic by engaging a profession that participates in the pain and trauma of others. These relational theories, however, emphasize the difference between neurotic masochism that seeks suffering to repair one's own irreparable injury from the value empathetic listening can have for repairing another's suffering. Compulsively engaging in acts that only seem altruistic or that seek reparation in oneself is different from becoming engaged as a bystander for another, to witness and heal alongside their injury. Constructive methods for those who practice these approaches are to bear witness, listen to testimonies, and becoming vulnerable with the other person to the point where self and other binaries are overcome for dynamism between these, as Sue Grand advocates.[2] Atonement occurs when the suffering, individuated ego is heard as a tone in the ears of another.

Donna Orange similarly recognizes the significance of witnessing another's injury that has the power to heal. There is an emotional understanding when one listens or recognizes the injury of another. When wounds are noticed, the therapist is not doing it for personal fulfillment as an ambulance chaser might seek to offer legal consultation to the injured parties. As easy as this reaction may be and as easy as it is to interpret all altruistic acts in this egoistic light, the meaningful possibility exists to witness, listen, and just claim "it is not OK for this to happen to anybody." A mutual passivity is acknowledged to both the persecution and injustices that can afflict the kind of subject who remains essentially vulnerable. Attempts "to be with" are sensitive to the violent attempt of "being within," for example made by the efforts of an analyst who claims to have privileged knowledge of another's suffering and so occludes the force of their subjective experience. There can only be here a shift in meaning and experience from Freud's understanding of the egoical self to a more relational approach, one that comes closer to Lévinas's understanding of the subject who is relational. Ultimately, it may be left to the conscience of each therapist to know their truest motivation between these two options, but we have to allow the second possibility that acknowledgment of another's trauma offers curative potential.

---

[2] See Sue Grand, *The Hero in the Mirror: From Fear to Fortitude*. See also Lou Agosta, *A Rumor of Empathy*; Donna Orange *The Suffering Stranger*, *Thinking for Clinicians: Philosophical Resources for Contemporary Psychoanalysis and the Humanistic Psychotherapies*.

Approaches in psychoanalysis that negotiate distances between the individuated desires of one's ego and those in the binding community have contributed two significant changes to Freud's psychoanalytic approach. The first is that the super-ego is amplified and believed to begin in earlier stages of the psyche's development. The ability to negotiate aggression felt in relation to others' expectations also begins earlier. Pre-reflective means, such as through empathy, tenderness, and care for managing interpersonal issues and adapting to these demands develop between the super-ego and individual drives in the early formation of personality. Some approaches have gone as far as eliminating the individuated ego altogether and only preserve the struggle between an id and super-ego.

Also, the development of libido in autoeroticism that aims at objects outside it does not have to resemble oneself for finding pleasure (Freud 1911, pg. 60). Infantile empathy confronts one with other types of subjects, as Ferenczi found in his clinical experience. Libidinal desire that is not based on what Freud called the narcissistic components of emotional life, which also form wider cultural bonds, is less likely to become frustrated and form delusions of persecution for the goal of psychic mastery.

The second big change in amplifying a super-ego that begins early in life is that the ego does not have a strong position outside its immersion in and with others. Instead of a heightened sense of aggression that results from transgressing social expectations, libidinal drives are always in negotiation with different contexts and environments. Like post-structural accounts of self, intersubjective psychotherapies have a view of a subject that is multifariously complex, negotiating its way through social and political matrixes of power.

Freud's work in psychoanalysis had a large influence during his time, and he always predicted that he would have a large impact on society. He worked at normalizing the sexual components of emotional and social life, while also treading carefully on the rigorous demands of scientific investigation as well as the norms of a polite Viennese society. Dying soon after his move to London, Freud's life ended with his own and his family's persecution. Freud did not have time to develop what moral possibilities can relieve the pressure of drives that are ambivalently related and that contributed to the events in his personal life and the catastrophic social reality around him. Though Freud died in a hyperbolic position that screamed of the impossibility of a moral life, we may see how similar events of persecution in the life of Emmanuel Lévinas lead to the opposite hyperbolic conclusion, namely, on the undeclinable necessity of leading an ethical life.

References

Ferenczi, S. (1949). Confusion of the tongues between the adults and the child (The language of tenderness and of passion). *International Journal of Psycho-Analysis, 30*, 225–230.

Freud, S. (1958). The standard edition of the complete psychological works of Sigmund Freud. In J. Strachey (Ed.). *The case of Schreber, Papers on technique and other works, ii-vii* (Vol. XII, 1911). London: The Hogarth Press and the Institute of Psycho-analysis.

References

Loewald, H. (2000). The waning of the Oedipus complex. *The Journal of Psychotherapy Practice and Research, 9*(4), 239–249.

Orange, D. (2015). *Nourishing the inner life of clinicians and humanitarians: The ethical turn in psychoanalysis*. New York: Routledge.

Stolorow, R. D., & Atwood, G. E. (1992). *Contexts of being: The intersubjective foundations of psychological life*. Hillside: Analytic Press.

Chapter 7
From Freud to Lévinas

Abstract This intermission recalls that I stage these characters according to a hermeneutical procedure, rather than providing a strict historical biographical study. I use these two figures nonetheless to chart the clash between moral skepticism and ethical subjectivity in order to recover a fundamental human concern for others, which I find that Lévinas develops in consideration of the kind of moral skepticism that Freud articulates.

Keywords Freud and Lévinas · Moral ambivalence · Freud's hesitations · Penumbra of ego · Autrui · The Other · Hostility and hospitality · Relational subjectivity · Otherwise than being · Empathetic relations · Anarchic goodness · Ethical subjectivity · Ethical substitution · Pre-ontological relation · Conflicting desires · Conflicting drives

Lévinas finds us already in the embrace of a stranger, while Freud is looking at the individuated ego of a subject and concludes that this embrace may not be possible. The *may not* that Freud compulsively repeats through his text leaves us room to explore the possibility initiated by Lévinas that "ethics is first philosophy" (1969, pg. 84). Like Freud, Lévinas was also acutely critical of moral imperatives such as the command to love all. For him, the dictum lacks the recognition of a singular *other* that we face in particular moral relations

Can Lévinas find a way toward a general ethic while preserving the singularity of each individual? Is it possible to have an egalitarian ethic without annihilating the singular, particular interests and drives in oneself, especially if one is tied to a threatening other through a brutal co-existence? Is love cheapened for those who deserve it by universally willing it to all, as Freud claimed? While Freud was concerned that the psyche and emotional life is too fraught with aggressive drives to peacefully co-exist with others and so cannot have a mutual moral ground, it seems as if Lévinas's ethic is ignorant of the psyche's conflicting nature.[1] However, it can

---

[1] Note that there are three kinds of conflicting relations in Freud. For Lévinas, ethical subjectivity is similarly constructed out of constant negotiations between totalizing aspects of self that is also infinite in itself, two aspects which are ambivalently related.

also be argued that it is precisely because of this tension revealed in Freud's work that the subject can become ethical in Lévinas's estimations. Only on these difficult grounds of an individuated subject struggling in an impossible isolation can Lévinas's ethical subject answer the call of a demand that is always difficult to answer.

By understanding these complexities inherent to the ego found in psychoanalysis, Lévinas develops the penumbra of an ego that is infinitely open to the other. A breathing shadow of the individuated ego is captured only in an approach and proximity to any possible knowledge, which flies under the radar even of the Freudian hermeneutics that is similarly suspicious of the psyche's (in)sufficiency to know itself. There is a splitting of Freud's voice throughout his work that culminates in *Civilization and Its Discontents* about loving the other like oneself, especially when the other does not deserve it. I find in these hesitating moments through Freud's writing an attempt to find a Lévinasian other, reminding Freud at a vulnerable time in his life about what lay *beyond* the libidinal and aggressive drives he writes about.

Lévinas catches site of a narcissism that amplifies its aggression in relation to others and speaks in terms of the ontological relation between these. The narcissistic circle is "[b]eing's interest [that] takes dramatic form in egoisms struggling with one another, each against all, in the multiplicity of allergic egoisms which are at war with one another and are thus together" (Lévinas 1998, pg. 4).[2] In this war, peace is sought through economic relations, rationality, and patience. Moral calculations ensue for the purposes of fair political relations, for example (Levinas 1998, pg. 192). But the picture does not stop only with this narcissistic egoism for Lévinas as it seems to do with Freud. Lévinas's *l'autre* is another other, an anti-egological, anti-empirical, and anti-logical alterity.[3] One is always also already committed by virtue of what Lévinas calls the approach of the other. The approach cannot be willed, or negotiated, away. Lévinas uses phrases like "pre-original saying," "proximity and approach," and "otherwise than being." These names are all also ultimately betrayals of that which must be presupposed for a cognition that commits each to an ability to respond to another's needs, a response-ability.

The common ground of the self and other is found in the mutual interpolation of a relational subjectivity. What may seem like an inconsistent or negligence in Lévinas's uses of *autre* (other), *autrui* (human other), and *l'autre* (the general other, or the Other of Alterity) can be understood as a deliberate ambiguity that illustrates the difficulty of sifting these out for one who is also always other. Most work on Lévinas comments on how otherness is used as a term, but I argue that to find strict designations forecloses the uncomfortable ambiguity of who the other is and the degree of their demand. Is it a particular person, is it a general designation for any other, or is it the alterity of an infinite God who is Other that another person can potentially hold when each is mutually made in its image? Ambiguity in his use of

---

[2] Brackets added.

[3] On Lévinas's *autrui* and the subject who is made in the affective proximity to the body of another human that suffers, but whose transcendent character is also as distant as the good beyond being, also see Adriaan T. Peperzak, "Transcendence" (1995).

these terms of a particular other, general other and God is, therefore, taken here as a literary device and hermeneutic procedure that iterates the most crucial point of Lévinas's approach on the ethical subject. The address from God is made in each demanding face as *visage* that comes from a particular person.

As difficult as the ethical relation is according to Freud, Lévinas emphasizes the inability to decline it. Two different and seemingly incompatible sets of language describe the ethical subject in what are considered Lévinas's two most influential works. His language refers to proximity and paradoxical antonyms that are contained in one and the same object, such as the infinite and totalizable qualities of a subject. A subject can host hostile and hospitable natures, and though many succumb to moments of the former with its clear benefits, we may assume that just as many have also succumbed to the later moments with fewer enjoyments for the self-sufficient ego. Similar to Freud, Lévinas develops these two as aspects of the ethical person that are ambivalently related. One aspect of the ethical subject is referred to as the individuated ego, and the other to the relational aspect of self that culminates in ethical subjectivity and co-constructed personhood. These aspects can also drive an individual to both desire and repel the same objects of their drives.

One methodology proceeds in the light of the kind of ego seen in Freud, an ego that is caught negotiating the influences that come from without and within the individuated self (Lévinas 2001, pg. 95). In Lévinas's *Totality and Infinity*, an individuated self is separated from the other who can still be "seen" through the face as *visage*, and through a non-erotic desire of the other. Alternatively, the ethical subject is also a creator of metaphysical relations that bridge from the self to the stranger, the orphan, or the widow. This self is not under the illusion of a moral life that can serve a self-interested fantasy of power, separation, and autonomy. It is another sensibility—the ethical one—which searches.

> The face, for its part, is inviolable; those eyes, which are absolutely without protection, the most naked part of the human body, nonetheless offer an absolute resistance to possession, an absolute resistance, in which the temptation to murder is inscribed. The other is the only being that one can be tempted to kill. This temptation to murder and this impossibility of murder constitute the very vision of the face. (Lévinas 1990, pg. 8)

According to Lévinas, to see the face is already to hear "Thou shalt not kill." Two aspects appear in the face: one is a personal desire and temptation to kill, to fight for one's individuated needs and libidinal desires, while the other aspect is a simultaneous vision that one cannot kill the other who is without protection.

Lévinas writes on substitution as a useful "trope of a sense that does not belong to the empirical order of psychological events, an *Einfuhlung* [empathy] or a compassion which signify by virtue of this sense" (Lévinas 1990, pg. 8).[4] The ability to substitute one's suffering for the other—to feel empathetic yet without sentimentality that is relative to an individual mentality, to offer bread even when I am just as hungry—presupposes a mutual vulnerability from which either an act of compassion or non-compassion can follow. In distinction from Freud, for whom projection and

---

[4] Brackets added.

transference can replace and impose one's object of love upon others, or where one's object of love may be substituted by more acceptable ones, substitution for Lévinas does not include any ontological ideation. A sense other than empirical and rational sensibilities opens to the individual needs of another when they arise. An anarchic shock that allows two particular individuals to relate takes over.

In *Otherwise Than Being, Or Beyond Essence*, Lévinas describes the egoical aspect of the subject as a sovereign that refers to its own saying and is a nominative self (1998, pg. 46–8). The second aspect is the relational one that is a personal pronoun, an accusative that is not derived from any nominative. This aspect does not stay identical to its internal processes, but in an ethical relation finds the unpredictable other in oneself and finds the self in another. When the demand of the other breaks through the synchronism of the self, then the relational self is in a relation of subjection (Lévinas 1998, pg. 125). The ability for a response—a *responsibility*—is granted from an "original goodness" that provides the openness necessary for any communication, while at the same time ensuring communicability (Lévinas 1998, pg. 121). Co-constitutionality by the other is the ability to create and become what you are without knowing in a rational sense what will develop. The egoical self does suffer in this relation that requires the other for its relational aspect, but it is for another aspect of self and the possibility of reaching a height in an ethical relation. The glimpses and traces received from others who have the possibility of offering bread in times of hunger and the ability to respond in the face of grave danger to the suffering of another are examples of an anarchic goodness.

In *Otherwise Than Being,* the individuated ego reaches the height of ethical subjectivity in the moment of substitution that is committed to another in preserving the vision of a face one cannot kill. Killing another goes beyond physical murder. The thought of humiliating another and drawing blood to their cheeks can be considered another form of murder that is sensitive to the judgments of a super-ego. Shame is murder of one's character, an ethical violation as murderous as physical death. Schreber's sense of shame and repression is illustrative of this character-soul-death inflicted by the psyche's mechanisms. Schreber's accusation against Flechsig was that he was committing soul murder, which for Schreber is exactly what his paranoid delusions did. Repressing his desire in shame resulted in the proverbial murder of his individuated psyche. Freud called this an internal collapse that causes a retreat of libidinal ties, which he personally experienced at the end of his life due to the death of family members, rampant persecutions in his hometown of Vienna, and eventual exile from what he considered his homeland.

For Freud, acts of sublimation and substitution preserve the social bond by redirecting feelings of aggression in the individuated ego. In *Beyond the Pleasure Principle* (1920), he tells the story of his 18-month-old grandchild who plays a "Fort-Da" game. For Freud, this game illustrates how sublimated aggression can turn into a cultural accomplishment. After experiencing the loss of a parent who walks out of the room, the child sends away his toy. In controlling the toy by bringing it back, the child achieves mastery of his aggression in a rule-bound activity. His aggression is articulated but redirected through this orchestrated game under his control. The ego regains its strength in substituting the object of his parents and the aggressive drive with the toy that he brings back. As such the individuated ego can preserve its stability in the face of loss. Mastery over the other, such as in delusions of persecution and in the rule-bound game, is required for preserving the egoical self, which is why Lévinas turns to notions of proximity in thinking about the ethical subject.

For the subject who is always intersubjective, always relational, the distance between each individuated self is significant for sensing the particular needs of the other. The ability to perceive someone differently from how they really are makes significant the "recourse that people have to one another for help, before the marvelous alterity of the Other has been banalized or dimmed in a simple exchange of courtesies which become established as an inter-personal commerce of customs" (Bernasconi 1988, pg. 165). The proximity between each isolated subject conditions the possibility of eliciting one's responsibility for the other's vulnerability. Lévinas's use of the non-empirical vision of a face solicits an idea that goes beyond the generalized ideas, or ideas one receives from cultural narratives that one can have of another who after all can still make a demand.

Proximate relations are neither to master the other, nor for earning reciprocity since calculative thought is not included. Additionally, proximate relations acknowledge the asymmetrical power relations that plague any relation. One's demands will not necessarily be seen, recognized, or appreciated. "The face is, from the start, the demand of which I was just speaking. It is the frailty of the one who needs you, who is counting on you. This is where the idea of dissymmetry – which is very important to me – comes from" (Bernasconi 1988, pg. 171). All are vulnerable to the frail face that makes a demand without offering a reward. Substitution as a pre-ontological condition is not a moral choice, act, or thought. Substitutability is an ontological fact that cannot be relieved, as much as one may feel uncomfortable with the infinite demand. Analogously, I do not grieve for the infinite demand to perceive the world around me, though it is similarly unsolicited. One needs to learn to discern what is important out of all the available data. Similarly, a moral sensibility that searches for what is important out of infinite data about a particular other is necessary for an appropriate response.

Where Freud asks if this ethical demand is humanly possible or even desirable, Lévinas asserts it is a necessary ability for a being that speaks and that demands a response. What do we do with the particular person who shows up defenseless? Freud insists on not knowing here and it may be due to his place and time in history, after the First World War, during the commencement of another, and a life that ends with a death in exile. Can we find that Freud only momentarily closed the possibility for a genuine ethical relation that exceeds narcissistic investment, which Lévinas later opens again? Does a hermeneutic of suspicion presuppose one of trust in order to interpret any language, symbols, and desires that can reflect a fragmented self at all? The openness to another that necessarily accompanies language prevents indifference to its power for shaping one's understanding of self and others. But I proceed to wonder in the next sections how moral freedom can count in preserving the life of the other in an ethic that considers it a demanding persecution to see the face of the other.

For Lévinas, the face makes a demand that a posteriori will always preserve the life of the other. How is moral freedom reconciled with this demand? Freud acknowledges this difficulty by considering the declining role of the rational agent's freedom in its moral life. Lévinas similarly sheds light on a psychic constitution that aggressively resents these internalized social norms and morals. Does Lévinas conceive of the individual drives that turn moral life into a masochistic pleasure, as Freud does, and if not how does he answer to this dilemma of conflicting drives and desires? The following sections that emphasize the cracks in identities and the value of epistemic gaps that cause unknowability will relieve a traditional value held for self-mastery and replace it with a value for vulnerability. I will extend Lévinas's suggestion of an intentionality of search to better understand what a vulnerable but ethical subjectivity is meant to do with the other that appears in a persecution of its egoistic aspect of self. Like the sections on Freud, three axes of unknowability, vulnerability, and relational subjectivity are used to understand the complex relationship between persecution and ethics.

References

Bernasconi, R. & David W. (eds.). (1988). *Provocation of Levinas: Rethinking the Other*. United Kingdom: Routledge.

Freud, S. (1955). The standard edition of the complete psychological works of Sigmund Freud. In J. Strachey (Ed.), *Beyond the pleasure principle* (Vol. XVIII, 1920). London: The Hogarth Press and the Institute of Psycho-analysis.

Lévinas, E. (1969). *Totality and infinity* (trans: Lingis, A.). New York: Duquesne University Press.

Lévinas, E. (1998). *Otherwise than being: Beyond essence* (trans: Lingis, A.). New York: Duquesne University Press.

Lévinas, E. (1990). *Difficult freedom: Essays on judaism* (trans: Hand, S.). Baltimore: John Hopkins University Press.

Lévinas, E. (2001). *Existence and existents* (trans: Lingis, A.). New York: Duquesne University Press.

Peperzak, A. T. (1995). Transcendence. In A. T. Peperzak (Ed.), *Ethics as first philosophy: The significance of Emmanuel Lévinas for philosophy, literature and religion* (pp. 185–192). New York/London: Routledge.

Part II
Emmanuel Lévinas

Chapter 8
Lévinas's Life and Work: A Historical Horizon

Abstract In this chapter, I consider the parallels between Lévinas's first major works on an individuated ethical subjectivity and latter ones that characterize ethical subjectivity as an ontological persecution. I find specific actions and personal friendships in Lévinas's life that stress the challenges that face a relational and vulnerable form of subjectivity that I advance here.

Keywords Ethical subjectivity · Ontological persecution · Ecole Normal Israelite Orientale · ENIO · Lithuanian Jews · Jewish Persecution WWII · Always already subjected · Persecution in Lévinas · Trauma of the face · Face-to-face relation · Relational subjectivity · Affective relations · Impinging relations · Ethical relation · Existential vulnerability · Intersubjective relations · Alterity of the other · Blanchot and Lévinas · Lévinas at Sorbonne · Master Chouchani · Phenomenology and the Talmud · Totality and infinity · Otherwise than being · Living in the margins · Lévinas's ethics

> "Is there sufficient pride, daring, courage, self-confidence available today, sufficient will of the spirit, will to responsibility, freedom of the will, for the 'philosopher' to be henceforth—possible on earth? Has all this really altered? Has that many-colored and dangerous winged creature, the 'spirit' which this caterpillar concealed, really been unfettered at last and released into the light thanks to a sunnier, warmer, brighter world?"
> —Friedrich Nietzsche, *Genealogy of Morals, E3 sect. 10*

What does this daring "will to responsibility" illustrated in a creatured spirit that soars in true freedom look like? From what is it unfettered: Could it be released from delusions, misguided moralities, or might it be a responsibility from other people? If Nietzsche intends the last, to what then does will respond? Does not a response presuppose an interlocutor, and so, therefore, imply that a release from misguided moralities is in order?

Like the logics of contradiction apparent in justifications for persecution that I tracked through historical and political theorists, and then in Freudian psychoanalysis, a logic of contradiction also appears in Lévinas's understanding of persecution (see Chaps. 1 and 2). I find that the logic of contradiction developed in Lévinas's work, however, is inverse to the one seen in Freud. Rather than projecting an interior idea onto an external object, for Lévinas projection becomes introjection without the possibility of declining this relation that persecutes the isolated ego. The ego is persecuted to go toward another in order to become an ethical subject. Subjectivity does not only constitute objects exterior to it, but other subjects also constitute another version of the self; this is a fundamentally dual relation. A reckoning about moral sentiments begins.

In his section titled "The Self" of *Otherwise than Being or Beyond Essence,* Lévinas characterizes persecuted subjectivity as

> The recurrence of the self in responsibility for others, a persecuting obsession, goes against intentionality, such that responsibility for others could never mean altruistic will, instinct of "natural benevolence," or love. It is in the passivity of obsession, or incarnated passivity, that an identity individuates itself as unique, without recourse to any system of references, in the impossibility of evading the assignation of the other without blame. The representation of self grasps it already in its trace. (1998a, pg. 111-2)

Subjectivity is always already in an ethical bind by virtue of persecutory demands imposed psychologically from within. One cannot decline psychological forces, but only on occasion choose how to respond to them. In order to understand how the persecutory subject as developed by Lévinas stands in contrast to Freud, I first explore how persecution is the binding force that is necessary for making the ethical demand. In Lévinas's life and work, characteristics such as unknowability, vulnerability, and relational subjectivity let us animate, postulate, and think through those aspects of his life that contributed to his notion of an ethical subject who is always capable of producing and suffering persecutions.

Emmanuel Lévinas spent the early years of his childhood in Kaunas speaking Russian and then Hebrew from the age of 6. He grew up in a traditional household that celebrated Jewish holidays; however, Lévinas's former student and biographer Salomon Malka writes in *Emmanuel Lévinas: His Life and Legacy* that the household, though traditional in practice, "was not excessively religious" (2006, pg. 6). The Lévinas family also had pride in Lithuanian culture and followed its developing involvement in traditional Judaism. The family's book collection was extensive, featuring authors such as Alexander Sergeyevich Pushkin, Fyodor Dostoyevsky, Nikolai Gogol, and Anton Chekov, who would make their way into Lévinas's theoretical work later in life.

A rise in anti-Semitism would lead to the family's exile several times in his youth, from Kaunas to Russia, to Poland, until finally the family returned to Lithuania. It was there, in 1920, that his father returned to owning a shop, and Lévinas was able to graduate high school. In a climate that increasingly divided between those who loved Slavic peoples and languages, *Slavophiles*, and those who were *Occidentalists* that loved Western cultures, Lévinas aligned himself with the "critical conclusion: Russia was entrusted with the sacred mission of reviving the religious intention at the heart of philosophy" (Malka 2006, pg. 9). These same ideological divisions were manifest in Freud's life, but as it was shown he fell on the other side of the rivalry as an Occidentalist. Dostoevsky was one paradigmatic author that Lévinas found engaging this mission of reviving the religious intention at the heart of philosophy. Using these terms, I find Lévinas's own path in this sacred mission was to revive not just the religious intention, but the persecuting demand of morality, as much as love, which sits at the heart of all philosophy. As such, Lévinas amplifies the persecutory demands of the other as ontological and existential, whereas Freud showed the persecuting relation as it pertained to psychological topographies, and moral and social commitments. Considering these impinging and affective relations, Freud stopped theorizing when it came to the difficult necessity of leading a moral life. He never found how to justify the origins of a moral sentiment in the human psyche, whereas Lévinas theorized about the binding necessity of living with others. What made them each reach such different conclusions about these moral possibilities?

During his life, Lévinas experienced a constant need—and resistance—to conform to whatever category made it easy to relate to another. Party affiliations, religious denominations, and class distinctions were some of the ID cards used in an era that was increasingly becoming massified and industrialized. Marketing, recruitment, and appeal to another were easier if each citizen fit into distinct categories. Like Freud, Lévinas grew up at a crossroads of culture, industrialization, and nation formation, as well as at a crossroad in the project of philosophy itself, which came into fuller fruition after Freud's death and during the postwar decades of the 1940s–1960s.

Like Freud, Lévinas did not feel limited by either rationalist, empirical, or phenomenological methodologies. Freud wanted to derive general impulses of the mind that used drives as a border concept, that "frontier-line between the somatic and the mental," that "psychical representative of organic forces" (1925, pg. 74). For Freud, there was the biological individual who both struggled for ego preservation and species preservation by way of libidinal and destructive drives. Lévinas also thought through the ways in which culture develops, considering a constantly looming barbarism that threatens to return. But, how can ethical standards be known? Is the "love" Lévinas writes about a mere feeling or sentiment of "love"? Closer to Freud's concept of libido, this notion of love for Lévinas is not one of an erotic and suffocating sentimentality, but is a metaphysical desire that builds cultural and ethical relations.

The universality of a hospitality and openness that comes with the capacity for language, in addition to the closed off character to which the form of a conflicted subject may succumb, is an idea that illuminates how transcendence in individuated identities develops through their relation. Language is one important way in which Lévinas found that selfhood is necessarily relational, or as Michael Fagenblat writes of Lévinas's concept of selfhood in *A Covenant of Creatures*, one who is "always already subjected" to others (2010, pg. 102). As anarchic as the shock and trauma of the face that calls one to respond, the beckoning of a face is the original form of discourse. The "authentic relationship with the other; it is discourse and more exactly, response and responsibility which is this authentic relationship" (Lévinas 1985, pg. 88). While one is always implicated in the very possibility of expression, of a saying in any particular language, Lévinas calls the "order of the said" that which "imposes a society with laws, institutions and social relations" that will always command one to consider another. Language, therefore, is the condition of possibility for identity as a relational subject.

The very possibility for language is also a feature in Lévinas's life that made him both esteemed and vulnerable throughout his academic career. He spoke Russian with his family and wife. He read Biblical texts in Ancient Hebrew. He also translated Husserl's German writings and lectures into French and as such had a claim to fame among existentialist thinkers like Simone de Beauvoir and Jean-Paul Sartre. While Lévinas's aptitude for learning languages benefited his early career, it posed a serious challenge later in his life. For example, eleven years after arriving in France, Lévinas became an administrative assistant in the education department at the *Alliance Israelite University*. Lévinas was a Lithuanian living in France, teaching Moroccan Jews how to assimilate to life in Paris. Neither French nor Moroccan, he led generations of students through this difficult project of negotiating cultures. Learning a French curriculum, students also received a religious education. These experiences, which show the malleability of language for Lévinas, grant power to transform the isolation of an individuated self into a reflection and into the various refractions of their social reality.

After publishing his first book, *De l'Existence à l'Existant*, Lévinas focused on earning a living for his family as director of the *Ecole Normal Israelite Orientale* (ENIO) (Malka 2006, pg. 147). He remained in that position until 1973 and finally left the school in 1979. Even as he worked in administrative roles at academic institutions, Lévinas regularly attended lectures by influential thinkers like Alexandre Kojève and participated in intellectual salons at the margins of university life, such as those hosted by Gabriel Marcel (Malka 2006, pg. 147). During this time after publishing his first work and acting as administrator, Lévinas was dissuaded from pursuing the most prestigious *agrégation* for teaching because of his accent. The advice came from several influential thinkers that Lévinas highly regarded (Malka 2006, pg. 148). Feeling comfortable and also utmost uncomfortable in language must be a jarring, ambivalent experience of deep alienation and dependency for a thinker who valued the role language has in developing oneself.

Later in life, when Lévinas's solitude from academia was credited as part of his search for a new language into the *terra incognita of thought*, he was still challenged by the voice through which his words would speak. Grasping a new language that pulled from his knowledge of lay Russian, German, French, and Hebrew, he spoke on the alterity of the other, sameness, and the third with trepidation in "a small voice, which made it hard for him to articulate himself … His language is certainly interesting although ultimately it was an artificial language, a bit fantastical" (Malka 2006, pg. 152). Imagine finding such an important ground in the capacity for language, while also feeling the isolation created by it. Eventually, Jean Wahl, a sort of mentor to Lévinas, would have to "go after him" to pursue his *doctorat d'état* with his work *Totality and Infinity* (Malka 2006, pg. 153). Only after this initiation, Lévinas became more known through his philosophical work and was invited to lecture at the Sorbonne in 1973 at the advanced age of 67.

Lévinas had a classical upbringing in the literature of his time, yet he maintained relationships with Maurice Blanchot, Mordechai Chouchani, and Jacques Derrida, thinkers whose work diverged from classical methods in significant ways. Lévinas's own work would produce new divergences from classical Jewish and philosophic inspirations, while maintaining various levels of proximity to each of them. As much as he was criticized for the work he produced in each field, his success was in maintaining only proximate distances from them.

Lévinas's friendship with Maurice Blanchot illustrates well the difficult task of only living in proximity to the other. Blanchot was Lévinas's friend from his early graduate days in Strasbourg during the 1920s. Malka writes that because of, and perhaps in spite of, political differences, "[t]he two men bonded very quickly, yet their friendship seemed improbable" (Malka 2006, pg. 26). Blanchot came from a privileged economic status and was inclined to support conservative political parties. On the other hand, Lévinas came from modest upbringings and, though a classist in literature, in all things political he remained on the left. Values of egalitarianism, and humane treatment of prison inmates, were issues Lévinas advocated for late into his life. They built a relationship based on vastly different approaches to matters each considered of utmost importance.

It would seem difficult that Lévinas could maintain a relationship with a social activist who "professed an aversion to democracy, parliamentarianism, capitalism, and communism," all qualities that, for Blanchot, were embodied in what he expressly called the "cosmopolitan Jew" (Malka 2006, pg. 29). Over the course of their lives a deep friendship developed between these two, a relationship that at the same time could be mutually injurious. I wonder what in Lévinas's understanding could justify such insufferable conditions; his approach to an infinite subjectivity will be further explored in upcoming chapters.

It could be argued his openness to different types of people is best understood through his post-phenomenological approach to writing and also in the ethical subjectivity apparent in his theoretical work. In his seminal book *Totality and Infinity*, Lévinas uses phenomenological language to go beyond a method restricted to psychological or ontological phenomenon. He uses it to develop a horizon of meaning that goes toward an unknowable self with a real, certain, and definite responsibility. The condition that "Goodness consists in going where no clarifying – that is panoramic – thought precedes, in going without knowing where. An absolute adventure, in a primal imprudence, goodness is transcendence itself" ensures the possibility of reciprocity and building larger cultural bonds beyond what one knows and is familiar with (Lévinas 1969, pg. 305). Still not in the erotic economies of self, welcoming the asymmetry in different types of moral responses that follow from contingent relations requires developing a kind of non-sensibility.

A new ability includes attunement to the particular other, which is necessary and necessarily varied according to contingencies in each; however, each person is equally formed out of these different vulnerabilities that are communicable through language. An ethical relation or general principle then cannot be given in advance but requires attunement to these asymmetries in power and abilities provided in each unique moment. Bearing witness, integration, and psychic reparation are ways that psychoanalytic therapy engaged Lévinas's ethics of substitution, a relation that values a disruption that comes from the other. Those approaches value a non-erotic proximity to the other as necessary, not for fulfilling the egoical need to repair trauma in one's ego, but precisely to disrupt the isolation of one's ego for finding a new self in the other. In injuring the egoical self in a realization of free communication, relational subjectivity reaches its ethical height in language with another.

Additionally, one lesson that stands out from Lévinas's writing that can help understand his openness to different types of people is that while one's identifications are necessary for building a self, those identifications are not enough for an ethical relation. Whether there is everything in common between two or they are totally dissimilar from each other, these only provide the platform for an anarchic push into the heights of ethicality. In one's openness to the alterity or infinite distance of the other, Lévinas insisted that any identifications whatever are never enough to represent the individual who is constituted by these varying identifications during their lives. In *Altered Reading: Lévinas and Literature*, Jill Robbins writes about Lévinas's thinking on responsibility that is helpful for understanding its anarchical aspect. Where there is a relation that does not hinge on any similarity between identifications, or emotions of desirability and love in the "economy of the same," alterity is glimpsed. There is necessarily an interruption and disturbance for both subjects in their response-ability. Again, the egoical subject who has identifications is a necessary condition for the relation, but they are not sufficient since the other must interrupt the self-enclosed interests of each.

Robbins continues to write of this form of reciprocity that glimpses "a deconstructive potential, for in identifying something like an internal division or border within the same that opens the same to the other, it achieves as it were a deconstruction of self, of self-coincidence, by the relation to the other" (Robbins 1999, pg. 30). A reciprocal need to find a border within each other in their asymmetrical relation obligates both to an infinite competition and infinite obligation to see the disruptive face of the other. The trace of the anarchical other appears as a face; to be stripped of all acquired identifications is to be "like a stranger, hunted down even in one's home, contested in one's own identity" (Lévinas 1998a, pg. 92). Sometimes all that is experienced is a disruption, a crack. We find that an "I" is a universal phenomenon for each body, while simultaneously each is also universally capable of breaking from itself. The self can also recoil to preserve itself over the other, eclipsing the other's needs. We may think that it was something of this understanding that enabled Lévinas's charitable and multifaceted relations.

It was ultimately beneficial that Lévinas did not limit his friendships only to those who agreed with his every perspective or reflected what he would call "the same" back to him. Blanchot, for example, would end up providing housing for Lévinas's wife and daughter during the Second World War (Malka 2006, pg. 30). The two found refuge in Blanchot's vacant house in France, while Lévinas was held in captivity as a prisoner of war at the camp Stalag XIB in Fallingbostel, Germany (Malka 2006, pg. 67). As much as these personal friends could stand in difficult relations to him, characterizing what could become hostile in their hospitality, Lévinas's own identity maintained these contradicting strands. Similarly, he stayed in dialogue with Catholic thinkers including phenomenologists Jean-Luc Marion and Paul Ricœur, and even Pope John Paul II. Agnes Kalinowska was Lévinas's student at the Sorbonne in 1975 and goddaughter of Pope John Paul II. Kalinowska arranged for their meeting, which would eventually lead to Lévinas's yearly invitations to speak at Castel Gandolfo, "the summer residence of the Pope located in the outskirts of Rome" (Malka 2006, pg. 229).

It was in his conversations with her that Lévinas made the infamous claim that philosophy is not only the love of wisdom but the wisdom of love (Malka 2006, pg. 228). A suffocating love, love that is too distant, or love that is too critical of the other are experiences that shed light on relations that have no wisdom in their relation—the two cannot relate to each other appropriately, whatever that measure may be between two particular people. With the *wisdom* of love in the background of their discourse, Kalinowska describes Lévinas as "essentially positive, open, [someone] who always saw the good side of things" (Malka 2006, pg. 228). In addition to being open to conservative thinkers, Catholic theologians, and phenomenologists of other religions, Lévinas was also deeply entrenched in learning the tradition of his ancestors. He was a devout student and was influenced by his teacher of the Talmud, Mordechai Chouchani. The strength of using phenomenology as a theoretical framework for these lessons in Talmud is that both these methods reject abstract concepts.

His scholarship would never be limited to what a "philosopher" might have implied at the time. For example, theology and religion were not tolerated in philosophical teaching at the Sorbonne, yet while he taught there, he also remained director of a Jewish school at the *Ecole Normal Israelite Orientale* (ENIO). Lévinas did not subsume one role into the other, but at times held them in critical proximities. In response to those who claimed Lévinas was a Jewish thinker, it was incumbent on him to remind them of the non-reducibility of his work and himself. If he accepted the identification imposed on him, then he would have a part in perpetuating the reduction. We see this responsibility in those who desire to fit into neat categories; some even work hard at receiving certain identifications from others or institutions like doctor or lawyer. We see this attitude as a persistent theme in Lévinas's own life. Reducing his identity to any one characterization or to any one aspect of his multifarious life is the violence of totalizing in one what remains infinite.

Lévinas refused to be totally identified in any particular way, whether it was as a Jewish philosopher or Talmudist, philosopher or phenomenologist, or even as teacher rather than administrator. The idea of being confined to any identification seemed reductive and, as such, violent (Malka 2006, pg. 269). Even as he was also tortured by the traumatic memories that he did not revisit often, we can see his appeal to the subject of *Totality and Infinity*, one who is open and welcomes the encounter in all its proven trauma.

Already in 1929 at a conference in Davos, Switzerland, with attendees such as Martin Heidegger and Ernst Cassirer, opportunities in philosophy began to open for Lévinas through the emerging field of phenomenology to speak about the ethical insights he found in lessons from the Talmud. Eventually, he managed to develop a language that imported insights of one framework to another:

> Lévinas was a known specialist in Husserlian and Heideggarian phenomenology. His modest publications up to that time did not suggest the impressive body of work that would make him one of the most important thinkers of the century. His contributions to philosophy were overshadowed by his writings on questions related to Jewish spirituality … and because he did not hold an academic position at a French university, his influence in philosophy was limited in comparison to his growing impact in the field of Jewish thought. (Lévinas 1996, pg. ix)

On the other hand, those who attended Lévinas's Talmudic lectures noted in various ways his non-fluency in these texts as well. In the introduction to *Nine Talmudic Writings*, translator Annette Aronowicz writes,

> In a sense, Lévinas's own life during this period best illustrates the contents of these essays, for while he was heading a Jewish school, writing essays on the Jewish tradition, and, from 1960, giving Talmudic commentaries at the yearly colloquia of Jewish intellectuals in Paris, he was also writing his great philosophical works, the works that speak to all human beings in "Greek," *Totalité et infini* (1961) and *Autrement qu'être out au-delà de l'essence* (1974), to mention the two generally recognized as his major contributions to the philosophical traditions. The Jewish subjects were fed by the philosophical work, and the philosophical work was fed by the contact with Jewish sources. The Jew and the "Greek" were in constant relation. (Lévinas 1990, pg. xiv-xv)

One tradition was not subsumed into the other, though one can legitimately ask how much these traditions could be separated. The Jewish particularism or specificity was not meant to replace the Greek method of searching for axiomatic generalities and abstractions. Indeed, a more pluralistic approach to knowledge and self can be gained if both are read alongside one another, as exemplified in Lévinas's two most popular works *Totality and Infinity: An Essay on Exteriority* (1961) and *Otherwise than Being or Beyond Essence* (1974).

For this goal, Lévinas wondered what the voice specific to the Rabbi's brings to notions of the human being, as such. What is unique in Talmudic readings, and where in this unique method and knowledge is there a lesson for all people, not just Jewish ones? By way of the particular embodiment of a Jewish identity, Lévinas made his way back to the philosophical in an attempt to speak with the Greek other.

In both his method and learning, Lévinas put a consistent emphasis on preserving a site that makes one's way back to an egalitarian ethic that must preserve the particular other. Rabbi Daniel Epstein, who translated *Talmudic Readings* into Hebrew, commented that Lévinas's approach to the Talmud could be a sort of phenomenological reading. Lévinas always had a constant need to avoid highly theoretical and conceptual language for returning to matters of everyday life, as is traditional for Talmudic discussions (Malka 2006, pg. 125). In typical fashion that avoids totalizing oneself to one label or another, Lévinas attempted to use the phenomenological method in his Talmudic lessons. Like Talmudic debate, phenomenology favors a return to everyday life, "to matters of human commerce, family relations, birth and death" (Malka 2006, pg. 125). Both the phenomenological and Talmudic approaches also overstep the often clumsy and artificial binary between subject-object, mind-body, and rationalism-empiricism.

In one and the same move, however, Lévinas managed to alienate Jewish scholars and phenomenologists alike. Prizing logic and scientific clarity in the attempt to systematize general structures of meaning and intentionality for everyday matters, the phenomenological method is anathema to Talmudic scholarship. Lévinas also alienated those academics that would immediately cast him as a religious thinker. For these reasons, he experienced alienation from a professional academic life early in his career in France. After publishing his first mature philosophical work *Existence and Existents* (1947), he next published *Nine Talmudic Readings* (1968) that were taken from keynote lectures given between 1957 and 1975 at the Colloquia of French-Speaking Jewish Intellectuals at the annual Paris meeting of the World Jewish Congress. His focus on Jewish writings for such a long period of time, especially when religion was restricted from academic learning, marginalized him from the secular, philosophical community.

In addition to what may have been an aversion from totalizing claims, perhaps the reason Lévinas continued engaging Talmudic and phenomenological approaches was because both emphasized a return to the things themselves. He could illuminate a sublime materialism and think through a theistic existentialism by "lighting up the hidden horizons of the text, the forgotten, the ignored, the obfuscated" (Malka 2006, pg. 125). Forgiveness, for example, holds the view up to oneself that no relation or character is fixed. In his Talmudic lectures, however, he admitted that it was possible to forgive many Germans for what happened during the Shoa, but that it was difficult to forgive his fellow phenomenologist Martin Heidegger. Here is a crack through which Lévinas could make infinity shine out of a wound particular to his life. The apparent fixed nature of history, despite Lévinas's understanding of history as something as open and evolving as subjectivity, overruled the possibility of forgiving Heidegger. In his unique readings, Lévinas also admitted a dread of facing superior scholars of the Talmud in his lectures (Malka 2006, pg. 33). Most Jewish scholars still do not accept Lévinas's interpretations. We can hear in this estrangement an echo of the same alienation that he must have felt from the philosophical community.

In the face of this dread, Lévinas worked hard on the lectures he gave. "[I]n each one of his discourses, he would make sure to inform everyone that he came to the Talmud quite late, and under the strict authority of a master, but that he was not a dilettante, a Sunday Talmudist. From time to time, he would explicitly pay homage to Chouchani" (Malka 2006, pg. 137). Lévinas felt and made his own vulnerability known. Luckily for Lévinas, or by no coincidence, his master in the Talmud also worked hard to go beyond traditional categories, meanings, and interpretations. Master Chouchani in many ways embodied what Lévinas would call the nontotalized subject. His name was not his own, his history is still largely unknown, and his wisdom was attested as limitless. He was not the typical teacher since he was nearly a vagabond with all the appearances of one; however, to anyone open to the other he would reveal a gem of intellectual vigor. Lévinas took his lessons and friendship seriously enough to compile his lessons with Chouchani into his book the *Talmudic Readings*.

Through his trepidation Lévinas embraced an open, dialectical relation to Talmudic texts in his use of contemporary events and modern literature. These new circumstances provide material for him as a reader to raise new problems about traditional concerns, like that of the "neighbor," or of the "other." The timid and inadequate place he felt in relation to these religious (and often also philosophical) circles is most apparent in the ambivalently related concepts he developed, such as a totality and infinity that structure ethical subjectivity.

Lévinas writes that when one is ethically committed it is in a "non-erotic proximity, to a desire of the non-desirable, to a desire of the stranger in the neighbor" (Lévinas 1998a, pg. 123). A desire that does not become fulfilled through pleasure makes a neighbor aware of their ethical being. Precisely in this move of substituting oneself with the other there is a moral awakening (Lévinas 1998a, pg. 123). An ethical relation cannot fall back into the ontological order of a narcissistic and egoical self even though each is confined to the imperialism of an egoical self. For this reason, Lévinas describes the anarchic face as a passivity that characterizes the ethical relation and elects its persons as hostages to a chosen claim. Relations of proximity that do not occlude oneself or the other can preserve indeterminacy of the self, but they happen mostly without a deliberate choice made. These proximate distances bestow the inspiration for substituting one's personal good or suffering for the other. His fraught relation to Heidegger, for example, was not part of the erotic economies of self that led Freud to conclude that all morality is a primary masochism. According to his writings, one's relation to the other, preserved as such, is always through trepidation. One cannot anticipate whether the other will appreciate the hospitality or become incited to hostility in response to another's openness and vulnerability. Both possibilities are available, and both are alienating for the other aspect of self.

Like the marginal status of Freud's psychoanalytic work to the positivists' method, Malka writes that Lévinas was a French philosopher who stood quietly on the margins, due to his "non-university status" (Malka 2006, pg. 115). Contrary to Freud, Lévinas's writing would not make a lasting impression at the time. Lévinas's son, Michael, went so far as to describe his father as a philosopher of the cracks (Malka 2006, pg. 263). It seemed, however, that Lévinas preferred to live in the margins of these dichotomous positions that too often become all consuming.

Already in his doctoral dissertation and first major work, published in 1947 as *Existence and Existents*, Lévinas shows how through these split identifications one can engage, not solely as confessional thinker, but as thinker more broadly, a thread which continues late into his life during his colloquia in 1989 (Malka 2006, pg. 138). Lévinas's intellectual engagements stood in contrast to Freud's relationships that ended in a rupture from those who disagreed with him. Lévinas was often more engaged in an intellectual hospitality to the other's thought, especially when they diverged from his own. But as both Freud and Lévinas built their theoretical insights, they could not be totally transparent to themselves. Persecuting impulses, when one becomes murderous of the other, despite explicitly held moralities, proves a useful wedge that makes clear the human vulnerability to commit these acts.

As he argued, so Lévinas fancied himself as never experiencing in his life "either true ruptures" or true "recoveries," but Freud's insight that conscious experiences cannot always reflect on its motives and actions applies equally to Lévinas (Malka 2006, pg. 159). Lévinas realizes that the past is always carried but argues that these always come with the renewed possibility of how to proceed for re-defining the present self. Two options are available for the self: either to assume that identifications are a bondage that restrict oneself, or to assert that there remains always a dynamic openness for many possible identifications. Maintaining view of the dynamic openness was an essential part of Lévinas's ethic, and its difficulty is illustrated in several relationships on which Lévinas turned his back, such as with Heidegger who, like him, was a student of the phenomenologist Edmund Husserl, but through his career as philosopher became rector of the University of Freiburg in 1931 during the Third Reich.

Limits and compromises in worldviews are a strength for what I will call the *relational aspect of self*, while the same compromises are perceived as a weakness for the egoical aspect of self. For Freud, individual desires were always "sacrificed" for maintaining cultural bonds. But is not the language of sacrifice only relevant for the egoistic aspect of self? Strength comes in the ethical subject when its relational aspect abandons the goal of mastery to welcome the other. The view here is of an egoical self that must contain an inherent openness. Openness in the self is the space where the possibility of an exchange of symbols and meaning in words can occur.

These words that are symbolic or representative of ideas and meaning can always induce closure toward the other, and for this reason, Lévinas distinguishes the order of the said from the very possibility of language, as such, in the saying. Conversation with many types, including someone like his mentor for Talmudic learning Chouchani who embodied a mysterious identity, is crucial for Lévinas. The ambivalent relation between these aspects in one subject could not have been more real than when he was treated as a philosopher one year, and in the next as a life not worth preserving as a common prisoner of war and despicable Jew.

However capable one is of sharing in enjoyments, the ethical relation contains the possibility of being berated, a valuable insight from Lévinas's reflection on a self that is structured on openness toward the other. Violence accompanies every word that can be heard, or idea attributed from one to the other. How upset does one become when they are mistaken for another person, another identification, or even when one's name is mispronounced? These identifications are taken seriously, but the egoical identifiers cannot occlude the openness in oneself and as such in the other. The essential openness of which any subject is capable must have given Lévinas an amount of confidence to step into these territories and develop a new language for expressing his concerns about a subjectivity that is relational.

Lévinas also finds that the ethical relation binds two subjects who are made of particular contextual attributions, such as mother, father, governor, artist, eldest child, prisoner, etcetera. These people are also never reduced to any of these attributes and qualifiers. Though everyone must begin with particular identifications that are chosen willfully or not, the other as such, remaining other in itself, is not mediated through any identification or context. As an anarchical rupture in being, Lévinas understands humanity as that which occurs in the sweeping motion of an infinite available to a particular kind of being.

I want to think about how Lévinas may have conceived, or felt through his life, the idea that the particular individual subject is always an inter-subject. How does one conceive of the idea that one is riveted to others in words, riveted to phenomenal representations, in addition to those non-phenomenal anarchic and immediate shocks received from seeing a face, without even noticing "the color of his eyes!" (Lévinas 1985, pg. 85–6). How can doubt arise for the self-sufficiency and infallibility of one's own thoughts, in the ability to choose with whom to have a relation? After all, this goes against the whole Western philosophical tradition that begins with the Socratic dictum to "know thyself" and which culminates in Freud's division of the self's psyche into parts that are opaque to itself.

In order to understand his radical ethics, it's possible to draw on Lévinas's experience as a prisoner of war at one point during his life and his life as a philosopher in another. For both identifications, others were required. Lévinas's subject who is in possession of an ego that is forced to engage an order of logic is also simultaneously under a "persecuting accusation" to "dispossess itself to the point of losing itself" from any logic for changing its essence (Lévinas 1998a, pg. 111). Vulnerability to that which conditions sensibility lies in one's relation to the "openness of thematization," or in what Lévinas calls bowing to "the identity of entities, poles of identifications" (1998a, pg. 80–1). In other words, each is related even to the other who cannot or has not yet appeared and is infinitely underdetermined because of their effects on each other in their relation. By necessity, the self remains open to the other who may finally appear. Like those who are de-humanized to filth at a given point in time, any "privileged" caste can also suffer the pain of embodied living in their own time.[1] Like everybody else, they must breathe and take in the world around them to survive. Breath is not consciously chosen at each inhale and exhale, but is more an obsessive, mindless activity. Whoever is contained by a body cannot remain there in itself as completely self-sufficient. A body requires what is external to it, namely, oxygen. Even if the external atmosphere has no regard for breaths that are necessary for the preservation of life, the body always relies on this relation for its very existence. Like the breath each body depends on for life, so each person depends on another for ethical life. Dependence on one for the other similarly yields life or death for the kind of self that is primarily ethical.

We may see in this elemental act of dependency between the outside world and the internal well-being of a body an illustration of one person in relation to others. According to Lévinas, where there is not another there cannot be oneself for the relational subject. Where there would be no language without the other's response, there is no self. The self is riveted to its created identifications made in community with others. A person, a name, a face is never a self-sustaining unity, but is broken

---

[1] An ethical relation that makes a demand from suffering in embodied life can extend Lévinas's ethic toward other–others, such as animals and ecology. The ethical relation is not the same with these because expression and language are not mutual; the face does not appear in the same way in the dog as it does in the store clerk. Still, more than language I believe that it is the vulnerability to suffer that justifies particular forms of the ethical relation, caring and taking care of the other's vulnerability.

as though "the atomic unity of the subject was exposed outside by breathing, by divesting its ultimate substance even to the mucous membrane of the lungs, *continually splitting up*" (Lévinas 1998a, pg. 107). Each stand in relations of ultimate dependency to what can never be totally one's own. And there were those who felt they could decide with whom to share the air. Hannah Arendt's condemnation of SS Lieutenant Adolf Eichmann in Jerusalem was, in Lévinas's opinion, the mistaken thought that one could choose with whom to inhabit the world, to somehow control the external that sustains the well-being of an internalized, atomized body.

It might be that Nietzsche's free spirit who dares to will his responsibility recognizes this burden and freely accepts the difficult fate of a constitutive dependency. By opening one's eyes, one is already committed to representations. Ears that are always open obligate one to an affectation that is caused by what is spoken and heard. In view of this, Lévinas worked toward these grounds that need to be presupposed for the ego to perceive any appearance of whatever, for a choice to appear, and a decision to be made. These grounds are beyond essence, where non-sense contains the possibility for a subject to have sense. The goal is not to argue for an irrational or romantic epistemology, but to recognize that any sense in its relationality requires an ethical precondition.

There is no exit from this burden to consider one's moral relations, even if one seems to be able to step away from their obligation, which lends the asymmetrical burden Lévinas must characterize in the relational subject. Nihilistic approaches to being, self, and ethics are only delusional about the self's exit from its relations because of an enclosed body, psyche, and its experiences of traumas private to an isolated ego. The asymmetrical relation is precisely the inability to remove one's need for another in creating, using, circulating, and repeating identifications about oneself. Rather than an abstract and philosophical claim, a relation is drawn between the weight of this burden Lévinas may have felt during his time in captivity, and a particular identification within a general category of "the dirty Jew."

The need to articulate the power of identifying marks could only amplify the ability—and later the explicit inability—to speak of particular relationships that were jeopardized by these fixed categories. This becomes an infinite need for Lévinas. How much of these ideas of an inferior humanity riveted Lévinas's own being as a Jewish person? Freud was similarly marked with a particular body in the general category of "the dirty Jew." Early in Freud's life, he did not understand why his Jewish ancestry would characterize him as inferior. Toward the end of his life, and as Austria continued to fight for Hitler's cause, he obsessively wrote a historic novel on Moses, a non-Jewish Arab, in an attempt to relinquish his characterization as "the other;" the Jew in its diminished worth.

If identifying categories and labels are made through language in community with others, is the implication that Freud, Lévinas, and any other Jewish person are complicit by accepting, tolerating, or remaining indifferent to identifications that make totalizing claims on the value of their life? Is the idea to dissolve these distinctions, as Freud tried in *Moses and Monotheism,* between the Jewish person and the Gentile? In accepting the marginal life, does not the relational subject become implicated in an injury inflicted by the other? Ontologically speaking, it is a great risk for oppressed societies to rebel. Often more lives are lost than saved. These questions will be addressed in later chapters with regard to the pre-ontological possibility of language and the inability to remain indifferent to personal identifications. The trace of a possibility denied, and inability to remain indifferent, speaks to the condition of an ethical subject for Lévinas that implicates any speaking subjectivity for the circulation and maintenance of identifying markers.

In Lévinas's thinking of a relational subject, the claim borrowed from Dostoyevsky that each one of us is guilty before everyone, and "I more than others," leads to the further claim that one takes responsibility for one's persecutor (Lévinas 1998a, pg. 146). We can see this not as a form of victim-blaming as much as bearing the weight of a co-constituted web of meaning. When sensibility "marks the absence of protection and cover … a being put in question by the alterity of the other … the restlessness of someone persecuted …. the groaning of the wounded entrails," then I cannot be sure the other will emerge from their egoical self for an ethical relation (Lévinas 1998a, pg. 75). If the burden is placed on each one as being more responsible for the other, then the indexicality of "self" and "other" still makes it a universal burden to avoid the injury. To add insult to this injury is the cold and real empirical fact that reward, honor, and gratitude need not follow in the asymmetry of these relations.

Acts of intentionality and contemplation occur in "the fabric of the same," where acts possess, affect, and reveal oneself in what is said or thought about "the order of things" through dialogues made up of answers and responses (Lévinas 1998a, pg. 111). I use the term *identifications* to encompass all these acts of a subjectivity engaged in intentional modalities. An unknowable subject is made up in its identifications, but also puts the recurring activity of an *ipseity* in the self to constantly question itself, according to Lévinas. Only in substitution with the other's suffering, in sensing or feeling it without the accompanying need to justify or make sense of it, can a self that is identified as individuated become inspired, inwardly spirited by the breath of the alterity of an external other, as an ethical subject (Lévinas 1998b, pg. 91–4).

Through his work, Lévinas aimed to contrast one form of an identifying "self"— one that is an ego preoccupied in thematization but that also resists these willful identifications—with another form of self-identification, which is still only potent, or a "being in potency," prior to its activity. While there is a need to logically order knowledge, there is an anarchical accusation that forces the self to detach from itself. Only in substitution, in the expulsion of the self from its identifications toward the other, can a responsibility prior to dialogue arise between two. In suffering for the other, one becomes a movement of recurrence out toward the other then back into the self. After the return to the self's enthrallment with its egoical identifications, the self that is traumatized by this persecution to find the other can then go back and question these affirmative claims again and again.

Why does Lévinas use this language of persecution to describe the ethical relation, and is it merely hyperbolic? This recurrence of going from self to other can be endured "only (by) the persecuted one who does not evade it, but is without any reference, any recourse to help (that is its uniqueness or its identity as unique!)" (Lévinas 1998a, pg. 111). Put another way, only by way of the self's unique identifications made by the ego, can it substitute itself for the other to become wholly other. (This will also be explored further later in the book.) First, however, there is a need to remember that these identifications do not constitute the self for the move outside oneself, and they always necessitate undoing their admittedly imperialistic hold on the ego. It is my argument that Lévinas's characterization of the individuated self as persecuted is not hyperbolic but speaks to how it feels to remove one's delusion of isolation from the other.

Caught between the totalizing tendency to make identifications and a pre-ontological relation to others that always remains infinitely otherwise, Lévinas finds the self a *persecuting responsibility* that requires and depends on others. This persecution is different from masochistic phantasies created by a super-ego against unacceptable desires since the adventure a subject must take with others does not repeat an original injury repressed in the ego. The injury to an egoical self for Lévinas is an interruption by an always new other. Persecution is then seen as a detached ego from others, rather than as the narcissist components of an emotional life that seeks what is the same. The subject is persecuted to seek that which remains other for its ethicality. The adventure toward the other for ethical subjectivity creates an infinitely new identity, highlighting a responsibility before the sensibility of *eros*. These ideas will be developed in the last chapters of this section on Lévinas.

Breaking relations of sameness is required for a constitution that is made with others. Freud's death drive may be thought of as one way for the psyche to undo the injurious and violent interpolated ideas that can be transferred from others. The psyche will find pleasure in this defense that saves itself from those injurious relations, even if the injurious relations are a product of the mind's neurosis. A way out from the disturbance of compulsively repeating those representations fixated to one's drives, however, was not found in Freud's analysis.

As hard as Lévinas's own experiences and traumas were, he concludes that the persecution of an ethical subjectivity must rest on goodness. Life is an enchantment with one's self-contained enjoyment. The inherent incapacity of any subject to also be indifferent—the necessity to address, to see, and even to repress—also reveals the value of living a life forged in these difficult relations. One can give to another bread when hungry and substitute one's suffering for another's.

After emerging from the horrors of the Holocaust, Lévinas describes this goodness as what can only remain as an anarchy that augments the individuated self. A non-deliberate affect that nonetheless arises from positioning oneself in this confrontation enables substituting one for the other: to give bread or act disinterestedly to those with whom we stand in relation (Lévinas 1998a, pg. 140). As a being who comes to know first through its skin, a sensual intuition, violence on an eidetic level is generated from that which occurs to the body. The sincere intentionality that Lévinas attributes to sensual perceptions of oneself makes embodiment and relationality central for thinking about vulnerability, which will be addressed in his hermeneutic of trust that goes beyond Freud's hermeneutic of suspicion.

A totalitarian effacement by a blank command to love everyone that often replaces the particular face of another justifies using others as a mere means for the fulfillment of an abstract moral universalism, as Freud showed. For Lévinas, in universal maxims the value of a demand that comes from a particular face in all its difficult complexities is lost. Freud's concern for the particular love I have for those who are important to me can be heeded here. It is precisely this kind of care and effort that avoids the erasure of another and is required for remaining modest about cultural norms, persons, and identifications. The need for presupposing sympathy with the other, or even understanding the other, even when the other is the self to the self, is decreased if the distance of an interruption is invoked and valued in this relation.

All are equal in their lifelong need to develop an individuated self. Each is also vulnerable to the particular details, labels, categories, and shifts in these identifications that they are forced to make through life. Epistemic gaps in knowledge that at the same time plague and bless each to an infinite openness are developed next as the kind of freedom a totalized and infinite subject enjoys, but which necessitate the other for mutually dis-identifying from its seemingly totalized identities. In other words, we all share the burden to both create and forge our identities while at the same time preserve the need to distance ourselves from them for our own personal and moral growth. Out of these considerations on a fundamental inability to know one's self, and the need to dis-identify with markers that can mistakenly totalize who one is, I find the need to develop a concept of freedom in the next chapter.

References

Fagenblat, M. (2010). *A covenant of creatures: Lévinas's philosophy of Judaism*. Stanford: Stanford University Press.
Freud, S. (1959). The standard edition of the complete psychological works of Sigmund Freud. In J. Strachey (Ed.), *An autobiographical study* (Vol. XX, 1925). London: The Hogarth Press and the Institute of Psycho-analysis.
Lévinas, E. (1985). *Ethics and infinity: Conversations with Philippe Nemo* (trans: Cohen, R.A.). Pittsburgh: Duquesne University Press.
Lévinas, E. (1969). *Totality and infinity* (trans: Lingis, A.). New York: Duquesne University Press.
Lévinas, E. (1990). *Nine talmudic readings* (trans: Aronowicz, A.). Bloomington: Indiana University Press.
Lévinas, E. (1996). In A. T. Peperzak, S. Critchley, & R. Bernasconi (Eds.), *Basic philosophical writings*. Chicago: Indiana University Press.
Lévinas, E. (1998a). *Otherwise than being: Beyond essence* (trans: Lingis, A.). New York: Duquesne University Press.
Lévinas, E. (1998b). *Entre Nous: Collected essays* (trans: Smith, M.B.). New York: Columbia University Press.
Malka, S. (2006). *Emmanuel Lévinas: His life and legacy* (trans: Kigel, M. & Embree, S.M.). Pittsburgh: Duquesne University Press.
Robbins, J. (1999). *Altered reading: Lévinas and literature*. Chicago/London: University of Chicago Press.

Chapter 9
Epistemic Gaps: Freedom and Mutual Dis-identification

Abstract In this chapter, I develop new yields to the concept of freedom that results from moral indeterminacy and gaps in epistemic knowledge, such as intellectual modesty instead of moral skepticism. After I emphasize the characteristic of unknowability in relational subjectivity and the vulnerability to foreclose its infinite dynamism, I explore a shift in ethics that impels dis-identifying from personal labels.

Keywords Unknowability · Relational subjectivity · Existential vulnerability · Infinite dynamism · Intellectual modesty · Dis-identification · Egalitarian particularism · Dynamic subjectivity · Passivity-activity alternative · Anarchic relation · Anarchical ethical relation · Proximate knowledge · Ethical subjectivity · Proximity of the other · Ethics of substitution · Lévinas on Hitlerism

Lévinas's approach to an ethical subjectivity that lacks any fixed ontic categories or identifications that can be essential to it, but who is present only as the events forged in it, provides the grounds to think through an egalitarian particularism that will not depend on any particular type of self. All conscious existents equally take their self very seriously; while at the same time, the particularity of their existence cannot be exhaustive or exclusive to all types of embodied existents that are preoccupied with the plenum offered in the sincerity of their own experiences. Each individual is not equal to every other, and so moral reciprocity and ethical obligations should not rest on this false presumption.[1] There is still a unifying characteristic for all that no one is equal to any other. I want to develop Lévinas's view of a dynamic subject that is

---

[1] See Kenneth Reinhard, "The Ethics of the Neighbor: Universalism, Particularism, Exceptionalism," (2005) for a convincing article on a universalism that is not opposed to and even promotes particularism in Lévinas's ethic. For an extended discussion on the role of the neighbor as representative of the other in Lévinas, also see Slavoj Žižek, Eric L. Santner, and Kenneth Reinhard, *The Neighbor: Three Inquiries in Political Theology* (2005).

constituted in multifarious sincere enjoyments, but who is also completely wrought by unconscious, primordial instincts that include an instinct for freedom.

Similar to Freud's view of "aliens" that are in the house of the ego, in *Existence and Existents,* Lévinas argues that a mind composed of conscious and unconscious aspects is a fullness that can "interrupt itself" and have recourse against itself (Freud 1918, pg. 143; Lévinas 2001, pg. 67). These two oppositional forces, however, are not only contrary to one another, but are also related in a sincere proximity to each other. Lévinas writes in language similar to Freud's, "[a]n abandoned temple is still inhabited by its god, an old house falling into disrepair is still haunted by the ghosts of those who lived there" (Lévinas 2001, pg. 26). A sincere intention can be enjoyed. A less allegorical example is when one is hungry, then one can eat.

In Lévinas's terms, the self is an existent who takes up existence in all its risks for delusion and illusion. Yet there is still always the possibility for Lévinas that "at the very moment when the world seems to break up we still take it seriously and still perform reasonable acts and undertakings; the condemned man still drinks his glass of rum. To call it every day and condemn it as inauthentic is to fail to recognize the sincerity of hunger and thirst" (Lévinas 2001, pg. 45). The sincerity and value inherent in everyday life leads Lévinas to conclude—somewhat different from Freud—that unconscious mental reservations are on the same spectrum as conscious ones. Conscious acts, then, are riveted; they are potentially interrupted not only by an unpredictable and somewhat trustworthy reality, but also by a mental life that is assured a measure of commensurability with the truthfulness of beings "outside" itself.

Language and one's mental image of the self can have sincerity to the degree that particular aspects of the self are illuminated, even in their error and delusion, since they represent the preoccupations of the imperialistic ego. Because Lévinas is as comfortable asserting conflicting characteristics in the subject as Freud is in his theory of drives, he can make the next claim that the present catches up with itself, but with a "lag behind itself, or effects a retreat, a rebound," in the affective relations through which the self is sincerely constituted (Lévinas 2001, pg. 68). Similar to the act of retreating into sleep, the unconscious does not have a separate existence from one's conscious life but is only enacted "beneath" it (Lévinas 2001, pg. 68). Although the unconscious mental life participates in the conscious one, it is never a present participation, similar to the way sleep does not remove one from existence, but is only a way of being that is inactive, passive: a "resting" that consolidates waking material (Lévinas 2001, pg. 689).

Pushing beyond the egoical self, Lévinas moves toward a "passivity that is prior to the passivity-activity alternative, more passive than any inertia, [and] is described by the ethical terms accusation, persecution, and responsibility for the other" (1998, pg. 121). Wherever these dichotomies (or antonyms) of passivity-activity are, the anarchical relation is not. Any activity that describes the imperialism of one's egoical self does not find the anarchical ethical relation. Lévinas develops language with an emphasis placed on proximate knowledge wherein any present participation of an existent's being and the preoccupations of its imperialistic ego are stunned. The ethical relation is not a negative moment, just as sleep is not a negative moment to the positive standard of wakefulness. In Lévinas's conception of ethical subjectivity, "this lag that occurs between a being and itself, which we have brought out as the principle characteristic of fatigue, constitutes the advent of consciousness, that is, a power to 'suspend' being by sleep and unconsciousness" (Lévinas 2001, pg. 30). Note Lévinas's use of quotation marks around the word "suspend" that has the power to create consciousness. Suspension from being is not possible alone, not in sleep and not in the unconscious but occurs with the interruption of the other. The mirage of an isolated being is suspended in a passivity that welcomes the other. Unconsciousness is equivalent to sleep in its evasion from the light of consciousness; however, the ability to suspend the connection between the unconscious and sleep from consciousness is a mirage, like the mirage that seems to suspend a fundamental relation between the self and another.

Whereas for Freud internal drives and their encounters with personal experiences principally motivate the development of an identity, for Lévinas, beyond the egoical self, there is an anonymous plenitude through which there is an infinitely renewable capacity to produce "oneself," to produce events. Lévinas calls the subject, or self, an infinite task that is given to an infinite regress where freedom is the very need to become identifiable (Lévinas 2001, pg. 84, 86). Contained in what is called the alterity of one's ego is the possibility of the ego's own shattering. Shattering the ego by moving into the proximity of the other, without the attempt to subsume the other, is exactly the risky business of the ethical relation. The relation is risky because there is no guarantee of acknowledgment or reciprocity from the other.

The shattering of one's ego does not resort to deeper sediment layers of the ways one is represented to the self or others, but rather is a preventative measure that bars any definitive identifier from encompassing the total person. Lévinas clarifies thus: "But what is the meaning of non-engagement within the ontological adventure? It is the refusal of the definitive. The world offers me a time in which I traverse different instants, and thanks to the evolution open to me, I am not at any moment definitive. Yet I always carry along my past whose every instant is definitive. But, there remains for me, in this world of light, where all is given but where everything is distance" (Lévinas 2001, pg. 84). One illustrative example is the quickness with which a radical racist may become tolerant of the very same racial group once hated. All that is required is to go out from the egoical self for an encounter, a moment in which the other is seen in a light where the represented identity as dirty, filthy, or unworthy is relinquished in a re-evaluation of their value. In the readiness with which one may abandon—or conversely adopt—a prejudice, the relative arbitrariness identifications can hold for the one conceiving them is most obvious. The proximate distance between these two is reduced into an affective change, an exchange.

The freedom afforded to any subject is contained in the impossibility of any identifier to totalize what one is. The stronger claim I find Lévinas making is that the ego is an event, an inherent violence forging a self that is vulnerable in this desire to totalize itself under identifiers, regardless of whether they are political, religious, or cultural affiliations. Ethical subjectivity, as such, is vulnerable to this desire. Pre-ontological persecution arises in the self that wants to be totalized in its identifications, but ultimately cannot in the process of becoming what one is: an ethical subjectivity. Though identifications constitute subjectivity, for better or worse, alterity and the ego's shattering preserve its freedom. For Lévinas, an ethical relation arises before any spoken word is even uttered, when the *visage* or face of another appears. Persecution in this sense is defined as the form in which the ego is affected to go outwards from itself and absconds from the light of an individuated consciousness (Lévinas 2001, pg. 101). The effect of persecution is an ethical subjectivity as such, and not only, as Freud argues, an affective relation experienced in the hatred by or for another.

Identity takes on new forms and meanings for Lévinas. One can ultimately never be identical with oneself because of the pre-ontological alterity of the subject. Many authors have difficulty reconciling how these two aspects—the pre-ontological and ontological forms of persecution—can reside within one subjectivity for Lévinas. Paul Ricœur calls this *the* difficulty of reading the otherwise in the title of Lévinas's work *Otherwise Than Being* (Ricœur and Escobar 2004, pg. 82–99). I will return to Ricœur's difficulty in the section on Lévinas's intentionality of search, but first instead of trying to solve this puzzle, I move forward in the assumption that the pre-ontological form of persecution is necessary for ethical subjectivity. The simultaneity of the ontological and pre-ontological forms of persecution allows each self to appear individuated, while also becoming scandalized by this individuation. According to Freud's understanding, those who are deemed other, along with moral norms, threaten psychic stability. While striving to uphold social norms, individual desires are frustrated, and social norms that begin with similarities to oneself villainize others that threaten these bonds of security. On the other hand, suffering a pre-ontological persecution for going toward another is scandalous because of the desire for an individuated self, but pose a necessary turn for the fulfillment of ethical subjectivity.

For Lévinas, the dynamism between a subject's infinite possibilities and totalized categories makes up every moment. This dynamism constitutes a dialectic rather than a linear sequence. A scrutinizing "primordial event of the present" is presupposed and later described as that which has decided, acted, resisted in "moments of the ontological adventure" (Lévinas 2001, pg. 34). Lévinas characterizes two aspects of subjectivity, where in one aspect there is action and in another servitude and subjection to the fullness of being as that which constitutes the existent that is an ethical subject.

Lévinas's unique sense of freedom is created for this structure of self that is prefigured with a fatigue and lag in its present participation that enables "taking charge of the present" from which an infinite number of particular identities can follow (Lévinas 2001, pg. 34). Any dislocation and disjunction of the self is not an aberration to be overcome. Neither can the lag become healed in the kind of analytic situation that Freud advocated early in his career as a psychologist, nor can a greater self-knowledge (like the Socratic dictum) prevent its inevitable partiality. Because the self is essentially an activity, and contemplation its action, then any intention or enjoyment does not constitute the ethical subject. Instead the responsible proximate distances that are kept between varied experiences lead to a mutual dis-identification for a substitution of both with their other.

The error lies in fixing an identity for that which can have no fixed identity, who requires another to develop oneself, and for who can be injured, suffer, go hungry, and die in their pain. One important moral consequence of taking the indeterminate and unknowable aspects of the persecuting subject seriously is that the pain of a suffering body should take precedence because it is more real and sincere than the veracity of any ideal. An ideal always requires a leap in judgment, in faith, and thus inherently lacks concrete justification for its belief. The most egregious error for ethical subjectivity comes from its conviction that any means are justified for convincing others of one's worldview. The error is most obvious when violent means are used to persuade others of a worldview that forgets the infinite alterity, or what Lévinas calls the face of the other. Freud is helpful for understanding the desire not-to-know one's perpetual partiality, as we saw in his reading of The Uncanny. Humility is an antidote for strongly held convictions that will be addressed more fully in the last section, concerning the intentionality of search.

One typical response in the history of philosophy has been to try and set thought itself on a more correct path to address its partiality. In response to the Eichmann trials, Hannah Arendt wondered whether the activity of correct thinking, as such, can condition men against evil-doing (2007, pg. 479). In response to this question, she develops an understanding of the banality of evil, which is characterized as having no rational justification for one's actions. Arendt characterizes the banality of evil as a form of rootless, superficial thinking that has no depth. As Arendt explains, "[w]e resist evil by not being swept away by the surface of things, by stopping ourselves and beginning to think, that is, by reaching another dimension than the horizon of everyday life" (2007, pg. 479). In order to prevent evil consequences that can result from partiality in one's thought, Arendt recommends avoiding becoming convinced by superficial representations that are attributed to the other. For Arendt, it was avoiding cliché and commonplace beliefs that replace genuine thought. Do not accept orders from authorities merely on the justification that it came from an authority. Do not believe the Jewish person is intrinsically greedy and dirty, or that every Muslim person is an irrational fanatical fundamentalist, or that every socially disadvantaged person is lazy, or that homosexual relations are perversions. These thoughts lead us to Point. To Laugh. To persecute, exclude, excommunicate, and to execute.

The evil represented in Eichmann's error, according to Arendt, was not rooted in an evil motive or intention, but just in accepting a banal order without much thought. Indeed, many if not all acts of persecution are rooted in a desire and intention to act for some concept of the good. Hobbes and Augustine, for example, justified political and religious persecution. Their political theories legitimized the zealous pursuit and persecution of those who were believed to threaten and pervert a social or divine norm. Chaos is perceived as an evil that needs a call to order at all costs, including banishing those who threaten social or religious orders (Christenson 1968, pg.

419).[2] Arendt's own advocacy for the execution of Eichmann, in spite of her critique that none are justified in deciding with whom to share the world, proves the extent reason can justify its own motivation to secure totalized explanations, as she herself found a way to justify with whom to share the world, and from whom the privilege should be withdrawn.

Most problematic in persecution is that thought cannot reflect on the motives, such as in cases of delusions of persecution. For Freud, an internal desire is projected outwards and becomes an external perception that is experienced as antagonistic. As a way of managing the conflict between desire and moral obligations, the other is sacrificed in the psyche's attempts to rid itself of unacceptable desires. The one persecuting, as much as the one who is being persecuted, cannot think the problem away. Neurotic delusions of persecution and real persecutions, such as those Freud experienced later in his life, are indistinguishable to the representing mind. Similarly, with Lévinas, persecution is that which makes one pursue egoical definitions, a necessary condition for having an ethical relation with the other. Lévinas emphasizes the need to ultimately relinquish, shatter, and dis-identify from these identifications for the ethical relation.

Undoing processes of identification on a regular basis would leave one without either thought or a self, which is not what Lévinas argues is necessary. Arendt addresses evil as if it were an effect of a conscious thought, albeit a lazy one. But this approach likewise does not address how delusional forms of persecution are an unreflective reaction to one's own guilt for failing to realize social standards. Seemingly rigid—but always only contingent—thoughts, moral ideas, and representations make up a fragmented self that includes traces of the other to justify its violent acts. Lévinas wants us to find fragments of the other in remembrance of epistemic gaps in any knowledge. Violent acts are accepted unknowingly as simply a part of cultural norms or the result of a rational process.

But where do these moral standards and cultural ideals come from, and who are the dominant groups that enforce them? I argue that these are as fluid as the identifications attributed to oneself, which makes anyone equally vulnerable to stand in relation of sameness or other to these ideals in different times and places. Historical testimonies and developed ethics may attempt to prevent persecution; however, the stronger these ethos are held, the more they inevitably become persecutory. The present study should also heed this warning about the possibility that any ethical conviction can become persecutory. There will always be the other for whom certain ideals will not apply, and those who will not willfully agree or comply. Until bodies are turned to dust, however, the unbearable knowledge for one's ability to use persecutory means is a fundamental vulnerability and a natural barbarism for the kind of identity wrought out of characteristics that are in conflict with each other that Freud and Lévinas describe.

In the next section I will continue to use Lévinas's work on *Hitlerism* in conjunction with stories from his personal life for understanding the conditions of this

---

[2] See Chap. 1.

fundamental existential vulnerability to persecute others. These stories undermine the traditional bifurcation between self-mastery and vulnerability, as if they were separable and as if vulnerability were eliminable. Similar to the way in which the biographical details of Freud's life were presented alongside his theoretical work, these stories from Lévinas's life are intended to inspire empathy with him as a complex human being. If moral blind spots are put in the fuller context of their lives, then we can bear witness to their vulnerabilities and redeem them from judgment.

References

Arendt, H. (2007). In J. Kohn & R. H. Feldman (Eds.), *The Jewish writings*. New York: Schocken Books.
Christenson, R. (1968). The political theory of persecution: Augustine and Hobbes. *Midwest Journal of Political Science, 12*(3), 419–438.
Freud, S. (1955). The standard edition of the complete psychological works of Sigmund Freud. In J. Strachey (Ed.), *A difficulty in the path of psycho-analysis* (Vol. XVII, 1918). London: The Hogarth Press and the Institute of Psycho-analysis.
Lévinas, E. (1998). *Otherwise than being: Beyond essence* (trans: Lingis, A.). New York: Duquesne University Press.
Lévinas, E. (2001). *Existence and existents* (trans: Lingis, A.). New York: Duquesne University Press.
Reinhard, K. (2005). The ethics of the neighbor: Universalism, particularism, exceptionalism. *Journal of Textual Reasoning, 4*(1).
Reinhard, K., Santner, E., & Zizek, S. (2005). *The neighbor: Three inquiries in political theology*. Chicago: University of Chicago Press.
Ricœur, P., & Escobar, M. (2004). Otherwise: A reading of Emmanuel Lévinas's otherwise than being or beyond essence. *Yale French Studies, 104*, 82–99.

Chapter 10
Freedom and Existential Vulnerability: Lévinas's Vulnerability to His Cultural Ideals

Abstract I provide examples in this chapter, such as Lévinas's relation to Palestinians and reflection on Hitlerism, that show Lévinas's difficulty upholding his notion of limited freedom and ethical responsibility. Considering what I describe is an existential vulnerability to foreclose infinitude in one's particular other, I impel the reader to reflect on their particular others and when they have been vulnerable to foreclose an ethical relation.

Keywords Vulnerability to cultural ideals · The face of the other · Pre-ontological persecution · Ontic persecutions · Existential vulnerability · Foreclosed ethical relation · Lévinasian ethics · Ethics of substitution · Alterity of evil · Ethical subjectivity · Israeli-Palestinian conflict · Reflections on Hitlerism · Dis-identification · Relational subjectivity · Precarious relationality · New moral horizons · Asymmetrical relation · Affective impingement · Existential freedom

The way I understand Lévinas is that the images one makes of themselves entails an existential vulnerability to totalize themselves and others in these images and identifications, which can only remain contingent markers for infinitely multifarious and diverse lives. Vulnerability is arguably the central task of Lévinas's work. Reading the biographical details of his life, where he spoke out against atrocities or left lingering silences, can illustrate the vulnerability he must have felt as a Jewish man raised in an increasingly anti-Semitic world before the World Wars. He also witnessed the development of a State of Israel and her relations to its neighbors. While the political considerations of how a state responds to violence are beyond the scope of this work, where the focus here is on the dyadic ethical face-to-face relation, the scholarship in Lévinas studies to decide how he personally handled these questions of political relations is instructive for the careful or suppressive tendencies each has with their private histories of trauma.

A task that I want to develop here, however, is to confront the full repercussions of thinking that vulnerability is an existential condition for everyone and what

© The Author(s), under exclusive license to Springer Nature Switzerland AG 2021
V. Giovanini, *Persecution and Morality*,
https://doi.org/10.1007/978-3-030-64664-6_10

responses are possible in its discomfort. Judith Butler writes in *Giving an Account of Oneself* on the helpful difference Lévinas makes between ontological and pre-ontological persecution that can also help understand existential vulnerability in Lévinas's life. Pre-ontological persecution in Lévinas is a precondition for all human beings that is made in the non-ontic "face," represented only in traces (Butler 2005, pg. 95). Butler writes that the pre-ontological address through a non-ontic face is an impinging relation that can come from "an idealized dyadic structure of social life," or it can come from "the voice of no one, the voice of God understood as infinite and pre-ontological that makes itself known in the face" (Butler 2005, pg. 90). Butler prefers to approach the other as coming from idealized dyadic structures of social life, but in my reading of Lévinas this places heavy ontic limits for relating to particular others. I may become convinced that anyone who is attributed with social labels like "Palestinian" or "rich" or "Republican" is automatically an alienated other for someone who is "Israeli" "poor" or "socialist." While exploring what the other means in terms of social relations is valuable, the address as a pre-ontological condition frees up the relation between any two individuals despite these idealized structures of their social life.

I prefer this reading of an address that comes as an impinging relation to any other, including those who may belong to social structures of sameness like one's family or kin. By taking up the prong of an impinging address that comes from one's particular face, an infinitude that is usually only attributed to God becomes imminently available in each person. Subsequently, the alterity of God and the alterity of an ethical subjectivity are complicated and not clearly delineated. We are required to reflect on the infinitude placed even on the most hated enemy. An impinging address, therefore, can come from anyone who seems outwardly to be my enemy, or another who belongs to the same people or relation of kin, which is consistent with Lévinas when he writes, "My people and my kin are still my neighbours" (1989, pg. 288). In other words, each is vulnerable to every other whether it is a Palestinian person to an Israeli one, or the Israeli person with another neighbor in Israel. After all, we are never replete of finding relations of enmity with anyone who happens to walk in my proverbial sun. What follows is that ethical subjectivity, though infinitely vulnerable to an other to realize its own subjectivity, must be weary not to occlude the other because of social, political, or historical contingencies in order to reduce the risk of inflicting ontic persecutions.

As much as I read the goal of Lévinas's theoretical work as advocating an understanding of the impinging but necessary ethical relation to the other, I wonder whether it is possible to remember this infinite responsibility always in one's life with the exigency it requires. If it is an impossible task, according to the way some have read Lévinas's interview on the massacre of Palestinian refugees in Lebanon, then he too can be seen as vulnerable to the conceits of totalizing himself as much as others.[1] Lévinas could not help but harbor certain traumas that may have pre-

---

[1] Read this controversial interview with Lévinas on the massacre in "Ethics and Politics" in *The Levinas Reader* (Oxford: Blackwell, 1989). Readers such as Martin Jay (1990), Howard Caygill (2002), and Judith Butler (2012) argue that Lévinas response was morally deficient, which can

vented his condemnation of the political leaders in Israel that did not intervene to prevent the massacres. Read another way, Lévinas was instructive in his caution not to quickly judge and condemn the still-unfolding complex, political situation. I will return to this incident later in the chapter, but the possibility to debate the appropriateness of Lévinas's response signifies the difficulty of an existential vulnerability that I aim to illuminate. I will not pick any entrenched side of the argument on Lévinas conduct nor attempt to reconcile Lévinas's position and statements to his philosophical work. Nor do I seek to condemn his personal character as complicit with racist or anti-racist sentiments. Instead I would like to see how these ambiguous lines can arise from his life's experiences. This is admittedly an imaginative endeavor, but the vast literature that attempts to arbitrate one way or other points to an essential ambiguity.[2]

The ambiguity more than any one position could also have been Lévinas's intention in that listeners would raise questions, discourse, investigate the facts, and decide what the correct ethical and political responses may be. As he repeatedly stated in the interview, none are indifferent to atrocities, all are responsible even before personal guilt shows up. I believe Lévinas would like to leave his listeners and readers with this impetus to investigate who are one's political allies and foes, which is a separate issue but grounded on the face-to-face encounter for ethical subjectivity.[3] I do wonder: what might be the limits, or allowances, perceived for oneself even while strongly believing in the need to welcome the stranger, or the unknowable alterity of the other, in order to become oneself as an ethical subject? Finally, how much more impinging does everyone become when their cultural ideal requires mastering through repression their vulnerabilities that arise from personal histories of trauma? At what cost do the ideals of omnipotence and omniscience come? Freud's development of one's desire not-to-know the other's vulnerability is useful for understanding the difficulty of Lévinas's ethic, exemplified in Freud's relation to people in Palestine that were hostile to increasing waves of Jewish refugees, and still perpetuated into Israel's existence during the latter part of Lévinas's life as a Zionist.

As a thought example, an image can be called to mind of Lévinas in a work camp looking at another's face emaciated in its suffering. An image of his family member called to mind in another death camp appears. There the smell of excrement lingers, along with the stench of countless murders and deaths. A non-phenomenal face can appear in apprehending the other's irreplaceability. He may see the face of another writhing on the floor, another who once had a family, belongings, desires, and simple delights. Once that face is gone, so is that world. It is easy to imagine that Lévinas was able to substitute himself for the other prisoner, or imagined family member, writhing on the floor. But according to his ethic, one or another's contin-

---

indicate shortcomings in his theoretical commitments on the ethical subject. Other readers such as Katz (2016) and Moran (2016) offer their defense of Lévinas and his work.

[2] See Katz (2016) and Moran (2016) for a list of the vast literature that open these questions.

[3] See Morgan Moran (2016) for more on this opportunity that Lévinas provides his reader, pg. 276.

gent identifiers do not restrict the spontaneous appearance of the face for an ethical relation.

The more difficult but relevant question is whether Lévinas could substitute himself for the Nazi guard standing outside his barracks (Malka 2006, pg. 68). Even if Lévinas's sense of substitution is pre-ontological, the implication that he could substitute himself with a Nazi guard would be at the very least insensitive and at the very worst an absurd question. The ontic relation between these prevents anyone from asking, expecting, or demanding that someone who endured such trauma could voluntarily inflict them. The possibility is violently removed from their horizon of meaning because of their particular experiences. Addressing the pre-ontological condition, however, enables a reflection on the limits of a dictum to love one's neighbor, the stranger, and the other. Those guards in whose hands Lévinas's life was trusted did not see his face, nor did they see his mother, father, and brothers with whose lives they were entrusted. Is it possible after this experience for Lévinas not to see the face of a suffering other, as the guards did not see in his younger brother, Boris?

The characteristic of existential vulnerability can show how it is possible even after such trauma to still inflict the same on another other. Freud found that this relation becomes more difficult the further one extends beyond narcissist ideals or qualities of sameness. Khazzoom showed an additional difficulty in that identities are formed out of personal traumas, which can also make one more vulnerable to repeat injurious experiences. For Freud, the repetition contributed to feelings of psychic mastery of trauma, while Khazzoom found how stigmas deeply resonate with the self's identity created thereafter. How much are these cycles of self-inflicted violence on oneself and others unavoidable or entrenched? I find in Lévinas work a way out of these relations, but only in anarchic glimmers whose opportunities must be seized by each individual.

Is it possible to think of these relations that constitute oneself as the ethical subject, always in proximity to the other, as retaining an amount of violence? An amount of personal trauma can lead to a foreclosure of the ethical relation. Defense mechanisms safeguard the egoical self from the other, whether in a consciously calculated manner or not. Ideals do motivate what they protect. These egological calculations lead to the conclusion that it may be best not to enter a relation. In relating to my neighbor, or the stranger, the ethical demand that persecutes the individuated self does injury to its egoical aspect of ethical subjectivity but at the same time seems to secure the physical survival of an embodied individual. Unknowingly or intentionally, this egoical interest injures ethical subjectivity by not entering the relation. Arguably, Lévinas's understanding of Hitlerism can also reveal his own vulnerability to foreclosing the possibility of an ethical relation with Heidegger as well as with his Palestinian neighbor.

In Lévinas's *Reflections on Hitlerism*, he articulates the underlying causes of what only appears to be a momentary contagion and madness of his day in 1934. Lévinas makes the strong claim that it was not momentary madness that led to the most destructive acts of his time, but rather concludes that "racism . . . is the very humanity of man" (Lévinas and Hand 1990, pg. 64). May this refer to a pre-original vulnerability for each to become racist? One is "vulnerable" to racism in view of a relational subject who requires the otherness of the stranger to become oneself. Lévinas finds that an original intuition is harbored in an "elementary feeling" that questions the very principles of civilization and implicates all as capable of becoming racist for undermining civilization (Lévinas and Hand 1990, pg. 64). Despite Lévinas's theoretical notions of vulnerability and substitutability, his humanity admittedly implicates that he is also capable of the same racist spirit, and a reading between the lines of his work and life's commitments confirms his own culpability.

There are two relevant points to make from his essay on Hitlerism in this section on Lévinas's personal vulnerabilities to the ideals of his time. The first relates to the generalizability of the claim that racism is a modification in the logic of universalism, namely, that racism expands force that is then used for racist ideals. The second relates Lévinas's concepts of vulnerability and substitution in the persecutory subject that arises from his life's horizon but that is not limited to him. For both, it will be relevant to draw connections between Lévinas's personal life and his political and social commitments, first in regard to Heidegger and Germany and then later to Palestinian Arabs and Israeli's support for using force to control their relations.

More than any materialism before, which in various ways preserved an amount of difference and thus freedom from destiny, Lévinas marks that at this time in Hitlerism the new essence of self is constituted in an appeal to heredity, to one's body as a vehicle for an "ineluctable original chain" (Lévinas and Hand 1990, pg. 64). Anchored in one's body, blood, or race, truth is under the constant need to propagate and universalize itself through these for creating a new world in the Aryan ideal. He found that Hitlerism was the attempt to find an identity between the self with a racial body. Against the classical interpretations that have sought to eliminate the effects of the body on a rational self, for Hitlerism the body becomes closer to oneself than any idea. The body physiologically controls its temperament and its activities as well as regulating its psychological health (Lévinas and Hand 1990, pg. 64). Lévinas adds that this claim of identity between self is also found in its intrinsic preoccupation with the body's death and sickness.

In beginning to describe the fluctuating concepts of man as free or beholden to a historical materialism, Lévinas also writes that Judaism bore the message about man's capacity to redeem history through remorse. The human being is not only reduced to personal whims; it is neither laid at the mercy of destiny, nor completely made of its social and material conditions. Even Marxism is not reduced to a strict materialism since the conscious revolt against one's social situation is to "free oneself of the fatalism entailed by that situation" (Lévinas and Hand 1990, pg. 67). He continues to argue that the modern concept of human spirit and the liberal notion of freedom in reason are all inherited from this Jewish notion that "man is not weighed down by a History in choosing his destiny" (Lévinas and Hand 1990, pg. 66). Jews are essentially ancestrally linked to this idea propagated through history. The only way to truly oppose this European notion of human freedom that stems from Judaism is to find identity between the self and body, toward which the Aryan ideal strives (Lévinas and Hand 1990, pg. 68).

In finding auxiliary support for this materialism in Hitlerism, it seems appropriate to ask Lévinas, for whom is this a "new conception of man"? Is it only for this "Hitlerism," as he accuses? Ironically, in the very same article that Lévinas traces the root of Hitlerism as an elementary feeling that on racial grounds as "expressing a soul's principal attitude towards the whole of reality and its own destiny," he writes on his own Jewish heritage that it bears a magnificent message on human destiny and freedom. Lévinas expresses his own racial bias and continues to place himself in the chains of his own tradition. The appeal to Jewish particularity and essence continues to persist through Lévinas's whole intellectual life.

Furthermore, the new conception of man sounds like Lévinas's own arguments in writing on the importance of one's body for subject formation argued in *Existence and Existents* (2001) and "Useless Suffering" (1998c). The difference is that Lévinas finds that Hitlerism propagates an idea of power in a certain type of Aryan body, while Lévinas propagates an idea of freedom as a legacy of the Jewish body. In the same article that Lévinas blames a new materialism as the cause of Hitlerism—the "biological, with the notion of inevitability it entails becomes more than an *object* of spiritual life. It becomes its heart"—he also writes on the liberal ideal for which the Jewish race of people was responsible (Lévinas and Hand 1990, pg. 69).

Lévinas's new concept of self stands in close proximity to those ideals of his time, as we saw in Freud's relation to the ideals in Austria during his life. The concept of self here in Lévinas is one that is constituted in an appeal to heredity with its body as its vehicle. Essence is not in a liberal freedom but a binding constitution of self in blood relations and a "society based on consanguinity" (Lévinas 2001, pg. 69). Lévinas continues that in Hitlerism, this new ideal of man brings new thoughts and new truth as much as leaving the space open for deceit. The Germanic ideal, according to Lévinas's analysis, is preoccupied with this possibility for deceit in moral and social ideals, and so refuses to commit to any spiritual truth that is not "anchored in his flesh and blood" (Lévinas and Hand 1990, pg. 70). As Lévinas understood, in Hitlerism social norms that build civilization then become an invasion of inauthentic substitutes for heroism, which is not far from Freud's sentiments about how culture is formed by sublimated aggressive drives.

Without explicit reference to Heidegger or his concept of existential authenticity, Lévinas writes that in Hitler's new ideal of society, only degenerate ideals can "promise sincerity and authenticity" (Lévinas and Hand 1990, pg. 70). Rather than revel in the effort of freethinking, this society enjoys aspects of an ideal that "make life easier. …Man no longer finds himself confronted by a world of ideas in which he can choose his own truth on the basis of a sovereign decision made by his free reason. He is already linked to a certain number of these ideas, just as he is linked by birth to all those who are of his blood" (Lévinas and Hand 1990, pg. 70). Hitlerism promotes a simpler mind, which does not have to freely choose between different abstract ideals and possibilities: birth and blood link these bodies to their ideals.

There are two problems with these last two faults Lévinas finds in Hitlerism in regard to his personal convictions, first that he advocated a similar suspicion in rationalism and second that he placed himself within a chain of hereditary lineage of beliefs in the Jewish people. As regards the first, what recourse does Lévinas have in the processes of "free reason" for ensuring a society that is not racist? Lévinas always expressed suspicion about the possibility for reason to reveal the truth of an ethically obligated subject. On the contrary, the processes of reason reveal dogmatic, partial, and illusory totalizing systems that lead to their own forms of violence. Additionally, within Lévinas's ethical theory, who is ever sovereign enough to make a free decision? Later in his life, Lévinas wrote a prefatory note to his *Reflections on the Philosophy of Hitlerism* (1990) stating that, led by logic, Western philosophy had not sufficiently insured against this elemental evil.

Lévinas's remarkable insight is his concept of self that is fundamentally relational, where the other is fundamentally and transcendentally always present in oneself. The forms of self that are characterized by Hitlerism have some of the same underlying assumptions that Lévinas presents. Lévinas argues for the particular values and insights that his race, heredity, and ancestry bequeathed to him, such as those seen in his *Talmudic Readings* and *Difficult Freedom*. The truths to which he is committed are anchored in his own Jewish heritage, inscribed in a body tied to his material lineage. There are important asymmetries between the racialized Jewish body and Hitlerism as a political position chosen and adopted. The comparison here is not to equate the two, but to show proximities between cultural ideals despite one's most earnest intentions of their difference. Furthermore, if race is primarily a social idea, then to a certain extent it is as amorphous as a political position. Lévinas's exact point is that any of these identifiers cannot lay total claim to what essentially one is. The matter of the extent to which race is a social construct scientifically or objectively is also not the issue here, in as much as whether Freud's psychoanalytic method objectively captures the truth of human nature or does not. These matters are important only to the extent that these positions are true for Freud and Lévinas, reflecting their standards of truth. Holding them accountable to their own psychoanalytic and moral theories proves more difficult than would be expected, a possibility that should make us all pause at the weight of convictions to safeguard any universal sense of "goodness."

Never capable of admitting these similarities, Lévinas finds a distinction between the two forms of universalism in Hitlerism and Judaism: the idea of expansion. Racism is the expansion and universalization of power and force based on heredity. The other legitimate form of universalism is the propagation of an idea rather than force, such as human liberty, as was done with the Jewish message of freedom.

I previously asked whether Lévinas would have to admit the possibility of his substitution with the Nazi guard and see here that it is possible. I find proximity in their thought. Ironically this proximity is in line with Lévinas's admission that this elementary feeling of racism constitutes the man in humanity. Admitted by Lévinas, the infinite subject also contains an alterity of evil (1998a, pg. 44). In the beginning of the essay, he reveals this "elementary feeling" in Hitlerism that is present in any soul (Lévinas and Hand 1990, pg. 70). If we move further along the timeline of his life, we can see this pre-ontological and originary possibility for substitution in an alterity of evil and, thus, where responsibility may be occluded in the context of his Zionism.

Racism is possible by a modification in the logic of universalizing truth, according to Lévinas. First, the logic of truth that is worthy of the name must be capable of going beyond the limited context in which it was conceived "to create a new world" (Lévinas and Hand 1990, pg. 70). There is universalism in the propagation of an idea that detaches from its point of origin and becomes a common heritage that is fundamentally anonymous. Since it is true for all, anyone who accepts the idea can master it. Many without force can create a community of individual peers in the propagation of an idea whose validity is strong enough for its wide acceptance. Universalism in the veracity of an idea, therefore, does not require external force or power for its propagation, writes Lévinas.

Lévinas provides an example of this kind of universal truth through the propagation of an idea in his text. It is freedom, liberal equality, and even Marxist materialism that preserves one's ability to revolt or find remorse, where "Man finds something in the present with which he can modify or efface the past. Time loses its very irreversibility. It collapses at the feet of man like a wounded beast. And he frees it" (Lévinas and Hand 1990, pg. 65). This idea of freedom has propagated into new ideals of freedom, such as the soul's freedom, and the freedom of reason. All these come as "peers" to the original biblical claim that all are created equal in the eyes of God without necessarily knowing to whom the credit is owed. Indeed, secular humanists today will accept the idea of freedom and equality despite its origination from biblical texts only because of its veracity and ability to sustain sociality (Nielsen 1990).[4]

Universalism rooted in racism, on the other hand, is an expansion of force. A universality that is compatible with racism universalizes force and becomes its method of propagation. Expansion for this universalism is of force "that constitutes the unity of a world of masters and slaves. Nietzsche's will to power, which modern Germany is rediscovering and glorifying, is not only a new ideal; it is an ideal that simultaneously brings with it its own form of universalization: war and conquest" (Lévinas and Hand 1990, pg. 74). At the time that Hitlerism propagated its racism, Lévinas saw justifications and a calculated apparatus for imprisonment and starvation for those who did not agree, or those who were not committed by blood to the universal order. Lévinas writes, "Universality must give way to the idea of expansion, for the expansion of a force presents a structure that is completely different from the propagation of an idea" (Lévinas and Hand 1990, pg. 70). Rather than call it universality, Hitlerism expands force and becomes "attached to the personality or society exerting it, enlarging that person or society while subordinating the rest" (Lévinas and Hand 1990, pg. 70). Distinguishing between the expansions of force from the propagation of an idea because of its own veracity, Lévinas finds that the expansion of force must attach to an individual person, dictator, or a society that upholds the idea of expansion that seeks to enlarge itself, while subjugating others.

---

[4] See Kai Nielsen's *Ethics Without God* (1990). These secularists accounts have been significantly rearticulated in a secular idiom through accounts of humanism and social contract theories.

If Lévinas finds here a fundamental principle that marks the humanity of men, what of the force used in Israel's Defensive Forces, the IDF, to keep its citizens safe at all costs? At the time of Lévinas's interview in 1982 about the massacre of Palestinian refugees in Lebanon, the State of Israel was still at the beginning of its use of militaristic force. However, the trauma of knowing that one's immediate family, and the Jewish people in general, was persecuted and slaughtered made it difficult, perhaps even impossible, for Lévinas to risk repeating his history in the new place of Israel. He may have desired not-to-know or see the face of the Palestinian other to immediately condemn the silence of the State's political leaders. Meanwhile, however, the expansion of military force that is arguably necessary for self-defense only heightened the precarious nature of the citizens of Israel's relation to their Palestinian neighbors. Both sides have become more vulnerable to injury by the other in the interest of their particular social, historical, and national interests.

The implication is not that Lévinas is a Nazi. The idea, however, is to show how easily one is vulnerable to justifying the use of force for preserving one's "self" or affiliated body politic. We can further see Lévinas's vulnerability in his commitments and social ideals. His desire-not-to-know, if we borrow the insight from Freud's analysis, made him vulnerable to appropriate the norms of his world's culture. Vulnerability as an existential condition is a theoretical insight that came out of the horizon of Lévinas's personal life, and reflects a similar vulnerability in Freud's life, such as moving out of Vienna, in spite of his theoretical awareness that desires and emotions can blind rational assessments. In Lévinas's reflections on ethical subjectivity, norms that were repudiated could not help but shape his own approach to life and knowledge.

These kinds of testimonies and actions in Lévinas's life force his readers to admit the high level of difficulty in the kind of responsibility he articulates and the heightened vulnerability to foreclose relational demands in the interests of an egoical aspect of self. Lévinas as a person was shaped by the experiences of his particular life, one in which he bore witness to his immediate family's life as persecuted Jews in Europe. Lévinas denounced Heidegger later in his life stating that it was possible to forgive many, but not Heidegger (Malka 2006, pg. 163). Lévinas also fulfilled his resolve never to step in Germany after the war, at times enduring lengthy travel detours to avoid stopping there. Still, these experiences did not mitigate the theoretical obligations he demanded from what he understood as the ethical subject. Rather what is apparent is these moments of foreclosure are moments of vulnerability to unethical relations that were possible even for an ultra-ethical writer like Lévinas.

In *Parting Ways: Jewishness and the Critique of Zionism*, Judith Butler problematized this issue of the difference between pre-ontological and ontological senses of persecution in Lévinas's writing. As I have understood the difference, pre-ontological persecution in the subject is the ubiquitous demand to oppress egoical self-interest in an effort to become ethical, substituting the egoical self in its relation to an individual other, regardless of what harm may have been inflicted previously between both. God's command for Abraham to "Go out, toward a/his self" in Genesis would be a pre-ontological persecution because the affective demand cannot be negotiated away, removes the individual's self-interest, and becomes applicable for all according to Lévinas's pre-ontological ethics of substitution.

On the other hand, the ontological sense of persecution appears in the varied phenomena of oppression through history, experienced by certain peoples at different times through different means and often by way of a logic of contradiction. Delusions of persecution are also ways for one to project aggression that arise from particular cultural norms and ideals that create guilt when the other is the one who seems to threaten the self. The claim that makes Lévinas's writing on persecution controversial for Butler is when ontological forms of persecution are equated to a pre-ontological "ultimate essence of Israel," which would legitimize using defensive force against enemies in its social and historical development (Lévinas 1990, pg. 225; Butler 2012, pg. 47). If the pre-ontological essence of people in Israel is to be persecuted on an ontic level, then any force used as self-defense is also justified.

Butler reads Lévinas as confounding the pre-ontological condition of persecution for any ethical subject to go toward another with ontic forms of persecution. Lévinas's silence about persecutions on an ontic level can then seem justified because of a pre-ontological condition, an essence of being persecuted. Israeli Jews feel justified in acts of "expulsion, killing, disenfranchisement" of those who threaten their safety, which simply cannot constitute justice for Butler (2012, pg. 34). Criticisms are launched against the State of Israel that justifies its use of force in the treatment of Palestinian citizens to ensure its security from the always-impending threat of another holocaust. However, to remain consistent with Lévinas's distinction between pre-ontological and ontological forms of social persecution, in a relation where the Jewish Israeli citizen who perceives justification to persecute their Palestinian-Israeli cousin, and vice versa, both sides remain faceless. Pre-ontological persecution, on the other hand, would require that both divest themselves in a dis-identification with all interests for the possibility of witnessing the other's vulnerability. Pre-ontologically, the humanity for both is removed during these ontic relations of persecution where the face of the other is not seen, and only one's trauma is represented. As each group appears in their totalizing aspects for the other, the more control and force are upheld as the only type of relation possible. Ontologically in the adventure in being, however, and through the ethical relation any social and political identifier can be broken, due to the pre-ontological vulnerability, so that the face of any other can be seen. Finally, Lévinas drew a distinction between the ethical relation that is between two from the political where a third intervenes for justice, and enables the always-available possibility to break social identifiers, and avoid the other's occlusion based on social contingencies.

Reading back to Lévinas, the infinite relation guarantees the possibility of breaking any of these totalizing identities. Butler's engagement with Lévinas's pre-ontology as idealized social structures inevitably leads to confounding ontic and pre-ontological forms of persecution since ontic relations are elevated to essential characteristics. By speaking of a pre-ontology that comes from an anarchic nowhere and proximate space between two particular faces, however, there are neither individual nor social essences for Lévinas. Here the ethical relation enters, prior to social ones, and what Moran argues is Lévinas's central theme—namely, to show the primacy of moral obligation to others over political or geographical considerations (2016, pg. 297). If there is no real otherwise to dyadic social categories in Butler's reading of Lévinas's understanding of Israel, then its social persecution must be read into the pre-ontological conditions that make it possible. But Lévinas constantly attempts to write on that which breaks beyond essence, as the title of his work *Otherwise Than Being, or, Beyond Essence* implies. Still, the theoretical division does not guarantee Lévinas and others would not personally suffer from this confusion due to each's particular history of trauma.

Untangling Lévinas's claims about persecution helps to develop the view of a relational self that becomes itself in relation to its neighbors. Returning to the relational aspect of ethical subjectivity that I will continue to develop in the last chapter, I can also reveal how Lévinas's own egoical, traumatic experiences prevented him from criticizing Israel's use of force against its neighbors. In exile, Jewish people never sought to convert or conquer the countries in which they dwelt. They were not imperialistic in attempts to make the other the same as them, but sufficiently maintained their status as other over more than 2000 year while in exile. These were not easy years and relations were almost never tranquil. Butler aptly recognizes the constructive nature inherent to these interruptive exilic relations (2012, pg. 38). Similarly, Israel as a state has been able to maintain peaceful relations with some of its neighboring Arab nations, such as with Jordan and at times with Egypt. Why then are "interruptive exilic relations" with a Palestinian person avoided for Lévinas (Butler 2012, pg. 38)?

Reflecting on the asymmetry of the inassimilable other who also constitutes the self, Butler writes:

> I want to suggest that the Lévinasian "interruption" by the other, the way in which the ontology of the self is constituted on the basis of the prior eruption of the other at the heart of myself, implies a critique of the autonomous subject and the version of multiculturalism that assumes cultures are constituted as autonomous domains whose task it is to establish dialogue with other cultures. (2012, pg. 38)

In this reading of Lévinas, Butler writes that the ethical scene to which Lévinas seems obligated is not limited "culturally and geographically," namely, only to Jewish Israelis (2012, pg. 38). As much as Lévinas himself may have experienced difficulty negotiating these lines, given certain personal traumas, his theoretical perspective of a subjectivity that is primarily unknowable, relational, and vulnerable would not have accepted rigid lines that limit autonomous, particular cultures and geographies. Even if this commitment is not exhibited in the calculated steps Lévinas took in speaking about the Palestinian neighbor, then the possibility of negotiating lines of identity was a meaningful enough idea for Lévinas to dedicate his life's work. Ultimately it is instructive that strong cases can be made that Lévinas was calculated not to outwardly condemn actors for the massacres out of shortsightedness (Caygill 2002) (Butler 2012) or out of caution that is consistent with his work (Moran 2016) (Eisenstadt and Katz 2016).

While Lévinas emphasizes the particular form of an exilic and persecutory essence of Israel, beginning with Abraham that was sent into exile to find himself elsewhere, Lévinas argues that everyone finds this archetype in themselves. Even if the requirement is not acknowledged, the requirement is that each remains open to the insight that one must go outside one's self in order to reach the height of ethical subjectivity. If the idea is lost, then one is led into the psychical territory of paranoiac delusions of persecution for repairing trauma where no relation is possible. Natural ethics is only based on retributive forms of justice, as Freud argued. In place of an irreplaceable face of the other who in the very temptation to kill becomes the one who cannot be killed, retributive calculations of justice give rise to a substitution in the alterity of evil (Lévinas 1998a, pg. 44). On the other hand, a self who is vulnerable to de-constituting its self-sufficiency in its relations is also always capable of undoing the "autonomous" cultural and social attributions as well for calculating retributive trauma.

In various times of Lévinas's life, it seems that he speaks offensively of "Arab neighbors" as if they cannot have the same ethical relation with those with a European sensibility. Lévinas refers to "the countless masses of Asiatic and underdeveloped peoples," those "for whom Abraham, Isaac and Jacob no longer mean anything," with "greedy eyes of those countless hordes," as "sects that devour one another," and he characterizes them as "a religious collectivity that has lost all political cohesion" (Lévinas 1990, pg. 165).[5] In a redeeming moment, and just as when Lévinas writes that the neighbor or the other can be his people and kin (1989, pg. 292), Lévinas also resists disqualifying humanity from those who subscribe to this type of "materialism"—an identifier that gathers all these descriptions together—so as not to denounce the aggression that arises from their legitimate discontent.

In another passage that reflects on who these "materialists" are, he writes that traditional Jewish thought, attributable to the three patriarchs, is a "framework in which to think of a universal human society that incorporates the just people of every nation and every belief, with whom it is possible to achieve the final intimacy" (Lévinas 1990, pg. 163). In other words, these "hordes" are made up of individuals that can be found in any nation or belief system who cannot achieve intimacy with those who are deemed incomprehensible others. These hordes must also be found in Israel and among the Jewish people. These masses can appear in any culture since it is the vulnerability of a subjectivity that receives pleasure in persecuting, and therefore, failing the ethical demand.

Lévinas's warning is that these "materialists" will push Jews and Christians alike, as he says, into the margins. The latter two have maintained an intimate relation with the other for Lévinas who studied phenomenology on a yearly basis with Pope John Paul II. Intimacy, after all, requires two who are separated from each other, not subsumed by the other, for a level of intimate proximity. An additional clue on who these materialists may be, those who are not limited to the social and

---

[5] It is worth nothing that Abraham was not originally a Jew or from the land of Israel. Abraham and Hagar gave birth to Ishmael who is believed to be the father of Islam. Not only is Abraham initially called an *Evry* (which means in Hebrew "from there" or "from elsewhere" or "otherwise"), he is also father to the Arab Muslim and Israelite Jew. These indicate a necessary proximity between Hebraic Jews and their neighboring Arab Muslim cousins. The close proximity of these identifiers should prevent totalized relations as enemy between them.

geographic location of "the Palestinian," can be found in his *Reflections on Hitlerism*. There he points toward the source of an elemental evil that occurs within the ontology of a being. For these materialists, there is no ethical subjectivity who comes already responsible for his neighbor as a revelation of their height, or an election that comes on behalf of an absent God. Even Western philosophy with its concept of liberalism is insufficiently prepared for this vulnerability in human nature to forget this height, a pre-ontological responsibility to be for the other on behalf of an anarchic other.

It may be tempting to fix these hordes as one distinct group of people, such as the Palestinians, which Butler indicates when she writes that, "For Lévinas, the prohibition against violence is restricted to those whose faces make a demand upon me, and yet these 'faces' are differentiated by virtue of their religious and cultural background" (2012, pg. 39). While Lévinas certainly admits here that there are others who are excluded from a relation, his ethic implicitly denounces totalizing these faceless hoards with any rigid or fixed ontic category and identifier of particular peoples or societies. Still, we see in these comments a Lévinas who was vulnerable to the possibility of effacing the other in given cultures due to the experiences of his own particular life's struggles.

Even if Lévinas's personal traumas led him to implicate certain groups in his Palestinian neighbor who did not value what he saw in the neighboring Israeli Jew, his ethics prevent a blanket condemnation of all "Palestinians" by emphasizing the anarchic and infinite face that appears in the face-to-face ethical relation. The anarchic and infinite distance that relates between two subjects does not only depend on those categories the ego makes for itself, but also on those used for shattering the self. Additionally, there is documentation of Lévinas's criticism of non-Palestinian Arab fascism, as well as his criticism of colonial traces in Israel's political maneuvers.

First, his disdain of these hordes is not restricted to those situated around and in Israel's borders, such as a person who is Palestinian. For example, his son Michael tells the story of how, during a visit to Morocco, they both fell ill. They witnessed a rise in frenzied beliefs and fundamentalism in support of the Shah (Malka 2006, pg. 260). Having witnessed the violence that results from these feelings during his youth in Europe, Lévinas became weary and fell ill. In this story, we see a Lévinas who does not restrict the ethical relations to individuals of a particular social, religious, or cultural background.

Additionally, it was not the status of the Arab as such that was offensive to Lévinas, but those who could not enter into dialogue or relation with the Jewish people returning to inhabit the land. On a trip to Israel in 1978, Lévinas went with a group of scholars to visit a Bedouin town. Upon learning that "Bedouins were required to burn their tents if they wanted to be eligible to receive stone houses from the government, Lévinas remained on the bus. 'It's colonialism!' he cursed" (Malka 2006, pg. 217). He defends here Bedouin Arabs who were generally more welcoming of the Jewish return to Palestine. In a small gesture, Lévinas protested their mistreatment by the Israeli state in remaining on the bus.

To say God, the good, the ethical, justice, or the face appears only for one group of people or excludes a whole kind of other people is to ignore the whole of Lévinas's corpus that emphasizes the infinite regress in ethical subjectivity that fights against the constant attempt to totalize itself. In one of the few comments Lévinas made about the Israeli-Palestinian conflict, he says:

> The Other is the fellow human being, the neighbor, not necessarily the near one, but the near one too. And in this sense, being for the Other, you are for your neighbor. But if your neighbor attacks another neighbor or is unjust toward him, what can you do? There, alterity takes on a different character, there, in alterity, an enemy can appear, or at least gives rise to the problem of knowing who is right and who is wrong, who is just and who is unjust. There are people who are wrong. (Malka 2006, pg. 296)

Lévinas admits in this relation of triangulation, in politics where there is more than just the self and other, an ability to be wrong. Although his limited remarks have earned him criticism, Lévinas never pretended these relations were easy, obvious, or fixed—even (and especially) for himself. Remaining alert is an infinite task and so his critics are also justified in their complaints and even obligated to make them, according to Lévinas.

After Arendt published *On Understanding Violence Philosophically and Other Essays* (1970), Glenn Gray reflects on *ekstasis*, a malicious form of rage that descends upon one that speaks to this alterity of evil. Like the point Freud makes in *Civilization and Its Discontents*, the same rage that motivates a passionate and violent response is the same source that drives the highest cultural achievements, such as science, art, and religion (Gray 1970, pg. 17). Similar to Lévinas, he writes that this form of ecstatic rage "grips us from without, takes us out of ourselves" and that these malicious "powers are not in us, but fall upon us," which is to characterize a form of alterity. Both Freud and Lévinas recognize ambiguous borders between self and other, between productive cultural growth and its source in a nature that is torn between individual and social interests.

Uncannily, Gray also uses a vocabulary close to that which Lévinas himself uses when he considers the face. Surveying the faces of docile students in the classroom, Gray explains:

> I need only close my eyes to imagine those faces contorted with hatred, those hands, feminine or masculine, clenched or clawlike, those bodies tensed and ready to spring, in order to realize that all of us conceal, half-knowing, powers that are at the furthest remove from the present setting. (Gray 1970, pg. 17)

It was in seeing the seated faces in a classroom that Gray need only close his eyes to imagine those same faces enraged. No one is immune to a violent passion and everyone can seem as removed from it as any other in their more civil moments. However, trauma by this alterity where the enemy appears presents the real possibility to prevent future ethical relations. Acting from one's desire not-to-know, a suppression of the other's suffering, is more commonly understood as moral negligence. Lévinas's choice to delay speaking against or naming the perpetrators of the slaughter of Palestinian lives seems to fit this charge.

Lévinas can be accused of speaking rarely on these challenges that Israel and its citizens faced during its formative years. He seemed to remain indifferent to the violence inherent in occluding the place of the other, which was taken to be his

10 Freedom and Existential Vulnerability: Lévinas's Vulnerability to His Cultural Ideals

ultimate task where Europe was concerned. One can see this as a result of the events of his life and the precarious status of Jewish people there. Ultimately nothing secures history against the repetition of those events he witnessed or against the return of a natural barbarism in being (Lévinas 1998b, pg. 187). We may still accuse him of turning a blind eye and thus of ignoring the persecution of an ethical life that would obligate him to act with these new neighbors in Zion precisely because it was so difficult.

These impasses in Lévinas's personal ethical optics are like Freud's relationships and the intertwining of his life and theory. Freud also read his life into his theories, which limited and circumscribed them when his personal fears and traumas became too pressing. These are most apparent in his relation to Fleiss. As previously discussed, Freud's repressed feelings toward Fleiss led to the misinterpretation of a dream that conveyed Freud's guilt for misdiagnosing a patient (the titular "Irma") in order to preserve Fleiss's character. The truth that Freud kept from himself would only be revealed to him later in his life.

There is no way to avoid becoming convinced by fancies of the mind, including these two thinkers who were most critical of the usual ways in which the mind conceals its desires. With their intimate knowledge of how one categorizes and represents others to themselves, each man could still not relate in ways that overcame the shortcomings they understood in theory. Even with a horizon of persecution in their own lives—either because of their Jewish ancestry or because of the work in which they were involved—neither could prevent committing the same injury toward others.

All too acute for Lévinas, who was a prisoner of war, was the ability for the cultured, philosophical thinkers who are obligated to moral injunctions to forget embodied people who can suffer as ends in themselves. The cultured is most vulnerable to forget the referents in those moral injunctions, the human being intrinsically worthy of respect. In addition to the vulnerability of avoiding the face and humanity of the other, it is also all too easy to become the other who is vulnerable and faceless. In order to stun the paralyzing effects of trauma and the persuasion of identification, what Lévinas calls "substitution" is one way of escaping the self to find oneself in another. I argue that an overall shift in value from self-mastery to a precarious relationality can help usher new moral horizons. Substitution for Lévinas is not limited to the Freudian sense of replacing an unconscious object or desire with a different conscious representation in the psyche's defensive struggle. Different from the substitution of psychic images and representations such as in dreams, and in Schreber's ontic substitution of a real Dr. Flechsig with his own neurotic delusion of Dr. Flechsig, Lévinas points to an ethical demand that is always between two particular individuals. The pre-ontological relation in substitution between two is always an anarchical shock to their histories of trauma that render each relation asymmetrical in unique ways and an affective impingement on both when it is welcomed in an openness.

Turning away from the neighbor because of an upsurge in a traumatized ego can lead to justifications, or seeming negligence, toward the other's suffering. This is the basic and fundamental vulnerability Lévinas's life articulates for the ethical subject, which recalls what Freud understands as repression for desiring not-to-know one's own moral failings and projecting internal aggressions onto another. Lévinas addresses the relative ease of turning away from the other that depends on degrees of proximity from specific to more general demands. Freud was also concerned with the limits of libidinal investment for which Lévinas articulated as a non-erotic relation that comes from the passivity of a pre-ontological alterity in each. What about the alterity of a different character where the enemy appears? Is it always in the other? But what if the other is in oneself? Does the alterity of the enemy simultaneously appear in my own face? Are there degrees of proximity that reside in the self's relation to itself?

The following final section develops Lévinas's work on an intentionality of search for attuning the self in its existential freedom to the ethical relation, rather than suffer the foreclosure of an ethical moment. Paul Ricœur's challenge that Lévinas's pre-ontology has no language for practical morality and that his ethic based on persecution has no ontic efficacy is redressed. The pre-ontological conditions for ethical subjectivity provide the possibility for the plurality of moral responses rather than condemn them to silence. Lévinas's language is also necessary when the point of view of an egoical self that has been traditionally valorized shifts to a priority for the relational self that is impinged by the other but finds a new height in them.

References

Butler, J. (2005). *Giving and account of oneself*. New York: Fordham University Press.
Butler, J. (2012). *Parting ways*. New York: Columbia University Press.
Caygill, H. (2002). *Lévinas and the political*. London: Routledge.
Eisenstadt, O., & Katz, C. E. (2016). The faceless Palestinian: A history of an error. *Telos, 174*, 9–32.
Gray, J. G. (1970). *On understanding violence philosophically and other essays*. New York/Evanston/London: Harper & Row Publishers.
Lévinas, E. (1990). *Difficult freedom: Essays on Judaism* (trans: Hand, S.). Baltimore, MD: John Hopkins University Press.
Lévinas, E. (1998a). *Otherwise than being: Beyond essence* (trans: Lingis, A.). New York: Duquesne University Press.
Lévinas, E. (1998b). *Entre Nous: Collected essays* (trans: Smith, M.B.). New York: Columbia University Press.
Lévinas, E. (1998c). Useless suffering. In R. Bernasconi & D. Wood (Eds.), *Provocation of Lévinas: Rethinking other* (pp. 156–167). New York: Routledge.
Lévinas, E. (2001). *Existence and existents* (trans: Lingis, A.). New York: Duquesne University Press.
Lévinas, E., & Hand, S. (1990). Reflections on the philosophy of hitlerism. *Critical Inquiry, 17*(1), 62–71.

Lévinas, E., Finkielkraut, A., & Malka, S. (1989). "Ethics and Politics". In S. Hand (Ed.), *The Lévinas Reader* (trans: Romney, J.) (pp. 289–297). Oxford, UK: Blackwell.

Malka, S. (2006). *Emmanuel Lévinas: His life and legacy* (trans: Kigel, M. & Embree, S.M.). Pittsburgh, PA: Duquesne University Press.

Morgan, M. (2016). *Lévinas's thical Politics*. Bloomington, IN: Indiana University Press. Retrieved July 5, 2020, from www.jstor.org/stable/j.ctt1c3gwwz.

Nielsen, K. (1990). *Ethics without God* (3rd ed.). Buffalo: Prometheus Books.

Chapter 11
Intentionality of Search: Vulnerability, Persecution, and the Ethical Bind

Abstract In this chapter, I develop Lévinas's intentionality of search, which does not require a fully rational agency but instead values a form of intentionality that constitutes an ethical subjectivity in a mutual apprehension of the other. To propose an egalitarian particularism, I introduce qualities like passivity and anarchy in the creation of ethical subjectivity that supplies each with a constant plenum of moral possibilities.

Keywords Vulnerability to cultural norms · The face of the other · Pre-ontological persecution · Existential vulnerability · Foreclose the ethical relation · Lévinasian ethics · Ethics of substitution · Alterity of evil · Anarchic alterity of the other · Saying vs. said · Atonement · Bear witness

This last section responds to the oft-heard criticism of Lévinas's language on a pre-ontological form of ethical persecution that it is hyperbolic and has no real ontic efficacy, as represented in Paul Ricœur's article "Otherwise: A Reading of Emmanuel Lévinas" (2004). I will begin by showing how Lévinas's hyperbolic language is appropriate when there is a switch in perspective and value from the individualized ego to relational subjectivity. He also calls these two *modalities of obsession*, of a self that goes toward itself and a modality of obsession by each monad of all the others, the latter of which illustrates his ontology in an ethics of substitution. Lévinas's distinction between the totalizing, egoical self, and the relational self is a persecution for the egoical aspect of self but is what exactly enables relational subjectivity to develop beyond it and move toward a form of self that responds to the other's particular needs. A pregnant body who cannot explain away the use of her organs, yet can accept the appropriation of her resources in moments of hostility or hospitality will be used as an image for the persecuting relation that can welcome a mutual dis-identification in order to become ethical. Using this image, I develop what the relational subject entails and finally illuminate why this ethical orientation through the malice and persecution of a subject is not as paradoxical as readers like Ricœur contend, but requires a shift in understanding subjectivity as unknowable, relational, and vulnerable.

The claim here is not that the persecutory relation is the only possible bind that can relate two ethical subjects, but that where there is a persecutory relation, there is the possibility for an ethical relation at the same time. If there is the phenomenon of persecution, then one is necessarily implicated in their ability to respond. Responses can be indifference, caring, to act, bear witness, remain skeptical, and, of course, perpetuate ontic forms of persecution that occludes the other. In spite of the constitutional vulnerability for becoming enchanted with individual fulfillment and mastery, Lévinas's work in light of Freud's moral skepticism can be used to motivate an intentional of search for an egalitarian particularism that values sensing the suffering of a particular other and that, at the very least, can prevent gratuitous measures of suffering.

Traditionally in phenomenology, different forms of intentionality constitute perceived objects. In an approach that goes "back to the things themselves," the real world offers itself in the intuitive presentation of its objects (Husserl 2001, pg. 168). Lévinas writes on Edmund Husserl's *Logical Investigation* that it is a method that proceeds from access one already has to an object as constituting a real part of the object's being (Lévinas 1998a, pg. 95). The meanings and description of phenomenon disclose the existence of an object in the synthesis of its moments, or aspects, with the one who conceives them. Phenomenology thus overcomes the traditional and awkward gap between subject and object, the antithesis of idealism and realism.

In what is included under the intentionality of search, Lévinas inverts the constituting gaze, which comes from the external other to constitute oneself. Intentionality is not the bedrock for constituting essences and identities of external objects; more fundamental is this relation between subjective intentionalities that constitute one another. Lévinas writes about the "full phenomenological" method, which, "aims to discover, for relations of knowledge, the foundations that properly speaking lack the structures of knowledge. These foundations impose themselves without certainty, but because they are anterior to and condition the structure of knowledge as such, they are more certain than certainty, more rational than reason" (Lévinas 1998a, pg. 101). Here is a glimpse of the Lévinas who goes beyond Husserl's logical foundations. But, then how does Lévinas defend the ability to apprehend unknowable conditions that are more "certain than certainty" (Lévinas 1998a, pg. 101)? Lévinas supports this claim in the non-conscious event of an obligation, apprehended first in a non-indifference to the other. The limits of knowledge are unavoidable as well as the persecutory bind that any other being places on the self. These acts restrict or enable oneself in varied and particular ways and are presupposed as affective for delineating oneself among others.

When shocking language such as "hostage" or "persecution" is used to express this relation that culminates in the ethical subjectivity, then it is adopted from the point of view of the egoical self that is looking at a relational self who is involuntarily vulnerable to the other. Traditional moral and political philosophies have been dominated by the illusory view of an isolated rational perceiver that must justify its relation to all others. Relational subjectivity, however, is constituted in a response to what Lévinas calls the interruptive face of the other. Vulnerability as it is understood in Lévinas's *Totality and Infinity* presents the reader with a non-phenomenal face of the other who must be preserved in their non-phenomenal strangeness (1969, pg. 73). Lévinas's idea of the face as *visage* means that the other appears without even registering the eyes' color or the nose's contours, but instead becoming attuned to a particular infinitude by "negating its finitude" (Lévinas 1969, pg. 196). The plurality of each particular person is not smothered but rather originates in this face-to-face encounter, which preserves separation and openness in a desire to go toward the other, each beyond their separate being.

In an "alterity of the-one-for-the-other, responsibility before eros," Lévinas articulates this relation that is beyond sensual pleasure, where persecuting and erotic aspects are ambivalently related for a being that has language (1989, pg. 137). Composed of its significations, identifications, its speech, and distance, each can be host to the other (Lévinas 1989, pg. 299). I will eventually show how Lévinas gives priority to the aspect and "resolution" of oneself in substitution where a relation to the neighbor is required to constitute oneself, but first two forms of obsession for ethical subjectivity can show how hard it is to make this shift in perspectives and priorities. Lévinas's personal relation with Heidegger shows how the traumas in his life prevented hosting another in substitution, as he would describe the ethical relation.

Lévinas writes that even if the face as *visage* has no representation, each finds in themselves an obsession that forces and persecutes going outside oneself. An interesting distinction is made between modalities of obsession where the self goes toward itself, where the ego "like a relation between monads prior to the opening up of doors or windows" is in "nowise a development of this (ethical) relationship" (Lévinas 1989, pg. 192). The modality of obsession of the self with itself can be seen to culminate in Freud's view of a psyche that develops through an autoerotic position. Morality in view of this enclosed psyche is the consequence of repressed aggression and a psychologically violent apparatus that develops for the material purpose of living a social life with others. A culture dominated by taking "selfies" that are shared with others illustrates this ego that is obsessed with itself.

Freud compulsively repeats this paradox where loving one's neighbor is a form of masochism. Moral pleasure is derived from the super-ego's harsh admonishments of individuated desires. Individuated desires are sacrificed for living with others. Without proper "windows or doors" that open to the other, morality is nothing more than this masochistic pleasure that comes from sublimating one's aggression toward others for social protection. The modality of obsession of the self that goes toward itself is what Lévinas calls an "erotic alterity": that is, the pleasure found in compulsively engaging one's psychic traumas, as Freud illuminated in his theory of the death drive in which a psyche seeks to master trauma and excessive excitations through repetition. The more one goes toward another who is not like oneself, the greater the risk for bigger disturbances and disappointment because the other becomes less psychically manageable. The other risks one's self-mastery and the ego's desire for omnipotence.

The subject who is intersubjective, who develops in relation to others, is key for understanding the shocking language Lévinas uses in his chapter on substitution.

Lévinas calls the "modality of obsession" that appeals to the relational self a pre-ontological ethical dimension of subjectivity. The condition of any ethical subjectivity is where "[t]he expression by each monad of all the others refers to substitution, in which the identity of subjectivity is resolved" (Lévinas 1969, pg. 297). Remember that the term expression, for Lévinas, reflects the capacity to reveal through other mediums than ontic speech the concerns, worries, desires, and ethical responsibilities of its speaker (1998b, pg. 297). Concerned with all others, ethical subjectivity is "resolved" only as traces that return from its encounters with the other (1998b, pg. 297). It is itself only as a response that can never fulfill the demand in the approach of the other. The demand made by the other breaks the synchronicity of the enclosed ego grounded in empirical impressions, rational, and unconscious processes. An ability to respond in the relational subject does not follow from what it *ought* to do but is an anarchic and asymmetrical relation that preserves the alterity of the other. From the point of view that values the relational aspect of self, every egoical fulfillment remains only partial.

In order to better understand the other that gestates in the same, Lévinas works under the image of "maternity, which is bearing par excellence, bears even responsibility for the persecuting and persecutor" (1998b, pg. 75). The immediacy between a mother and child borne out of the body signifies her vulnerability. The analogy to maternity is the strongest for a body that creates out of its resources another, and in following degrees of parenting that bear another who is seemingly autonomous. A body pregnant with another life cannot explain away the use of internal organs as it is shared with the fetus. As the female body breathes, the fetus is affected.

In the modality of obsession where the self goes toward itself and is seen from the perspective of an isolated ego, the fetus is a hostile parasite that greedily absorbs her resources. Nutrients are taken from the mother and used for the fetus's bodily development. She becomes sick if the fetus is not nourished. Her health is at risk due to the health of the fetus. The fetus limits its mother from reaching egoical and ontological fulfillment from its earliest phases, and ultimately in pursuit of the other's life can neglect whatever potentialities existed before its arrival. In this modality, asymmetry exists in the mother's ultimate passivity to this impinging relation. Her inability to escape from or decline the weight of this commitment to the fetus's demanding need, dependence, and relation persecutes her. The use of her resources affects her in a most personal way in the same measure that this appropriation also cannot be explained away to her dependent fetus. Eventually, this fetus will also grow to walk, seemingly as its own person, into the world without her, capable to forget all this relation entails.

Once the fetus develops and is born, she is also presumed to be responsible for the child's upbringing and holds a limitless, pre-ontological obligation. She is responsible for the child's life, even if the mother's individual ego obsessed with itself may become convinced that it is not responsible for it. Nonetheless, it was her originating body that threw it into existence. It is fair to warn that maternity as an analogy for the persecuting ethical relation breaks down in its limited view of one sex. Namely, it would be wrong to say that only females (or only those reproductive bodies capable of becoming pregnant and giving birth) bear ethical responsibility for their children. Obsessed by any other, the pre-ontological ethical dimension of subjectivity is also not restricted to specific sexed or gendered relations (Lévinas 1998b, pg. 192). It would also be incorrect to say that a mother bears the responsibility for everything the child will do, even though she will often feel it is the case. The pre-ontological demand of this persecuting relation makes it just as incorrect to say that a female mother is the mere facilitator of the ethical possibility that her male child can bear, as some feminist critiques of Lévinas's view of maternity have argued (Brody 2001). The analogy between ethical subjectivity and maternity breaks down in these cases because, for Lévinas, the intersubjective vulnerability that maternity paradigmatically illustrates is common to any ethical subjectivity.

The egoical aspect of the self—a relation with the other that goes through the self, or the same as the self—is necessary for an ethical relation; however, the egoical self is not sufficient in Lévinas's view of the persecuted subject that is passive in the need to prioritize preserving the other, as such. Both the self and other risk becoming lost in identifications that are made and projected onto one another. Similarly, the child does not represent the alterity of a general other, but rather bears the development of a more difficult relationship with a particular other. The child is anticipated to share traits with the body in which it gestates and so is projected to share some of its same qualities. Still, the example is helpful for understanding the dynamic dichotomy that structures the relation between the ontological and egoistic sense of self with the pre-ontological, relational, and ethical one.

Switching modalities from the ontological interest of an individuated self to the ethical (and taking the point of view of the relational self in the modality of the one-for-the-other), the mother perceives herself as a host to the fetus.[1] Expanding from the female body to parenthood and personhood, maintaining her health is in substitution for the other in her, a child who is encouraged to become independent. The fact of its growth and eventual departure is of no importance to the hospitality she offers. She will even take pride in empowering the child to lead an independent life despite her individual loss and, as such, she will expose the immediate vulnerability of her egoical self to the other, individuated self. The mother's passivity to the other that gestates in the same is not carried out in order to preserve what she knows of herself, nor is it valued as reflecting her accomplishments. Though these egoistic considerations often motivate a mother's actions and care at various moments, a dialectic between selflessly working for the other arises from an anarchic passivity of being affected at all (Lévinas 1998b, pg. 121). It is this dynamic between a con-

---

[1] The opposite claims can be made, namely, that the modality of a self that is interested with itself can also choose to carry the fetus to affirm her own religious, social, and personal biases that occlude the interests of her fetus and vice versa. In the modality of obsession of one with all others, she can choose to terminate the fetus in its interest, for example, if it will be born into deprived conditions. It is important to note that this paper makes no claim about the freedom a female has in relation to the fetus her body carries and the appropriate relation. Furthermore, the thrust of this work declares the impossibility of deciding in advance that a relation is either wholly hospitable or hostile to the other. Nuance and attunement to the particular situation is the highest goal of ethical subjectivity.

cern for oneself and for the other in oneself that this work aims to emphasize for a shift in moral values and priorities.

Instead of the egoistic concern, empowering the other is done for their well-being. Lévinas continues to write on the second modality of obsession, "[t]he ego obsessed by all the others, supporting all the others, is an inversion of intentional ecstasy. In passivity the ego is a self under a persecuting – accusation of a neighbor" (1969, pg. 297). By becoming obsessed by all others, the isolated self cannot help but become impinged upon. The egoical self feels itself persecuted in its simultaneous need to obsess over others, for the mother in obsession with itself her fetus is hostile. Intentional ecstasy, or *ekstasis*, undergoes an inversion here since it is not directed from one perceiver toward an external object. Instead, inverted intentionality is an affective relation between two subjects that mutually constitute them as ethical. Even if it is difficult to empirically verify when each of these modalities is engaged, it is reasonable to imagine that the mother's "being is put in question by the alterity of the other, before the intervention of a cause, before the appearing of the other"—that is, even before the child is born (Lévinas 1969, pg. 75). She suffers risks to her individuated health and well-being, which is similar to the ambivalent relation between a self and other that is also not clearly delineated. The passivity inherent in her vulnerability to this particular fetus already bears her ethical responsibility; after this, any further moral judgment may follow in their particular ontic relations.[2]

The exteriority that constitutes ethical subjectivity enables the ego's movement into an abyss that separates isolated individuals but that brings them into a proximate distance, a space of relatability. Broken off from participation with the infinite through their individuated embodiment, a movement into what is called the abyss is always capable of shattering their separation. Lévinas writes in *Totality and Infinity* that the abyss vertiginously sweeps along the subject who is incapable of stopping itself from this movement (1969, pg. 93). Movement into the abyss also signifies infinity, which breaks open enclosed and isolated egos, rupturing the totalized self. Rather than conceive of the infinite—the movement of the abyss—as some abstract metaphysical realm, it is more useful to consider the movement into the abyss as signifying a particular space and configuration between two for grounding the ethical relation. The infinite is found in another and moves when two reach each other despite their totalizing isolation.

Richard Cohen's article "Some Notes on the Title of 'Totality and Infinity'" shows how Lévinas's pairing of these two terms already provides a clue to the concepts on which his ethics will depend. If we take seriously the claim that Lévinas's whole endeavor was to rethink the concept of vulnerability, then the title that

---

[2] Better to imagine that no body that bears another is either wholly hostile or hospitable to the fetus. A dialectic across moments, as Lévinas and this paper argue elsewhere, implies that every pregnant body relates in both ways through the term of a pregnancy or parenthood. The general position that no one is either wholly hostile or hospitable can support the further claim that all readers can sympathize with both positions at different times. What becomes important are the values and standards that are held in social norms that enable human flourishing.

includes an infinite against totality begins with the ethical decree "that impels thinking and being (that) is not wonder or disclosure but closer to the bone, as it were, it is human vulnerability and the moral responsibility it elicits" (Cohen 2010, pg. 112). In other words, moral obligations and responsibility have recourse to a particular body that houses an infinite subjectivity that is beyond any totalizing claim, ideal, or maxim. An existential vulnerability to totalize oneself and others that leads to ontic forms of persecution requires thinking: What are my ideals? Who is excluded from these totalized ideals? And what impinging relations result from this closure of seeing infinitude in the other?

Shrouded in an ego that asserts itself in the play of a totalizing ontology, there is an *originary* or infinite aspect of self that is prior to the ego, where "to communicate is indeed to open oneself, but the openness is not complete if it is on the watch for recognition. It is complete not in opening to the spectacle of or the recognition of the other, but in becoming a responsibility" for them (Lévinas 1998b, pg. 119). The original *we* occurs in the upsurge of the ego behind *de facto* communication that uses symbols and signs. This communication is always risky, uncertain, and adventurous, going into the dangers of living with a particular other. One's vulnerability is an indeclinable responsibility, but one that can be refused by another in upholding their ego over the ethical subject. Various relationships that abruptly ended in Freud's life illustrate how prioritizing self-mastery prevents these relations that disrupt individuated concerns.

Cohen continues that Lévinas announces going toward the other person who remains un-subsumed, truly other "in a love thy neighbor" that does not follow from love of the self but that "is" the self, the true self. This love is a non-erotic, unsentimental form of love. Often called an interruption, the "metaphysical desire" implicit in one for exteriority, for the other, inherently throws the totalized self and its self-sufficiency into question (Lévinas 1969, pg. 82). In an always-renewed reversal of the priority that had hitherto determined philosophy, it is "love of wisdom" for an individual serving the "wisdom of loving" another (Cohen 2010, pg. 113). It is to put the morality and suffering of the other before one's own—such is the imperative that drives ethics, such is the non-totalizable infinity of *Totality and Infinity*.

Understood under a rubric of the relational subject who is ruptured, the interruption is not only to be healed into a totality with the other, but a mutual *inter* of each ruptured ego into a relational intimacy with another. Here is not an altruistic or self-flagellating self. The constant watch over language, identifications, and the kinds of relations that make the other into the same all exhibit the basic vulnerability of this ethic. How do we keep watch over this new type of difficult freedom that does not serve an egoical self, but that also does not occlude the other in their relation?

Lévinas's chapter on substitution is central for his overall project of catching sight of the ethical subject. Although the ego posits itself as totally unified, it cannot rest there. The ego finds no rest and must be "cored out" of its nucleus, for example, by tearing away bread from one's own mouth for the other (Lévinas 1998b, pg. 64). These kinds of acts that are not motivated by recognition are easier for some than others and not always distinguished one from the other. Communicating and helping those who are considered enemies happens enough to consider them emblematic relations, rather than anomalous. For example, in recent protests against Dakota Access Pipeline, Army veterans came to protect peaceful protestors. These veterans swore allegiance to the commitments of their country represented by their commanding officers and superiors. The Army Corps of Engineers was responsible for breaking up protestors, but recognition by veterans of a persecution perpetrated against rightful claims to protect U.S. land made them act in the interest of the vulnerable community. An unlikely alliance was made between these two groups of people during this exchange. For Lévinas, those veterans embraced a new meaning. It is precisely in these times of difficult communication that awareness of the recurrence of persecution that always waits to bear responsibility for the other remains.

For ethical subjectivity, a constitutional vulnerability rests in the individual that has the choice to value and act as an individuated ego or relational person. Responsibility for the other rivets the egoical subject in an accusation and a wounding. Wounding, however, is only for the aspects of self that are reduced to its thematized, egoical, and self-sufficient aspects. For the relational person, responsibility is the way of existing with, safeguarding, and being safeguarded by the other. The relational aspect of the self is present as a trace that returns to itself only by way of the other (Lévinas 1998b, pg. 64). Various recent interviews of teachers who were protesting for higher wages in Oklahoma City spectacularly highlight this relational aspect of self.[3] Many worked as a teacher for decades with minimum income, or a 25% pay decrease over the previous 10 years, while they were also expected to pay for student resources in the classroom. Even while their personal interests were deprived for so many years, the idea of leaving the profession made them feel guilty. The value of these student and teacher relations was prioritized for so long that several teachers felt as if they were abandoning their students by leaving their teaching profession. These interviewees make clear that it is possible to value another over one's personal interests.

Language is a sufficient condition to implicate an ability to respond and, as such, to have freedom in the type of response offered. The choice to respond, however, cannot be declined in virtue of the possibility afforded by language, which comes from an embodied subject. Acknowledging that one always contains an element of alterity, an unexpected and unpredictable surprise, putting one's life in the hands of another is a great risk. But as Lévinas articulates, the individuated self is persecuted in the need to take this adventure toward the other where the self is exposed as delusional about itself, as much as the other remains otherwise. The "adventure of life" is such because while each can be confined to the egoistic self as Freud surmised with horror, at the same time, as Lévinas makes clear, the adventure can also be a privilege. It may be that Freud's theoretical framework is incapable of reaching this conclusion about the ethical nature of subjectivity, or that Lévinas could articulate this necessity only because he emerged from the horrors of both World Wars. Both,

---

[3] https://news.vice.com/en_us/article/vbqy9d/we-talked-to-18-teachers-in-oklahoma-who-just-cant-anymore

however, led persecuted lives whose theories took seriously the conflicted nature of an individuated subject who cannot help but remain riveted to others.

At the risk of qualifying the important relation between political power relations and what has largely been considered the personal domestic spheres, a large goal of this work is to restore personal (responsibility) that is reflected in political relations of power (Hanisch 1970). How public policy, social, and historical contingencies make up each individual is important so long as it is remembered that at the same time the person in the "personal" also effect political structures. Instead of eviscerating ethical subjectivity to socially contingent contexts where there is no individual responsibility, or in a hermeneutic of suspicion where the self cannot trust itself as Freud does, Lévinas creates a near impossible ontology for ethical subjectivity that is formed out of these demands that conflict with each other. When the imperialism of ego does not cover over the self, the uniqueness of the self that can act for the other can also work to find political resolutions by means of two inter-subjects (Lévinas 1998b, pg. 112). In the space between two, each person with the other can affect change in their political lives.

The need to engage in fanciful machinations—to explain away and justify any suffering with narratives like "it's too far from me," "I don't know these others who are suffering," and "their suffering is deserved"—is already to respond to the demands that suffering makes on each relational individual. The only condition that makes this ethical orientation possible is the bare suffering of a body that unexpectedly crashes into another's reality. Veterans responding to protestors are an example of a suffering that crashed into the sensibility of another, where the face of the other unavoidably appeared, like the fetus's use of the host's organs. If suffering and pain can flood sensibility, then each is obligated to respond. The appropriate question then becomes: When will each host in hospitality or hostility the other who gestates in the formation of oneself?

Normally each response is subject to moral scrutiny, typically according to a rational standard. Only after morally scrutinizing the vulnerable body that is capable of finite thought are amounts of suffering justified and negotiated to figure out when protection is deserved. For the relational self, however, a pre-ontological relation "is a relationship without any *a priori* which arises from a spontaneity, not from that which ontology requires in a finite thought. For, in order to welcome entities in finite thought, a pure receptivity, [sic] must operate as a transcendental imagination, formative of the imaginary" (Lévinas 1998b, pg. 194). Though indifference is always an *a posteriori* option, recognition of the other and remaining in one's difference is a necessary condition for any response whatever.

Lévinas accepts much of Freud's view of the egoical self that is articulated at the end of *Civilization and Its Discontents*. Like Freud, there is the totalized self, the egoistic self, but then for Lévinas there is also the infinite aspect of self. The ethical subject contains an infinite alterity that cannot be totalized in any form of knowledge. A deep conflict characterizes Lévinas's infinite subjectivity who is also persecuted in an ontology that demands totalizing descriptions and attributes. The anarchic alterity of the other, which makes up the relational self, makes it so that the subject as ethical always demands the preservation of otherness. Before arriving at

Paul Ricœur's critique of the pre-ontological commitment to the other in Lévinas that is paradoxically both a persecution and an ethical obligation, I would like to show how Lévinas amplifies the guilt that Freud was concerned with and how an intentionality of search finds a way out through to the other. My response to Ricœur that Lévinas's ethics are not separated from ontology, but ethics as the very expression of ontology is set up by this discussion about the way out of an imperialistic ego from itself through the other and remembered by an intentionality of search, which if forgotten risks stalling moral breakthroughs between two.

If ethics is an optical lens through which to see every interaction, then demands, judgments, and disappointments are possible in every relation. Lévinas comes close to Freud in thinking about guilt in the cultured ego who has the possibility for increasing amounts of guilt as civilization grows. Similar to Melanie Klein's and Sándor Ferenczi's work, Lévinas imbues the subject with guilt from the beginning, as soon as there is a body and eyes to perceive. Lévinas often emphasizes the need to protect the widow and orphan, the poor, the stranger, and any other whose life is precarious and lacks resources. Significantly, caring for these amplifies the demand since everyone at some point will fall into most of these categories. Additionally, evasion is not possible when the self is forged out of its relations. A self that is limited in resources could not possibly fulfill the demand that arises in each particular circumstance. The cry from Dostoevsky's *Brothers Karamazov*, "Each of us is guilty before everyone, for everyone and for everything, and I more than the other," comes from the overwhelmed position of realizing the obligation of this kind of unceasing demand (Lévinas 1996, pg. 18). However, it does begin one's moral adventure from the beginning of their life. Here is where I find Lévinas approaching intersubjective psychoanalysis that realizes a deeply contextual nature that then also forms reparative ways for negotiating these contexts.

Guilt cannot be expiated when the other is imposed upon by the self's impressions and desires. Externalizing guilt as in delusions of persecution, for example, cannot be an appropriate process of the ego's recovery since the other is not allowed to remain other in the process of projection. New time is not created with another here, but only repeats an internal trauma. If the other is a mere projection that allows me to develop a mastery over my trauma, then there can be no change for both. Rebuilding social relations through what remains the same for oneself are processes the ego reconstructs for a recovery of libidinal cathexes to the social world, but that is not to stand in an ethical relation with the alterity of the other.

To be clear, the anarchic alterity of the other does not come from a transcendent God, at least not directly. Anarchic alterity comes from the face of the other, their embodied life, experiences, passions, and traumas. Theodicies that resign to violent relations and apologize for God's silence are negligent reprieves from the real and often painful demands made by the anarchic alterity that comes from the other person. Historical and material redemption can only come between people who responsibly face those who carry an injured past. Lévinas's understanding of the ethical subject was all too aware about this obligation and called it a persecution of the egoical self. An additional difficulty arises when the other can be heard or seen; this depends on the space between two and not on intentions and actions of each in isolation.[4]

Judgment revealed in the eyes of the other silently expresses an unlimited and increasing responsibility that also comes with "an accusation of my guilt (that) call me forth to justice without end" (Peperzak 1993, pg. 103).[5] Becoming totally overwhelmed with guilt in the face of an infinite responsibility that could never be fulfilled is not resolved in Lévinas's work, much like Freud. The infinite obligation and unavoidable guilt produced in this responsibility is also the main issue readers of Lévinas have with his ethic. But the guilt remains and amplifies in an imperialism of the ego and in advocating for the self's mastery. Masochistic pleasure from an admonishing super-ego results from repeating one's injury for self-mastery, which is always delusional. There is no isolated self that can be mastered. Freud was right to be dismayed in his search for a means for psychic control of its ambivalent drives. On the other hand, through an intentionality of search the relational subject that can never be mastered preserves the space to find the other. Needless amplification of the guilt that Freud found so problematic can be managed and psychically atoned for in the sense of finding a tone in its recognition by another.

To a certain extent, Lévinas removes the individual's choice and the identity of a person from consideration in an ethical exchange. Instead, an emphasis is placed on a psychic or constitutional vulnerability that opens to create the ethical encounter. The doers have no place to choose to do the right thing; rather, they are always already vulnerable, chosen, or elected to have the encounter. Like a dual turnkey that requires both parties to unlock a vault, so here do two people have to be open in the moment of election for an ethical relation. Lévinas's ethics are the condition that allows for the possibility of various articulations of moral theories, various turnkeys, by placing us in certain kinds of relations with the other. While the condition of ethics Lévinas emphasizes as a pre-ontology does not necessitate an action done by oneself or any single other, such as unlocking the vault by way of a two-partied turnkey, the pre-ontological condition presupposes that one can be attuned for keying into the moral possibilities in each particular circumstance when the other appears.[6] Any morality whatsoever is an expression of an originary care for the other, but the pre-ontological condition can be forgotten.

For Lévinas, an important distinction that opens the ethical possibility is the difference between the ego, on the one hand, and the self as relational subjectivity, on

---

[4] Reference to the space between two that contains an element of radical freedom resembles what Arendt describes in *The Human Condition* (Arendt 1998) and Michel Foucault in *Power/Knowledge* (Foucault 1980). Details for a comparison between these ideas are beyond the scope of this paper.

[5] Parenthesis added.

[6] In order to avoid ontologizing the ethical subject, the ethical condition will be referred to as pre-ontological or alterity. For the similar attempt not to phenomenologize the trace, relations of proximity, and the face as *visage*, we will develop an intentionality of search. Lévinas is careful not to imply that the face phenomenally appears, but rather arises in a relation anarchically. The search in this intentionality is one that requires another object to constitute the self. The self is obsessed in finding itself through the other, which in this intentionality of search will suggest processes of attunement to find the particularities of another.

the other. Freud only conceived of the first. The ego can perceive itself free from moral obligations because of its super-individuated identity. The play of ontic categories and identifications appears most important for this ego. There are only what Lévinas calls *proximate* relations between any two where attention is given to a pre-natural form of signification. People, strangers, neighbors, and kin must stand in relation for an ethical encounter like two who stand on a cliff waiting to catch what the other throws. Any signification presupposes an abyssal sensibility that is "vulnerability and signifyingness […] before it gets bent into *perseverance in being* in the midst of a Nature" (Lévinas 1998b, pg. 68, 81–94). Proximity of the other that allows for an immediate sensible relation while also preserving the uniqueness of each raises the question: Where does the direct line between the two come from and how does the other know how to catch what is thrown? The answers are in Lévinas's notion of *passivity* in subjectivity and in the notion of a *saying* against the *said*.

Over and against the super-individuated ego, there is the embodied self as a subject who, like the mother with her fetus, is exposed and passive to an encounter. Preoccupied with its own skin, Lévinas locates the "hither side of identity," where there is an *anarchy* that resists thematization (1998b, pg. 108). The anarchic movement is prior to the substantiation of anything said, any event and avatar. It never appears as a certain determinate object. In contrast, the self is only a potential ethical subject who is always held hostage to the certainty of determinate objects and remains in oneself without rest until the approach of another. The emphasis on approach helps prevent thinking of a relation to the other that subsumes and projects each identity into the other. First, because no fixed identity exists and, second, because an infinite and unbridgeable distance exists between each subject. But then how is the relation achieved?

Ricœur explains why many have abandoned Lévinas's ethics as capable of informing any normative moral theory or standard. There is no simple way to accept this infinite guilt and responsibility as pre-ontological, to accept persecution as a necessary condition for ethical subjectivity. If ethics is only a particular moral standard that is universalized, then we should all be scandalized. A utilitarian can see how Kantian deontology is partial and vice versa. On the other hand, if the ethical subject is pre-ontologically grounded, then it is hard to see how this would speak to any particular life and face. Along with Ricœur, I wonder how this call to passivity, which is disconnected from ontology, bears on one's particular moral strength. How can one be morally praiseworthy if one does not *choose* the ethical relation? It is worth reviewing the full passage where Ricœur expresses his outrage at Lévinas's claim:

> The Self occupies the place of the other without having either chosen or wished to do so. The "despite oneself" of the hostage condition signifies the extreme passivity of the injunction. This paradox – of an *inhumane condition* called upon to say the ethical injunction – should be shocking. The non-ethical says the ethical solely by virtue of its excess. If substitution must signify something irreducible to a will to suffer, in which the Self would recovery mastery over itself in the sovereign gesture of the offering, of obligation, then it must remain an "expulsion of self outside of itself [. . .] the self emptying itself of itself" (*OB*, 110-111). In short, it must be by its "very malice" that persecuting hatred" (*OB*, 111) *signifies* the "subjection through the other" of the injunction under the aegis of the Good. I

> wonder whether Lévinas's readers have assessed the enormity of the paradox that consists in having malice say the extreme degree of passivity in the ethical condition. It is "outrage," the height of injustice, that one asks to signify the call to benevolence: "It is through the condition of being hostage that there can be in the world pity, compassion, pardon, and proximity" (*OB*, 117). That is not all, the "trauma of persecution" (*OB*, 111) must also signify the "the irremissibility of accusation" (*OB*, 112), in short, limitless guilt. Here Dostoyevsky takes over from Isaiah, Job, and the Koheleth. Here we have a kind of crescendo: persecution, outrage, expiation, "absolute accusation, prior to freedom" …. Does this not constitute an admission that ethics disconnected from ontology has no direct appropriate language of its own? (Ricœur and Escobar 2004, pg. 92)

Ricœur understands that an ethical ground rooted in such a hyperbolic position of passivity and an impingement from without is an admission that there is no way to speak, know, and develop moral lessons. These ethical grounds have no ontology. Ricœur attempts to mitigate Lévinas's position through its implications for a politically just life in the rest of his article (Ricœur and Escobar 2004, pg. 92). I take another tack to preserve the extreme language of ethical subjectivity, however, by using the two modalities of an egoical and relational subjectivity just articulated. The paradoxical ethical condition that rests on this extreme degree of passivity, persecution, and hostage-taking requires shifts in perspective from the egoical self to the relational, vulnerable subject as a way of understanding Lévinas's claim.

From the perspective of the egoical subject, it is indeed an outrage to be hailed into responsibility since each is self-sufficient in providing for itself. From this perspective, the requirement of another for one's own self-realization is an outrage, a persecution. Why should anyone have to endure an expulsion outside the (egoical and partial) self toward the other (egoical and partial) self? However, it is not really an "expulsion" so much as a going toward the relational self to constitute the ethical subject. The exilic condition enables finding oneself in the other; the real sense of self—ethical subjectivity—requires its others.

To proceed through Ricœur's charge, the condition of taking the egoical self as a hostage for the relational self is not "inhumane" but provides grounds for both aspects of self. Passivity in the alterity of each explains the unavoidable capability of sensing another's suffering while at the same time implicates each in what is *more* humane. From the perspective of a relational self that requires the other for any self-fulfillment as ethical, it is the egoical self-sufficiency that is an outrage. How can one become what one is *without* a passivity in alterity that welcomes the irreducible difference of the other? *A posteriori* the passivity can become either hostile or hospitable to the other, but the adventure is worthwhile if it means reaching a new height of intersubjectivity. If I am reminded of this passivity, my capability to sense the other's suffering, then a dialogue begins in myself as other. Ethics is not disconnected from ontology as Ricœur argues, but is the articulation of ontology where the possibility of infinite normative moral standards arises. Passivity here is not a call to benevolence, which already names a normative standard, but instead passivity is the grounds that provides any morality, sensibility, and thought that must be in conversation with what is otherwise from a self that is only obsessed with itself.

As Lévinas writes, "[t]he recurrence of the self in responsibility for others, a persecuting obsession, goes against intentionality, such that responsibility for others could never mean altruistic will, instinct of 'natural benevolence,' or love" (2001, pg. 112). The self can only proximately grasp the other in indirect traces for which an intentionality of search is necessary. Each is responsible for remembering their free and unique ability to respond. There are many direct and contextually sensitive standards that are articulated through language that follow from this bare realization of a subject who is both persecuted to live with others, but who also always pursues particular configurations of a moral life. Crystallizing any one standard or aspect of self as self-sufficient for a subject who can be moral in many different, ambivalently related ways is to do an injustice to the ethical ground of the self. It is to forget the self as ethically response-able.

There are normative standards that Ricœur names in the passage as if they were the pre-ontological grounds Lévinas writes about. He names the altruist who chooses to willingly suffer for the other and as such "recovers mastery" of the egoical self (Ricœur and Escobar 2004, pg. 92). We also hear an egalitarian vulnerability in the need for all selves to empty their (egoical) self, as well as finding an ethics of virtue in the possibility of recovering mastery of the relational self in a "sovereign gesture" (Ricœur and Escobar 2004, pg. 92). Note these consistent references to an individual self who assumes total control and power for passivity. But these are different forms of passive normative morals and not the passive grounds by which each individual negotiates these different forms of moral standards. Additionally, a "limitless guilt" sounds like the ascetic who is never complete in releasing its individual self from sensual pleasures all through life. Here again Ricœur confounds an ascetic normative standard acted upon by an egoical aspect of self with the pre-ontological grounds that condition these different ways of relating with others.

Each cannot choose to decline their totalized identifications, and as such pursue and are persecuted by the infinite ability to remain other in oneself. On the other hand, the relation between two infinite subjectivities also always remains "unassumable like a persecution" since the particularity of each relation is unique and never to be repeated again (Lévinas 2001, pg. 87). The multifarious ways in which relations are forged, such as those Ricœur names, are so preoccupying that the bare ability to navigate them is taken for granted. But how many times have dialogues halted because each side perceives itself incapable of conversation with the other? Without remembering our search of the other, even in oneself, peace among people like an Israeli Jew and Palestinian Arab will forever remain halted. But, if the passive grounds are preserved for remembering one's personal freedom to choose from many moral possibilities, then the self can also be for the other. In being for the other, here one is also for the self. In one sly move, altruism and egoism are preserved by modalities that are preserved and ambivalently related in an ethical subjectivity. However, the anterior condition in this ethic resides in the self's capacity also to delude itself about its egoical self-sufficiency and has carried moral discourses to disastrous ends for too long.

An egalitarian morality can help articulate the ways in which all are equally vulnerable to the demand a particular face makes. The face does not appear in any phenomenal terms, such as shape, size, color, or a configuration of its parts. If one is capable of suffering, and suffering comes from the exposed body, the demanding face can be sensed and gives rise to a response and as such, responsibility. However, an egalitarian response that sets the same response for everybody cannot be appropriate for the needs of each particular face. Each particular body and context require different aids, attention, and care. Let the minimum moral standard remain at the vulnerable body that is then capable of finite thought, capable of forming its existence through imagination, and deserving of protection.

References

Arendt, H. (1998). *The human condition* (2nd ed.). Chicago: The University of Chicago Press.
Brody, D. (2001). Lévinas's maternal method from "Time and the Other" through *otherwise than being*: No Woman's Land? In T. Chanter (Ed.), *Feminist interpretations of Emmanuel Lévinas* (pp. 53–77). Pennsylvania: The Pennsylvania State University Press.
Cohen, R. A. (2010). *Lévinasian meditations: Ethics, philosophy, and religion*. Pittsburgh: Duquesne University Press.
Foucault, M. (1980). In C. Gordon (Ed.), *Power/Knowledge: Selected interviews & other writings 1972–1977*. New York: Pantheon Books.
Hanisch, C. (1970). *"The Personal Is Political." Notes from the second year: Women's liberation; Major writings of the radical feminists*. New York: Radical Feminism.
Husserl, E. (2001). In D. Moran (Ed.), *Logical investigations* (Vol. 2, 2nd ed.). London: Routledge.
Lévinas, E. (1969). *Totality and infinity* (trans: Lingis, A.). New York: Duquesne University Press.
Lévinas, E. (1989). In S. Hand (Ed.), *The Lévinas Reader*. Oxford: Blackwell Publishing Ltd.
Lévinas, E. (1996). In A. T. Peperzak, S. Critchley, & R. Bernasconi (Eds.), *Basic philosophical writings*. Chicago: Indiana University Press.
Lévinas, E. (1998a). *Discovering existence with Husserl and Heidegger* (trans: Cohen, R.). Evanston, IL: Northwestern University Press.
Lévinas, E. (1998b). *Otherwise than being: Beyond essence* (trans: Lingis, A.). New York: Duquesne University Press.
Lévinas, E. (2001). *Existence and existents* (trans: Lingis, A.). New York: Duquesne University Press.
Peperzak, A. (1993). *To the other: An introduction to the philosophy of Emmanuel Lévinas*. West Lafayette: Purdue University Press.
Ricœur, P., & Escobar, M. (2004). Otherwise: A reading of Emmanuel Lévinas's otherwise than being or beyond essence. *Yale French Studies, 104*, 82–99.

Chapter 12
Conclusion

Abstract In this final chapter, I recount significant experiences that supported and complicated both Freud's and Lévinas's theoretical conclusions on morality. In my conclusion, I suggest that one possible ethical safeguard includes turning away from traditions that value self-mastering individualized egos because this risks losing site of an underdetermined, particular self that requires others to constitute itself.

Keywords Ethics reconsidered · Relational person · Ethical subjectivity · Horizons of meaning · Self-mastery · Social bonds · Relational psychoanalysis · Intersubjective psychotherapy · Object relations psychoanalysis · Reparative relations · Empathic relations · Egoical self · Existential vulnerability · Ethicist · Phenomenologists · Psychoanalysts · Unknowability · Relationality · Underdetermined psyche

Ethics Reconsidered: Always Only a Proximate Response

Both Lévinas and Freud were highly suspicious of universalizing moral theories that disregarded emotional and contextual complexities. Both articulated their views on the egoical aspect of what is at its core relational persons who can doubt their moral obligations while also seeking to live among others. The constant attempt to simultaneously preserve common social norms with egoical demands commits the persecutory subject to an ethical life. I have tried to characterize the persecutory subject across these authors' works and lives in order to find how these binds can forge, risk, circumvent, and enable ethical subjectivity. The personal lives of Freud and Lévinas created horizons of meaning that extended their theoretical work on persecution. In seeing how these two were persecuted in their lives—and how they then reflected on and wrote about these experiences—I showed how they negotiated these aspects of self that were in conflict.

Freud's life included both prolific writing and extensive travel as he circulated letters to friends and colleagues alike and embarked on many research trips throughout Europe and the United States to discuss his work. He formed committees and gave lectures in his home. Freud would call these efforts "libidinal investments" that are one means to master aggression. Of course, my analysis follows Freud's own perspective and method. Whether Freud's method is objectively true is irrelevant to the truth it held for him. Delusions of persecution were one way that Freud found that the psyche defends itself against individual desires that are socially unacceptable. In the extreme example of the paranoid subject, the other is imagined as persecuting the self since the self can project an unwanted desire onto the other as a way of maintaining internal equilibrium. Meanwhile, the unsuspecting other onto whom the paranoid subject projects guilt is occluded, avoided, and can persecute in retaliation. Both the persecutor and the persecuted are sacrificed to the demands of a moral super-ego. Negotiating between individual desires against internalized social norms, the super-ego creates large amounts of guilt only to ultimately repeat the psychic aggression it aimed to avoid. Much of Freud's writing is laden with traces of his guilt from a desire to challenge cultural norms while also abiding to the strictest norms.

The masochistic pleasure, the enjoyment in persecuting oneself, and the enjoyment of persecuting others seem to have two recourses in action, according to Freud's final reflections and writings. On the one hand, mastery of the self can build a social bond that integrates different individuals into one group. The unified group becomes the goal for which individuality must be sacrificed. On the other hand, another option Freud articulates for making a social bond among many is to create a unified group out of many individuals wherein the social goal is to preserve the particularities of its members. The former course of action included the destructive, cannibalistic tendency to consume the other, subsuming differences for one common ideal. The ideal is usually unattainable, like Plato's ideal forms of the good or Aristotle's contemplative man. Norms that are identified through a super-ego always risk producing a neurotic compulsion to attain whatever its goal at any cost, such as grinding others to dust. An exaggerated form of morality in a social bond among a diverse group of mastered individuals can produce an illusion of equality or exaggerated forms of care for the other. Another exaggerated form of morality is a high level of self-involvement with one's delusions and minimal care for others. Freud's understanding of Nathanael in "The Sandman" was a literary example of the capacity to castigate oneself and others for individual traumas. Schreber was his real-life example for this delusional capacity to recover from these individual experiences of trauma.

Freud's latter course of action, however, which aims at creating a unified group out of many individuals, would have to negotiate between different and ambivalently related interests, ideals, and values. In order to preserve difference, the particularity of the other (which can jeopardize one's sense of harmony and unity) must be preserved. The unexpected, dangerous, and traumatic compulsions that come from real confrontations with the other would be taken as a platform to develop one's moral sensibility. Responding to these differences would receive the highest value for making social life and bonds bearable and can thus be understood as an egalitarian particularism. Relations among many individuals without an idyllic social bond would always remain highly precarious. Everyone is equally particular and requires due diligence to prevent subsuming differences in a zealous pursuit of private, individual ideals. Prioritizing difference calls for an ethics of proximity that prizes an unknowable response between two in a relation over mastery of the self; it is admittedly, by both Lévinas and Freud, the more difficult approach to build ethical relations.

Freud was important to this investigation because he clearly explicated delusions of persecution. In a certain sense, he demythologized what is often viewed as innately or inherently evil in those who have paranoiac delusions or those who persecute for an introjected ideal. Instead these are means by which the ego repairs itself. Understanding persecution in this way, however, also leaves open the question of how to conduct a moral life when the persecutory relation is not voluntary. The ambivalent relation between psychic drives that grows with the demands of cultural life preoccupied much of Freud's theoretical work, but when it came time to acknowledge the underdetermined character of moral standards in his work on "The Uncanny," Freud repressed this repression.

The important point of etymological ambiguity in moral and social norms was made at the beginning of his text on the uncanny feeling, only to be abandoned by Freud at the end of his essay. Economies of masochism grip the moral life in cultural development with no clear way of resolving the increasing amount of guilt created by super-egoical demands. In *Moses and Monotheism*, one of his last works, Freud aimed to dissolve the difference between the Jew and Gentile in writing on an Egyptian Moses. Even if the account is not historically accurate, the urgency with which he wrote this at the end of his life—during Nazi persecutions in Vienna—reveals his attempt to relieve the persecutory forces that resulted from his disqualification of an Aryan cultural ideal.

Repressing the difficult impingement of others is one of the ways that Freud personally dealt with persecution and with his fear that the persecutions may in large part be delusional. As a Viennese Jew, his social life included daily acts of persecution, though he feared some internal perceptions were unjustified. I also find that Freud's desire for acceptance from a reluctant positivistic-scientific community reveals another particular source of vulnerability in his life. Developing his own method and creating a field of psychotherapy is the fervent attempt to master this vulnerability. His work, which investigated the life of the mind through non-empirical means, was a source of pleasure as much as guilt. However, his attempt to master this difference only perpetuated the guilt he would feel when oppression was felt from others. His correspondences with Zweig indicate an amount of animosity toward a Jewish heritage that was always second to his love of Viennese and German belonging, which made their rejection of him especially traumatic.

His work and life show how difficult it is to find ways to negotiate this desire for mastery with colleagues; they explain his lifelong doubt about the possibility of a "natural ethic" that would only increase aggression when he did not meet social expectations. Moving from Freud to relational psychotherapy, I considered how Freud's approach to a moral life becomes less severe if we do not begin with the ideal of the individual's ego-drive that through guilt must be repressed and aggressively sacrificed for social bonds. These relational, intersubjective approaches remove the interior ego-drive all together. The intersubjective psyche always develops in relational contexts, and the break from individuated desires early in life becomes necessary for developing real relationships with others.

Intersubjective and relational approaches in psychotherapy begin with the assumption that the self always develops in a context. There cannot be an isolated ego to analyze. At the heart of subjectivity in relational psychotherapy is an inclusion of the other. Moving from ego psychology to object relations psychoanalysis, Melanie Klein's research found that the aggressive drive begins in early infancy. The individuated ego is not primarily contending with its aggressive and libidinal drives but is most concerned with the objects at which desires are driven. Guilt begins earlier in life as much as the reparative possibilities for the individuated psyche that always aims at other objects. Klein went as far as characterizing these earliest stages in infancy as persecutory and thus the most significant stage for reducing aggression in adulthood.

She did not, however, provide reparative measures as much as Sándor Ferenczi, who helped pave a way to intersubjective approaches in psychoanalysis. Ferenczi, a member of Freud's inner circle of colleagues, placed special importance on the empathetic relation for reparative relations between therapist and the one who comes for treatment. He found that clinical settings alienate this relationship, prevent empathy between two people, and further prevent a real possibility to acknowledge a repressed trauma. Hans Loewald was similarly concerned with the fabrication of an isolated ego and the theoretical difficulty of alleviating its mounting aggression. Loewald argues in "The Waning of the Oedipus Complex" that an infant's need to psychically "kill the parent" contributes to its developing a sense of responsibility. Morality is not a neurotic compulsion, but critical self-reflection that forms a self who lives alongside others. The other is not represented and internalized merely for narcissistic-masochistic means, but rather is preserved in a relation that keeps its distance.

In acts of reparation, contexts and relationships take precedence in the developing psyche over the pleasure or aggression (or in certain instances, pleasure *and* aggression) of isolated desires. The self is always interpersonal with another and so, even if unpleasant, any other contributes to psychic maturity. George E. Atwood and Robert Stolorow are contemporary relational psychotherapists whose goal for the inter-relational subject is to harmonize a subject's fragmentary psychic parts rather than cure them. By approaching psychoanalysis through its contemporary intersubjective orientations, there is the possibility of developing a resonance between the psychoanalytic method and Lévinas's ethic.

Relations are impinging and always require negotiation. Sharing particular traumas, bearing witness, and suffering alongside another are some ways to negotiate moral relations that exceed masochistic economies. Intersubjective and relational approaches in contemporary psychoanalysis also help find ways for the ego to negotiate its ability to respond in these demanding and persecutory relations. Donna Orange's work is a convergence between psychoanalytic views of a self that culminates in a Lévinasian injunction, especially for those who are caretakers of others. Advances in these concepts of self are evident in language that is used to refer to *patients*, and *objects*, later switched to *clients*, then changed to refer to actual *peo-

ple. This is one small but significant change to approach the other in the context of psychotherapy.

These strategies were used to show how less dependency on notions of mastery can reduce super-egoical demands for a reduction in masochistic pleasure as well as avoid the psychic use of delusional perceptions as a form of repair. A mature ethic accepts vulnerability and unknowability. The relational person can navigate dynamic contexts while negotiating personal desires and social expectations, similar to the Lévinasian form of pre-ontological persecution that prompts a contextualized self who is also individuated. These developments in psychoanalysis are like the moves Lévinas makes that encourage speaking against totalized forms of the self from which fixed relations emerge. Rather, a flux and co-constructed reality are the basis for the self that can relieve standards that make the individual feel guilty. There can also follow an increase in the possibility for an ethic that is neither neurotic nor masochistic. Freud's psychoanalytic insight began this trajectory that led into relational and intersubjective psychoanalysis and landed in Lévinasian ethical territory.

The violence inflicted through the two modes that cohabit the ethical subject is not ignored in Lévinas's ethic. Moral credit is given to ethical subjectivity when it expertly navigates these two conflicting modes. In order to become attuned to the particularities of another, the egoical self must not be fragmented but must have an integrated sense of self. I used the term egoical rather than egoistic to show how the individuated ego can welcome the other. The egoical self is made up of its identifications that are used as the platform through which one breaks, and makes, its ethicality. Egoical is also different from Freud's use of egological since these impinging relations of persecutor to persecuted are not logical and cannot be reflected on, prevented, or healed through reason. If identifications are held in a flexible relation to what one is, then the egoical is the necessary beginning from which a relation itself becomes possible.

Both thinkers were born and grew up in Europe yet also lived under an undeclinable relation to their Jewish heritage or lack thereof. Especially at the beginning of the twentieth century, these often-conflicting allegiances created clashing senses of identity that lead to questionable loyalties. For Freud, these conflicts in identity associations often lead to delusional sympathies for his Austrian roots that in reality were not justified in his time, while for Lévinas he was forced to turn a blind eye to horrors perpetrated against those he considered enemies to his Jewish allies in Israel. The experiences of their lives can help readers relate to how ontic forms of social persecutions can foreclose ethical relations, and how the fear from delusions of persecution can arise.

Knowing these abuses, we may think of responsibility and vulnerability in ways that are particular to each and unique to every relation. Everyone's vulnerabilities are different and particular; they are unique to the contingent histories of upbringing and trauma. Instead of hiding one's vulnerability because it makes one appear weak, one can elevate their vulnerabilities to embrace the other. Unique vulnerabilities have the power to elicit unique responses.

Re-signifying the term vulnerability also requires thinking about privilege differently. One's "privilege," which prevents one from seeing another's suffering, is not beneficial for the ethical subjectivity and is thus not a privilege at all. *Privilege* is the biggest shortcoming for the ethical subject, though the individuated ego desires its own privilege. Seen from the point of view of the relational subject, one's supposed privilege deprives the self from relating to the other and so prevents the realization of a truly ethical self. When the other is sacrificed for oneself, this is not a privilege but an egoical travesty. On the other hand, when attuned to the other, both individuals (individuated egos) emerge as responsible persons. The one who exposed their vulnerability, and the other who was attuned to its reception, opened a space for alterity to move them both out of themselves.

Lévinas showed that the persecutory relation already begins in the conditions of a subject who must identify among others while also simultaneously remain free in an infinite alterity. The other of alterity to which one must relate, however, does not reduce or harmonize guilt, which was the question Freud pursued. The relational subject obligates one to another in being for the other on behalf of an alterity that is infinitely distant, like an absent God. Lévinas increases the demands and obligations to produce an infinite guilt. This infinite guilt, however, is an equal burden each particular subject must bear individually with another, not in the mastery over another.

Lévinas and Freud both felt the confines of an identity formed through the forceful expectations of others. According to Lévinas, the subject is persecuted in its bodily existence that takes the space of another. One's body always obligates its subject to impinge on others while it also requires that one live a sensible life among them. In his personal life, we find more negotiations with colleagues and friends than in Freud's life, but not without an amount of bias toward particular types of identifications. Lévinas felt tension from the religious community in which he taught because of his phenomenological approaches to Talmudic texts. He also experienced resistance from the broader philosophical community because of what was perceived as his overtly religious approach to ethics and ontology. With a cautious and soft voice, he constantly negotiated the ways in which he was identified. In both circles, he always insisted that he could not be totalized by either of them.

These personal experiences provided grounds for theoretical work that was committed to maintaining the conjunction in a subject that is both totalized by historical contingencies and infinitely open for creating new possibilities. When friends and philosophers took divergent approaches, Lévinas attempted to remain unconstrained by these changes. His mentor Chouchani, the nomadic Talmudic scholar who strived not to fix identity, is an embodiment of Lévinasian ideals for negotiating these aspects of the subject.

All of this, in turn, raises intriguing questions about the three conditions of a persecuting subjectivity in regards to its ethical relationships. What makes probing these conditions of unknowability, existential vulnerability, and relationality such an interesting problem for ethicists, phenomenologists, and psychoanalysts is the fact that each must consider the effects of an underdetermined psyche for its ontological condition. So long as experiences are shaped by a reflection on effects of a life lived with others, recognition of an elemental ignorance is liberating as much as it is terrifying. There is still the need to consider the importance of this under-determinacy on political, social, and legal frameworks for protecting those who are most vulnerable. While this book engages the personal lives of Freud and Lévinas, and those effects on their theories, readers must also ask themselves how their personal lives effect their ways of being with others—and more importantly, ways of avoiding their others. My aim throughout has been to explore what happens when these interrelated components are not reflected upon, and the dangerous consequences that can follow. But another aim has been to explore the strength of thinking about proximate relationships, the power of language to commit each to an ability to respond to hospitality with simultaneous hostility toward the other, in a culture that prizes individualism at any and all costs.

By probing toward these conditions that make the persecutory subject possible, we can begin to understand the underlying causes of the many types of ontic persecutions that have existed in history. My step toward a moral philosophy opens a dialogue about possible ways of developing from egoical selves that seeks mastery and self-sufficiency to relational subjects that come into being by responding to the needs of particular others.

There is gravity here in a relational subject who seriously contends with the unavoidable necessity of responding to another's suffering in every present moment. Imprisoned by identifications made among others, the ethical self seeks to escape the ego. Since nothing can totalize, confine, or suspend its participation in infinitude, and as partial as any identification must remain, the ontological adventure for every one is the position of holding the world on its shoulders. Relations to others are difficult. Ambiguities abound in how the other makes its demand, since for Lévinas it cannot depend on any empirical signs and relations of sameness, yet nonetheless these demands are made. Just as the use of imagination in perception is unavoidable, so it is impossible to evade one's ability to respond, to have responsibility (1998, pg. 111). Like an unavoidable chain, the subject is persecuted in this relation, but as Lévinas argues, the burden is always already shouldered together with others.

Reference

Lévinas, E. (1998). *Otherwise than being: Beyond essence* (trans: Lingis, A.). New York: Duquesne University Press.

Postscript

After Trump's presidency, it is harder to be baffled by what happened in Germany. The excitement to vilify "the other" has reached fever pitches all over the USA and across the world. Once again synagogues were burnt, lynching appeared on the California landscape, and migrant women and children were kept in locked cages in the USA. The enthusiasm to persecute those who are vilified appeared again, like what can be seen in black and white pictures from the 1940s. All those who acted, served, obeyed commands, or stayed silent had justifications for their acts by some imagined good, or did so through apathy. Trump appealed to single issues, such as protecting the Jewish State of Israel, America first policies like walling off immigrants. He endorsed pro-religious freedoms and anti-women's rights that emboldened many to defend these ends by any means necessary. With these very scary tendencies to fight for what is perceived as right, however, now comes our renewed opportunity to evaluate ourselves and the barbaric tendency to persecute others for moral ends. The fact has crashed into our realities, and one way to move forward is to deal with this threatening relationality and unavoidable connectivity.

At the same time, nothing is so abundantly clear during COVID times as the importance of our relations and interconnectivity. My mere breath could potentially harm, maybe even kill, you and your loved ones. Some people have been reluctant to adopt new norms such as distancing, masking, and washing. Research has shown that these tend toward individualistic ideologies, which at this current moment puts their own lives as well as those of others at higher risk for infection. Unchecked individualism no longer makes sense when it is exactly on those terms that the virus is propagated. It has become harder to insist on being unaffected by others. On the other hand, protestors from all colors, creeds, religions, and nationalities took to the streets to insist exactly on their realization that everyone deserves to breath freely among others. People voluntarily sacrificed their ability to freely breathe, wearing masks in the streets with others, to show solidarity for the injustice in George Floyd's murder.

Those who will make it through this pandemic can engage a new understanding of how we affect each other, and to think through how porous we are to one another. The uniqueness of a pandemic in this digital era is the ability to show in images the traces of our actions and speech. After some reflection, a new understanding of ourselves can emerge—one that heeds the call and vulnerability of one to the other rather than flaming a desire to persecute them. The matter is not if a new morality will be ushered, but how and in what spirit it will be done.

Los Angeles, 2021

Bibliography

Adorno, T. (1998). *Aesthetic theory* (edited: Hullot-Kantor, R.). London & New York: Continuum.
Agamben, G. (1998). *Homo sacer: sovereign power and bare life* (trans: Heller-Roazen, D.). Stanford, CA: Stanford University Press.
Agamben, G. (1999). *Remnants of Auschwitz* (trans: Heller-Roazen, D.). New York: Zone Books.
Arendt, H. (1970). *Introduction to J. Glenn Gray: The warriors: Reflections on men in battle*. New York: Harcourt.
Arendt, H. (2007). *The Jewish writings* (edited: Kohn, J., & Feldman, R. H.). New York: Schocken Books.
Arendt, H. (1970). Thinking and moral considerations: A lecture. *Social Research, 38*(3), 417–446.
Arendt, H. (1998). *The human condition* (2nd ed.). Chicago: The University of Chicago Press.
Aristotle. (1897b). *Nicomachean ethics*. Book 2 (trans: Weldon, J.). New York: Macmillan.
Aristotle. (1987a). *A New Aristotle Reader* (edited: Ackrill, J.L.). Princeton, NJ: Princeton University Press.
Bataille, G. (1987). *Eroticism* (trans: Dalwood, M.). New York: Marion Boyards.
Bataille, G. (1988). *Inner experience* (trans: Boldt, L. A.). Albany: SUNY.
Bataille, G. (1989). *The tears of eros* (trans: Connon, P.). San Francisco: City Lights.
Becker, D., Isabel, C. M., Elena, G., Juana, K., Elizabeth, L., & Michael, V. (1989). Subjectivity and politics: The psychotherapy of extreme traumatization in Chile. *International Journal of Mental Health, 18*(2), 80–97.
Benso, S. (2000). *The face of things: A different side of ethics*. Albany: SUNY Press.
Bergo, B., & Stauffer, J. (2009). *Nietzsche and Lévinas: 'After the Death of a Certain God'*. New York: Columbia University Press. eBook.
Bernasconi, R. (1988). *The Provocation of Lévinas: Rethinking the Other*. London\New York: Routledge.
Bernasconi, R. (1995). "Only the persecuted...": Language of the oppressor, language of the oppressed. In A. T. Peperzak (Ed.), *Ethics as first philosophy: The significance of Emmanuel Lévinas for philosophy, literature and religion* (pp. 77–86). New York: Routledge.
Bernasconi, R. (2002). What is the question to which 'substitution' is the answer? In S. Critchley & R. Bernasconi (Eds.), *The Cambridge Companion to Lévinas* (pp. 234–251). Cambridge: Cambridge University Press.
Bernasconi, R. & David Wood (eds.). (1988). *Provocation of Levinas: Rethinking the Other*. United Kingdom: Routledge.
Blanchot, M. (1993). *The infinite conversation*. Minneapolis, MN: University of Minnesota Press.

Brody, D. (2001). Lévinas's maternal method from "Time and the Other" through *otherwise than being*: No woman's land? In T. Chanter (Ed.), *Feminist interpretations of Emmanuel Lévinas* (pp. 53–77). Pennsylvania: The Pennsylvania State University Press.
Buber, M. (1987). *I and Thou* (trans: Smith, R. G.). New York: Macmillan Publishing Company.
Buckle, H. T. (1878). *History of civilization in England*. Book 1 of 3. Toronto: Rose-Belford Publishing Company.
Butler, J. (2004). *Precarious life: The powers of mourning and violence*. London: Verso.
Butler, J. (2005). *Giving and account of oneself*. New York: Fordham University Press.
Butler, J. (2009). *Frames of war: When is life grievable?* London/New York: Verso.
Butler, J. (2009). Ethical ambivalence. In J. Stauffer & B. Bergo (Eds.), *Nietzsche and Lévinas: 'After the Death of a Certain God'* (pp. 70–80). New York: Columbia University Press.
Butler, J. (2012). *Parting ways*. New York: Columbia University Press.
Burnham, J. (ed.) (2012). *After Freud Left: A Century of Psychoanalysis in America*. Chicago: The University of Chicago Press.
Caputo, J. D. (1993). *Against ethics. Contributions to a poetics of obligation with constant reference to deconstruction*. Bloomington, IN: Indiana University Press.
Christenson, R. (1968). The political theory of persecution: Augustine and Hobbes. *Midwest Journal of Political Science, 12*(3), 419–438.
Cohen, R. (1991). God in Lévinas. *Jewish Thought and Philosophy, 1*(2), 197–122.
Cohen, R. A. (1985). *Face to Face with Lévinas*. New York: SUNY Press.
Cohen, R. A. (2010). *Lévinasian meditations: Ethics, philosophy, and religion*. Pittsburgh: Duquesne University Press.
Confino, A. (2014). *A world without Jews: The Nazi imagination from persecution to genocide*. New Haven: Yale University Press.
Craig, E. (1998). Vulnerability. In *Routledge encyclopedia of philosophy*. New York: Routledge.
Critchley, S. (1992). *The ethics of deconstruction. Derrida and Lévinas*. Oxford: Blackwell Publishers.
Critchley, S. (1999). *Ethics, politics, subjectivity: Essays on Derrida, Lévinas, and Contemporary French Thought*. London: Verso.
Critchley, S. (1999). The Original Traumatism: Lévinas and Psychoanalysis. In R. Kearney & M. Dooley (Eds.), *Questioning ethics: Contemporary debates in philosophy* (pp. 230–242). New York: Routledge.
Danieli, Y. (Ed.). (1998). *International handbook of multigenerational legacies of trauma*. New York: Springer.
Derrida, J. (1987). *The post card: From Socrates to Freud and beyond* (trans: Bass, A.). Chicago: University of Chicago Press.
Derrida, J. (1978). Violence and metaphysics. In *Writing and difference*. Chicago: University of Chicago Press.
Derrida, J. (1999). Hospitality, justice and responsibility. In R. Kearney & M. Dooley (Eds.), *Questioning ethics: Contemporary debates in philosophy* (pp. 65–83). New York: Routledge Press.
Doukhan, A. (2012). *Emmanuel Lévinas: A philosophy of exile*. UK: Bloomsbury Studies in Continental Philosophy.
Ettinger, B. (2006). In B. Massumi & J. Butler (Eds.), *The matrixial borderspace*. Minneapolis: University of Minnesota Press.
Fagenblat, M. (2010). *A covenant of creatures: Lévinas's philosophy of Judaism*. Stanford: Stanford University Press.
Farrell, J. (1996). *Freud's paranoid quest: Psychoanalysis and modern suspicion*. New York: New York University Press.
Ferenczi, S. (1949). Confusion of the tongues between the adults and the child (The language of tenderness and of passion). *International Journal of Psycho-Analysis, 30*, 225–230.
Fiske, J. (1881). The philosophy of persecution. *The North American Review, 132*(290), 1–17.
Foucault, M. (1980). *Power/knowledge: Selected interviews & other writings 1972–1977* (edited: Gordon, C.). New York: Pantheon Books.

Freud, S. (1953a). The standard edition of the complete psychological works of Sigmund Freud. In J. Strachey (Ed.), *The interpretation of dreams (second part) and on dreams, i–iv* (Vol. V, 1900). London: The Hogarth Press and the Institute of Psycho-analysis.

Freud, S. (1953b). The standard edition of the complete psychological works of Sigmund Freud. In J. Strachey (Ed.), *Notes Upon a Case of Obsessional Neurosis* (Vol. X, 1909). London: The Hogarth Press and the Institute of Psycho-analysis.

Freud, S. (1953c). The standard edition of the complete psychological works of Sigmund Freud. In J. Strachey (Ed.), *Three essays on sexuality and other works, i–iv* (Vol. V11, 1901–1905). London: The Hogarth Press and the Institute of Psycho-analysis.

Freud, S. (1955a). The standard edition of the complete psychological works of Sigmund Freud. In J. Strachey (Ed.), *Totem and taboo* (Vol. XIII, 1913). London: The Hogarth Press and the Institute of Psycho-analysis.

Freud, S. (1955b). The standard edition of the complete psychological works of Sigmund Freud. In J. Strachey (Ed.), *An infantile neurosis and other works* (Vol. XVII, 1918). London: The Hogarth Press and the Institute of Psycho-analysis.

Freud, S. (1955c). The standard edition of the complete psychological works of Sigmund Freud. In J. Strachey (Ed.), *A difficulty in the path of psycho-analysis* (Vol. XVII, 1918). London: The Hogarth Press and the Institute of Psycho-analysis.

Freud, S. (1955d). The standard edition of the complete psychological works of Sigmund Freud. In J. Strachey (Ed.), *Clinical Notes on Obsessional Neurosis* (Vol. XVII, 1918 [1914]). London: The Hogarth Press and the Institute of Psycho-analysis.

Freud, S. (1955f). The standard edition of the complete psychological works of Sigmund Freud. In J. Strachey (Ed.), *Beyond the pleasure principle* (Vol. XVIII, 1920). London: The Hogarth Press and the Institute of Psycho-analysis.

Freud, S. (1957a). The standard edition of the complete psychological works of Sigmund Freud. In J. Strachey (Ed.), *On narcissism* (Vol. XIV. 1914a). London: The Hogarth Press and the Institute of Psycho-analysis.

Freud, S. (1957b). The standard edition of the complete psychological works of Sigmund Freud. In J. Strachey (Ed.), *Instincts and their vicissitudes* (Vol. XIV, 1914b). London: The Hogarth Press and the Institute of Psycho-analysis.

Freud, S. (1957c). The standard edition of the complete psychological works of Sigmund Freud. In J. Strachey (Ed.), *Repression* (Vol. XIV, 1915). London: The Hogarth Press and the Institute of Psycho-analysis.

Freud, S. (1957d). The standard edition of the complete psychological works of Sigmund Freud. In J. Strachey (Ed.), *Mourning and melancholia* (Vol. XIV, 1917). London: The Hogarth Press and the Institute of Psycho-analysis.

Freud, S. (1958). The standard edition of the complete psychological works of Sigmund Freud. In J. Strachey (Ed.). *The case of Schreber, papers on technique and other works, ii–vii* (Vol. XII, 1911). London: The Hogarth Press and the Institute of Psycho-analysis.

Freud, S. (1959). The standard edition of the complete psychological works of Sigmund Freud. In J. Strachey (Ed.), *An autobiographical study* (Vol. XX, 1925). London: The Hogarth Press and the Institute of Psycho-analysis.

Freud, S. (1961a). The standard edition of the complete psychological works of Sigmund Freud. In J. Strachey (Ed.), *The ego and the id* (Vol. XIX, 1923). London: The Hogarth Press and the Institute of Psycho-analysis.

Freud, S. (1961b). The standard edition of the complete psychological works of Sigmund Freud. In J. Strachey (Ed.), *The economic problem of masochism* (Vol. XIX, 1923). London: The Hogarth Press and the Institute of Psycho-analysis.

Freud, S. (1961c). The standard edition of the complete psychological works of Sigmund Freud. In J. Strachey (Ed.), *Neurosis and psychosis* (Vol. XIX, 1923). London: The Hogarth Press and the Institute of Psycho-analysis.

Freud, S. (1961d). The standard edition of the complete psychological works of Sigmund Freud. In J. Strachey (Ed.), *Civilization and its discontents, and other works* (Vol. XXI, 1930). London: The Hogarth Press and the Institute of Psycho-analysis.

Freud, S. (1964a). The standard edition of the complete psychological works of Sigmund Freud. In J. Strachey (Ed.), *New introductory lectures on psycho-analysis and other works* (Vol. XXII, 1936, pp. 1–267). London: The Hogarth Press and the Institute of Psycho-analysis.

Freud, S. (1964b). The standard edition of the complete psychological works of Sigmund Freud. In J. Strachey (Ed.), *Why war?* (Einstein and Freud) (Vol. XXII, 1933 [1932]). London: The Hogarth Press and the Institute of Psycho-analysis.

Freud, Sigmund 1955c. The standard edition of the complete psychological works of Sigmund Freud. In J. Strachey (Ed.), *Recapitulations and problems* (Vol. XVII, 1918 [1914]). London: The Hogarth Press and the Institute of Psycho-analysis, .

Freud, Sigmund 1955e. The standard edition of the complete psychological works of Sigmund Freud. In J. Strachey (Ed.), *The uncanny* (Vol. XVII, 1919). London: The Hogarth Press and the Institute of Psycho-analysis, 1955.

Freud, S., Strachey, J., Cixous, H., & Dennomé, R. (1976). Fiction and its phantoms: A reading of Freud's Das Unheimliche (The "Uncanny"). *New Literary History, 7*(3), 525–645.

Freud, S., Zweig, A., & Freud, E. L. (1987). *The letters of Sigmund Freud and Arnold Zweig.* New York: New York University Press.

Gay, P. (1988). *Freud: A life of our times.* New York/London: W.W. Norton & Company.

Gibbs, R. (1992). *Correlations in Rosenzweig and Lévinas.* New Jersey: Princeton University Press.

Goffman, E. (1963). *Stigma: Notes on the Management of Spoiled Identity.* Englewood Cliffs, NJ: Prentice Hall.

Gray, J. G. (1970). *On understanding violence philosophically and other essays.* New York/Evanston/London: Harper & Row Publishers.

Halevi, Y. K. (2018). *Letters to My Palestinian Neighbor.* New York: Harper Collins Publishers.

Hanisch, C. (1970). *"The Personal Is Political." Notes from the second year: Women's liberation; Major writings of the radical feminists.* New York: Radical Feminism.

Hathaway, J. C., & Foster, M. (2014). *The law of refugee status* (2nd ed.). Cambridge: Cambridge University Press.

Hazony, Y. (2012). *The Philosophy of Hebrew Scripture.* New York: Cambridge University Press.

Heidegger, M. (1962). *Being and time* (trans: Macquarrie, J., & Robinson, E.). Oxford & Cambridge: Blackwell Publishers Ltd.

Heidegger, M. (1988). *The basic problems of phenomenology* (rev. ed.: Hofstadter, A.). Bloomington: Indiana University Press.

Husserl, E. (1982). *Ideas pertaining to a pure phenomenology and to a phenomenological philosophy* (trans: Kersten, F.). The Hague: Nijhoff.

Husserl, E. (2001). *Logical investigations.* (edited: Moran, D., 2nd ed. Vol. 2). London: Routledge.

Husserl, E. (1970). *The crisis of European sciences and transcendental phenomenology; an introduction to phenomenological philosophy.* Evanston, IL: Northwestern University Press.

Kant, I. (1997). *Critique of practical reason.* (edited: Gregor, M.). Cambridge, UK\New York: Cambridge University Press.

Kant, I. (1998). *Critique of pure reason* (edited: Guyer, P., & Wood, A.). Cambridge: Cambridge University Press.

Kant, I. (2000). *Critique of the power of judgment.* (edited: Guyer, P.). Cambridge: Cambridge University Press.

Kant, I. (2008). *Fundamental principles of the metaphysics of morals* (trans: Abbott, T. K.). New York: Cosimo Classics.

Karlsson, G. (2010). *Psychoanalysis in a New Light.* New York: Cambridge University Press.

Kearney, R. (1989). *Dialogues with contemporary continental thinkers: The phenomenological heritage. Paul Ricœur, Emmanuel Lévinas, Herbert Marcuse, Stanislas Breton, Jacques Derrida.* Manchester: Manchester University Press.

Khazzoom, A. (2003). The great chain of orientalism: Jewish identity, stigma management, and ethnic exclusion in Israel. *American Sociological Review, 68*(4), 481–510.

Klein, M., & Riviere, J. (1946). *Developments in Psychoanalysis: Notes on Some Schizoid Mechanisms* (edited: Heimann, M., Isaacs, S., & Riviere, J.). London: Karnac Books.

Klein, M. (1984). *Love, guilt, and reparation, and other works*. New York: Free Press.
Klein, M., & Reviere, J. (1937). *Love, hate and reparation: Two lectures*. London: Hogarth.
Klein, M., & Riviere, J. (1964). *Love, hate and reparation*. New York: W.W. Norton & Company, Inc..
Laplanche, J., & Pontalis, J. B. (1974). *The language of psycho-analysis*. New York: Norton.
Lévinas, E. (1969). *Totality and infinity* (trans: Lingis, A.). New York: Duquesne University Press.
Lévinas, E. (1985). *Ethics and infinity: Conversations with Philippe Nemo* (trans: Cohen, R.A.). Pittsburgh: Duquesne University Press.
Lévinas, E. (1987). *Time and the other* (trans: Cohen, R.). Pittsburgh, PA: Duquesne University Press, .
Lévinas, E. (1987). *Collected philosophical papers of Emmanuel Lévinas* (trans: Lingis, A.). The Hague: Martinus Nijhoff.
Lévinas, E. (1989). *The Lévinas reader* (edited: Hand, S.). Oxford: Blackwell Publishing Ltd.
Lévinas, E. (1990a). *Difficult freedom: Essays on Judaism* (trans: Hand, S.). Baltimore: John Hopkins University Press.
Lévinas, E. (1990b). *Nine talmudic readings* (trans: Aronowicz, A.). Bloomington: Indiana University Press.
Lévinas, E. (1994). *Beyond the verse: Nine talmudic readings and lectures* (trans: Mole, G. D.) Bloomington: Indiana University Press.
Lévinas, E. (1995). *Theory of intuition in Husserl's phenomenology* (2nd ed., trans: Orianne, A.). Evanston, IL: Northwestern University Press.
Lévinas, E. (1996). *Basic philosophical writings* (edited: Peperzak, A. T., Critchley, S., & Bernasconi, R.). Chicago: Indiana University Press.
Lévinas, E. (1997). *Proper names* (trans: Smith, M. B.). Stanford, CA: Stanford University Press, .
Lévinas, E. (1998). *Of god who comes to mind* (trans: Bergo, B.). Stanford, CA: Stanford University Press, .
Lévinas, E. (1998a). *Discovering existence with Husserl and Heidegger* (trans: Cohen, R.). Evanston, IL: Northwestern University Press.
Lévinas, E. (1998b). *Entre Nous: Collected essays* (trans: Smith, M. B.). New York: Columbia University Press.
Lévinas, E. (1998c). *Otherwise than being: Beyond essence* (trans: Lingis, A.). New York: Duquesne University Press.
Lévinas, E. (2001). *Existence and existents* (trans: Lingis, A.). New York: Duquesne University Press.
Lévinas, E. (2001). *Is it righteous to be? Interviews with Emmanuel Lévinas* (edited: Robbins, J.). Stanford, CA: Stanford University Press.
Lévinas, E. (2003). *On escape* (trans: Bergo, B.). Stanford, CA: Stanford University Press.
Lévinas, E., & Hand, S. (1990). Reflections on the philosophy of hitlerism. *Critical Inquiry, 17*(1), 62–71.
Loewald, H. (2000). The waning of the Oedipus complex. *The Journal of Psychotherapy Practice and Research, 9*(4), 239–249.
MacIntyre, A. (1999). *Dependent rational animals: Why human beings need the virtues*. Chicago: Open Court.
Mackenzie, C. (2013). *Vulnerability: New essays in ethics and feminist philosophy*. New York: Oxford University Press.
Malka, S. (2006). *Emmanuel Lévinas: His life and legacy* (trans: Kigel, M., & Embree, S. M.). Pittsburgh: Duquesne University Press.
Mensch, J. R. (2000). *Postfoundational phenomenology*. University Park, PA: Pennsylvania State University Press.
Nielsen, K. (1990). *Ethics without God* (3rd ed.). Buffalo: Prometheus Books.
Nietzsche, F. (1886 [1966]). *Beyond good and evil: Prelude to a philosophy of the future* (trans: Kaufmann, W.). New York: Vintage Books.

Nietzsche, F. (1967). *On the genealogy of morals and ecce homo* (trans: Kaufmann, W., & Hollingdale, R. J.). New York: Random House.
Nietzsche, F. (1968). *The will to power* (trans: Kaufmann, W., & Hollingdale, R. J.). New York: Vintage Books.
Nietzsche, F. (1974). *The Gay Science: With a Prelude of Rhymes and an Appendix of Songs* (trans: Kaufmann, W.). New York: Vintage Books.
Nietzsche, F. (1983). *Untimely meditations* (trans: Hollingrale, R. J.). Cambridge: Cambridge University Press.
Nussbaum, M. (2006). *Frontiers of justice: Disability, nationality, species membership*. Cambridge: Harvard University Press.
Orange, D. (2009). Intersubjective systems theory. *Annals of the New York Academy of Sciences, 1159I*(1), 237–248.
Orange, D. (2011). *The suffering stranger: The hermeneutics for everyday clinical practice*. New York: Routledge.
Orange, D. (2015). *Nourishing the inner life of clinicians and humanitarians: The ethical turn in psychoanalysis*. New York: Routledge.
Peperzak, A. (1993). *To the other: An introduction to the philosophy of Emmanuel Lévinas*. West Lafayette: Purdue University Press.
Peperzak, A. T. (1995). Transcendence. In A. T. Peperzak (Ed.), *Ethics as first philosophy: The significance of Emmanuel Lévinas for philosophy, literature and religion* (pp. 185–192). New York/London: Routledge.
Reinhard, K., Santner, E., & Zizek, S. (2005). *The neighbor: Three inquiries in political theology*. Chicago: University of Chicago Press.
Rempell, S. (2013). Defining Persecution. *Utah Law Review, 1*, 283–344.
Richardson, W. J. (1995). The Irresponsible Subject. In A. T. Peperzak (Ed.), *Ethics as first philosophy: The significance of Emmanuel Lévinas for philosophy, literature and religion* (pp. 123–131). New York\London: Routledge.
Ricœur, P. (1967). *The symbolism of evil* (trans: Buchanan, E.). Boston: Beacon Press.
Ricœur, P. (1970). *Freud and philosophy: An essay on interpretation*. New Haven/London: Yale University Press.
Ricœur, P. (1975). Phenomenology and hermeneutics. *Nous, 9*(1), 85–102.
Ricœur, P., & Escobar, M. (2004). Otherwise: A reading of Emmanuel Lévinas's otherwise than being or beyond essence. *Yale French Studies, 104*, 82–99.
Robbins, J. (1999). *Altered reading: Lévinas and literature*. Chicago/London: University of Chicago Press.
Ronell, A. (2003). *Stupidity*. Chicago: University of Illinois Press.
Rosenzweig, F. (1955). *On Jewish learning* (edited: Glatzer, N.). New York: Schocken Books.
Rosenzweig, F. (2005). *The star of redemption* (trans: Galli, B. E.). Madison: The University of Wisconsin Press.
Scholem, G. (1976). *On Jews and Judaism in Crisis. Selected essays* (edited: Dannhauser, W. J.). New York: Schocken Books. Inc.
Shuster, M. (2010). Philosophy and genocide. In *The Oxford handbook of genocide studies* (pp. 217–235). Oxford: Oxford University Press.
Sorel, G., & Jennings, J. (1999). *Reflections on violence*. UK: Cambridge University Press.
Stolorow, R. D., & Atwood, G. E. (1992). *Contexts of being: The intersubjective foundations of psychological life*. Hillside: Analytic Press.
Strhan, A. (2009). And who is my neighbour?: Lévinas and the commandment to love re-examined. *Studies in Interreligious Dialogue, 19*(2), 145–166.
Tauber, A. I. (2009). Freud's philosophical path: From a science of mind to a philosophy of human being. *The Scandinavian Psychoanalytic Review, 32*, 32–43.
Tauber, A. I. (2010). *Freud, the reluctant philosopher*. Princeton University Press.
Turner, B. (2006). *Vulnerability and human rights*. University Park, PA: Pennsylvania State University Press.
Weber, S. (1987). *Institution and interpretation: Theory and history of literature*. Minneapolis: University of Minnesota Press.

Index

A
Affective impingement, 145
Affective relations, 109
Aggressions, 6
   and guilt, 85
Aggressive, 29, 30, 33, 35
Aggressive desires, 81
Aggressive impulse, 82
Aggressiveness, 82
Aggressive super-ego, 86
Alterity of evil, 137, 142, 144
Alterity of the other, 110, 112, 120
"Always already subjected", 109
Ambiguities, 171
Ambiguity, 57, 133
Ambivalence, 86
Ambivalent aggressions, 93
Ambivalent drives, 37, 39, 42, 44, 45, 50
Ambivalent love and hate, 93
Ambivalent relation, 90, 92
Anarchical ethical relation, 124
Anarchical relation, 124
Anarchic alterity of the other, 152, 157, 158
Anarchic face, 116
Anarchic goodness, 102
Anarchic movement, 160
Anarchic shock, 102
Antagonism, 93
Anti-Jewish, 72
Anti-Jewish persecutions, 31
Anti-Semitism, 108
A posteriori, 161
Asymmetrical relation, 145
Atonement, 159

Autobiographical study, Freud's, 39,
   47, 49, 74
Autoeroticism, 96
Autre (other), 100
Autrui (human other), 100

B
Bear ethical responsibility, 152
Bear witness, 150
Beyond the Pleasure Principle (1920), 40
Biographical truth, 29
Bio-medical research, 65
Bisexuality, 28
Blanchot, Maurice
   and Levinas, 110–112

C
Child's emotional development, 93
Chouchani, Mordechai, 110, 113, 115, 117
Civilizations, 4
Cixous, Helen
   uncanny, 56, 62–64
Cold War, 86
Colonialism, 143
Communal feelings, 85
Condensation, 42
Conflicting desires, 30, 99
Conflicting drives, 104
Conservative super-ego, 82
Constitutional vulnerability, 156, 159
Contemporary psychoanalysis, 168
Cosmopolitan Jew, 111

Coterminous self, 93
Criticisms, 140, 143, 144
Cultural attitude, 86
Cultural expectations, 81
Cultural expression, 84
Cultural progress, 68

D
Daniel Schreber's delusions, 44–46, 49
Darwinism, 38, 54
Defiant mood, 78
Delusions of persecution, 27, 43–46, 50, 56, 59, 65, 68, 75, 78, 140, 158, 166
Dis-identification, 140
Disjunction, 126
Dislocation, 126
Distantiation, 19, 20, 80
Dyadic ethical face-to-face relation, 131
Dynamic subjectivity, 123, 126
Dynamism, 126

E
Ecole Normal Israelite Orientale (ENIO), 110, 113
"Economy of the same", 112
Egalitarian ethic, 114
Egalitarian morality, 162
Egalitarian particularism, 123, 150, 166
Egalitarian vulnerability, 162
Ego, 64, 65, 79
    cultural life, 81
    exercises standards, 66
    ideal, 66, 83
    moral masochism, 83
    psychic constitution, 82
    sadistic super-ego, 83
Egoical, 169
Egoical self, 13, 17, 18, 125, 139, 146, 157, 161, 169
Egoical self-sufficiency, 161
Egoistic, 13
Eichmann trials, 127
Elemental altruism, 93
Elementary feeling, 135–137
Emmanuel Levinas: His Life and Legacy, 23
Empathetic relations, 92, 101, 168
Empathy, 91, 93
Enthusiasm, 77
Epistemic error, 2
Epistemic gaps, 122
Erotic alterity, 151

Ethical injunction, 160
Ethicality, 169
Ethical relations, 2, 11, 12, 21, 109, 111, 116, 117, 120
Ethical responsibility, 154
Ethical responsiveness, 10
Ethical subject, 101–104
Ethical subjectivity, 11–13, 15, 17, 22, 23, 90, 101, 102, 111, 121, 123, 125–127, 132–134, 139, 141–144, 146, 151–154, 156, 157, 160, 165, 169, 170
Ethicists, 170
Ethics, 34, 35
Ethics of proximity, 167
Ethics of substitution, 139, 140, 145, 149
Ethnic cleansing, 6
Etymological ambiguity, 167
European civilization, 79
European culture, 72
European Jewry, 72
European sensibility, 142
Existence and Existents (1947), 115
Existential authenticity, 136
Existential freedom, 146
Existential vulnerability, 12, 74, 129, 131–134, 155, 170
Externalizing guilt, 158

F
"Face" as visage, 16
Face of the other, 140, 150, 157, 158
Face-to-face ethical relation, 143
Farrell's criticism, 50
Ferenczi, Sandor
    infantile empathy, 96
    intersubjective approach, 90
    intersubjective ego, 90
    narcissistic identification, 92
    professional hypocrisy, 91
    psychosis and neurosis in adult sexual life, 92
    relational approach, 93
    super-ego in infancy, 91
    terrorism of suffering, 93
    therapist's care, 92
    traditional psychoanalytic method, 91
Foreclosed ethical relation, 134
Forgiveness, 115
Fragility, 17
Freedom to choose, 35
"Frenemy", 54, 62

Index

Freud
　and Einstein correspondence, 50
　in *Kristallnacht*, 77
　and Levinas (*see* Lévinas, Emmanuel)
Freudian psychoanalysis, 13
Freud's Autobiographical study, 39, 47, 49
Freud's career, 39
Freud's correspondence Einstein, 85
Freud, Sigmund
　machinations, 3
　persecution, 19
　Psyche/Psychical Apparatus, 6
　skepticism, 23
　subjectivity, 3
　super-ego, 7
　suspicion, 19
Freud's insight, 29
Freud's life
　bisexuality and homoeroticism, 28
　forms of psychic conflict, 30
　homoerotic narcissism, 28
　letter to Zweig, 29
　neurotic and psychotic symptoms, 28
　"paranoid", 29
　self's motivations, 29
　vulnerability, 30
　work in psychology, 28
Freud's method, 166
Freud's *Moses*, 67, 69
Freud's positivism, 39
Freud's Schreber case, 44
Freud's the Uncanny, *see* The Uncanny
Freud's vulnerability, 71, 77
Friend and enemy, 54, 62
Frustrated sexual desires, 28
"Full phenomenological" method, 150

G
German culture, 72
Guilt in Melanie Klein, 90
Gulf War, 86

H
Heimliche, 56, 57
Hermeneutical phenomenology, 14, 20–22
Hermeneutics of suspicion, 3, 7, 12, 17, 19,
　　20, 23, 29, 78, 80, 81
Heroism, 136
Hesitations, Freud's, 100
History of Civilization in England (1878), 4
Hitlerism, 128, 135–138

Hoffman, E.T.A., 55, 57–61, 63, 64
Homoerotic desire, 30
Homoeroticism, 28
Homoerotic narcissism, 28
Homosexuality, 68
Homosexuality in Freud, 43, 46
Homosexuality in libido theory, 39, 44
Homosexual relations, 127
Horizons of meaning, 165
Hostage, 150, 160, 161
Hostility and hospitality, 101
Humility, 127
Hyperbolic language, 149

I
Idealized social bonds, 34
Idealized standards, 31
Idyllic social bond, 166
Impinging relations, 109
Individual desires, 30
Individuated self, 30, 31, 33
Industrialization, 4
"Ineluctable original chain", 135
Infantile empathy, 96
Infantile tenderness, 92
Infinite dynamism, 126
Intellectual activity, 4
Intellectual violence, 85
Intentional ecstasy, 154
Intentionality of search, 150, 158, 159, 162
Internal catastrophe, 79, 80, 82, 84
Internal collapse, 78, 79
Inter-psychic guilt, 33
Interruptive exilic relations, 141
Intersubjective approaches, 23, 90–91
Intersubjective ego, 90
Intersubjective psyche, 167
Intersubjective psychoanalysis, 18, 169
Intersubjective psychotherapy, 91, 96
Intersubjective relations, 118
Intersubjective vulnerability, 153
Inversion of intentional ecstasy, 154
Irma's injection, 41–43, 46, 47, 50
Israeli-Palestinian conflict, 144
Israel's Defensive Forces (IDF), 139

J
Jewish intellectuals, 114, 115
Jewishness, 74
Jewish particularism, 114
Jewish persecution, 73, 78

Jewish Persecution WWII, 112
Jewish spirituality, 114
Jewish tradition, 114
Justified political, 127

K
Korean war, 86
Kristallnacht, 31

L
Language, 156
Lévinas, Emmanuel
 anti-Semitism, 108
 deconstructive potential, 112
 egalitarian ethic, 114
 ego in psychoanalysis, 100
 ethic, 100
 ethical demand, 103
 ethical relation, 120
 ethical relation, 14
 ethics of substitution, 111
 Existence and Existents, 116
 and Freud, 99–104
 Husserlian and Heideggarian phenomenology, 114
 Jewish particularism, 114
 language, 109, 110
 machinations, 3
 narcissism, 100
 narcissistic egoism, 100
 non-empirical vision, 103
 non-erotic proximity, 116
 non-university status, 116
 openness of thematization, 118
 persecuting responsibility, 121
 persecution, 19, 121
 proximity and paradoxical antonyms, 101
 radical ethics, 118
 relational subject, 120
 self-identification, 120
 sincere intentionality, 121
 at Sorbonne, 110, 113
 sovereign, 102
 subjectivity, 3
 suspicion, 19
 Totality and Infinity, 101
Levinasian ethics, 133, 134, 137, 140, 145, 159, 160
Lévinas on *Hitlerism*, 128
Lévinas's analysis, 136
Lévinas's ethic, 117, 168, 169

Lévinas's life and work, 108
Liberal equality, 138
Liberal freedom, 136
Libidinal attachments, 7, 44
Libidinal investments, 46, 165
Libido, 96
Limitless guilt, 161, 162
Lithuanian culture, 108
Loewald Oedipus complex, 90, 94
Love they neighbor, 83, 86

M
Marxist materialism, 138
Masochism grip, 167
Masochistic pleasure, 159, 166
Master aggression, 166
Materialism, 142
Materialists, 142, 143
Maternity, 152, 153
Medical-positivism, 38
Modalities of obsession, 149, 151
Modality of obsession, 152, 154
Monotheism, 67, 69
Moral ambiguity, 57
Moral ambivalence, 56
Moral credit, 169
Morality, 62
Moral masochism, 83, 86
Moral negligence, 144
Moral pleasure, 86
Moral scrutiny, 157
Moral sensibility, 103
Moral super-ego, 166
Moses, 67, 69
Mutual dis-identification, 89, 127
Mutual passivity, 95

N
Narcissism, 100
Narcissistic gratification, 84
Narcissistic identifications, 84
Narcissistic investment, 84
Nathanael's delusions, 61
Nathanael's general mood, 60
Nationalism, 54
Natural barbarism, 1, 128, 145
Natural benevolence, 108, 162
Natural ethics, 142, 167
Natural morality, 83
Nazi anti-semitism, 72
Nazi persecutions, 73

Neurotic paranoia, 27
New moral horizons, 145
Non-ontic face, 132
Non-phenomenal face, 133

O

Objection-relation school, 90
Objective memory, 91, 92
Object-relational psychoanalysis, 17
Object-relations psychoanalysis, 168
Oedipus complex, 90, 94
Ontic persecutions, 132
Ontological persecution, 109
Orange, Donna, 90, 93–95
"*Otherwise than being*", 100, 102, 108, 114

P

Paranoiac delusions, 21, 64
Paranoiac delusions of persecution, 43, 51, 53
Paranoid delusions, 27, 28, 44, 46
Paranoid delusions of persecution, 27
Paranoid disorders, 27
Passionate love, 93
Passive ego, 90
Passivity, 79, 81, 89, 124, 161
Passivity-activity alternative, 124
Paul Ricouer on evil, 78
"Pedantry and crudity of psychoanalytic terminology", 49
Penumbra of ego, 100
Persecuted subjectivity, 108
Persecuting obsession, 162
Persecuting responsibility, 121
Persecuting the other, 31, 32, 34
Persecution, 121, 126, 150
    as anarchic possibility, 14
    definition, 3, 12
    ethical relation, 2
    ethical subjectivity, 121
    intellectual and industrial capacity, 5
    in Lévinas, 107, 108
    mass scales, 5
    neurotic delusions, 128
    persecuting spirit, 5
    pre ontological, 15
    psychological and moral affects, 3
    real persecutions, 128
    Schreber's delusions, 50
    in social and political histories, 8
    sovereign's use, 6
    super-ego, 121
    torture, 8
Persecution to genocide, 72
Persecutory, 8, 80
Persecutory relation, 8
Persecutory subject, 21
Persecutory subjectivity, 9, 12, 16
Phenomenologists, 170
Phenomenology, 150
    and the Talmud, 113–115
Physical violence, 78
Pleasure, 84
Political philosophy, 5
Political power relations, 157
Positivism in Vienna, 37, 38
Positivist methods, 63
Precarious relationality, 145
Pre-ontological alterity, 146
Pre-ontological persecution, 132, 139, 140, 149, 153
Pre-ontological relation, 103, 157
Pre-ontological responsibility, 143
Pre-ontological "ultimate essence of Israel", 140
Pre-ontological vulnerability, 140
Primary masochism, 83
Privilege, 170
Professional hypocrisy, 91
Proximate knowledge, 124
Proximity of the other, 124, 125
Psychic conflict, 30
Psychic integration, 93
Psychic organism, 30
Psychic stability, 126
Psychoanalysis, 7, 22, 46, 49, 76, 78, 81, 87, 168, 169
    approaches, 96
    intersubjective, 91, 96
    objection-relation school, 90
    psychic integration, 93
    psychosis and neurosis, 92
    suffering, 95
Psychoanalysts, 170
Psychoanalytic method, 137
Psychological health, 135
Psychological poverty, 84
Psychotherapists, 168
Psychotherapy, 167–169
Punishment, 83

R

Racism, 54, 135, 137, 138
Radical inter-dependency, 90
Radical passivity, 94
Radical racist, 125

Reality principles, 53, 54, 62, 63
Reflections on Hitlerism, 134, 137, 143
Relationality, 9, 10, 12, 170
Relational persons, 165, 169
Relational psychoanalysis, 169
Relational psychotherapy, 167, 168
Relational subject, 171
Relational subjectivity, 18, 100, 108, 112, 135, 159
Relations of persecutions, 7
Religion, 113
Religious community, 170
Religious persecution, 127
Reparation, 90, 95
Reparative relations, 168
Responsibility, 156, 168, 169, 171

S
Sadistic conscience, 83
Sadistic super-ego, 83
Saying *vs.* said, 160
Schreber's delusions, 44, 45
Schreber's intellectual ability, 80
Schreber's paranoid delusions, 27, 30
Scientific psychology, 41
Self-diagnosed neurosis, 48
Self grasps, 108
Self-mastery, 166
Self's motivations, 29
Self-sufficient, 161
Sense of guilt, 80, 81, 83
Sense of morality, 83
Sexual-social desires, 30
Signifyingness, 160
Social bonds, 81, 82, 86, 166, 167
Social norms, 55, 57, 58, 61, 62, 65–67
Social persecution, 140
Social protection, 151
Social relations of persecution, 19
Social standards, 41
Sovereign gesture, 160, 162
Stigmas, 33
Stigma symbols, 33
"Strangeness keenly", 54
Structure ethical subjectivity, 116
Subject formation, 90
Subjective idealism, 21
Subjectivity, 9
　ethical bind, 108
　in intentional modalities, 120
　in positivist method, 37, 39
Substitutability, 103

Substitution, 103
Super-ego, 7, 54, 68, 86, 90
Super-egoical demands, 66
Super-egoical guilt, 86
Suspicion, 19
Switching modalities, 153

T
Tenderness and care, 91, 93, 96
Terrorism of suffering, 93
"The dirty Jew", 119
"The Economic Problems of Masochism" (1924), 83
The Ego and The Id (1923), 43, 83
"The irremissibility of accusation", 161
Theistic existentialism, 115
Theology, 113
The Philosophy of Persecution (1881), 4
"The Political Theory of Persecution: Augustine and Hobbes" (1968), 5
The Sandman, 55, 58, 59, 61, 64, 166
The Symbolism of Evil, Paul Ricœur, 78
The uncanny
　conflicting moralities, 59
　death, 63
　in Hoffman's story, 63
　"ought", 56
　"primitive" belief, 55
　psychoanalysis, 62
　sensation, 56
　social norms, 57, 58
"The Waning of the Oedipus Complex" (2000), 94
Totalitarian effacement, 121
Totality and Infinity, 110, 111, 113, 116
Traditional psychoanalytic method, 91
Trauma of the face, 109
Traumatic memories, 113
Trieb (Freud's), 39, 40, 51
Troubling desires, 68

U
Unbearable trauma, 94
"Uncannily", 54
Uncanniness, 55, 60–62
"Unconscious contradiction", 45
Unconsciousness, 125
Underdetermined psyche, 170
Understanding persecution, 167
Unheimliche, 56, 62–64
Universalism, 135, 138

Universality, 138
Unknowability, 169, 170
Unrealistic moral injunctions, 89
"Unselfish philanthropy", 5
"Useless Suffering", 136

V
Values of egalitarianism, 111
Viennese culture, 72–74
Vietnam War, 86
Violence, 8
Vocabulary, 144

Vulnerability, 9, 10, 12, 17, 30, 118, 131, 135, 139, 154, 160, 167, 169

W
Why War?, 50, 85, 86
"Will to responsibility", 107
Wish fulfillments, 42
Wounding, 156

Z
Zweig, Arnold, 72, 74–78

The manufacturer's authorised representative in the EU is Springer Nature Customer Service Centre GmbH, Europaplatz 3, 69115 Heidelberg, Germany. If you have any concerns regarding our products, please contact ProductSafety@springernature.com

Printed and bound by CPI Group (UK) Ltd, Croydon, CR0 4YY

25/03/2026

02078174-0002